I0112460

Neoliberalism and National Culture

Studies in Critical Social Sciences Book Series

Haymarket Books is proud to be working with Brill Academic Publishers (www. brill.nl) to republish the *Studies in Critical Social Sciences* book series in paperback editions. This peer-reviewed book series offers insights into our current reality by exploring the content and consequences of power relationships under capitalism, and by considering the spaces of opposition and resistance to these changes that have been defining our new age. Our full catalog of *SCSS* volumes can be viewed at www.haymarketbooks.org/category/scss-series.

Series Editor
David Fasenfest, Wayne State University

Editorial Board
Chris Chase-Dunn, University of California—Riverside
G. William Domhoff, University of California—Santa Cruz
Colette Fagan, Manchester University
Martha Gimenez, University of Colorado, Boulder
Heidi Gottfried, Wayne State University
Karin Gottschall, University of Bremen
Bob Jessop, Lancaster University
Rhonda Levine, Colgate University
Jacqueline O'Reilly, University of Brighton
Mary Romero, Arizona State University
Chizuko Ueno, University of Tokyo

Neoliberalism and National Culture

State-Building and Legitimacy in Canada and Québec

Cory Blad

Haymarket
Books
Chicago, IL

First published in 2011 by Brill Academic Publishers, The Netherlands.
© 2011 Koninklijke Brill NV, Leiden, The Netherlands

Published in paperback in 2013 by
Haymarket Books
P.O. Box 180165
Chicago, IL 60618
773-583-7884
www.haymarketbooks.org

ISBN: 978-1-60846-243-8

Trade distribution:
In the U.S. through Consortium Book Sales, www.cbsd.com
In the UK, Turnaround Publisher Services, www.turnaround-psl.com
In Australia, Palgrave Macmillan, www.palgravemacmillan.com.au
In all other countries by Publishers Group Worldwide, www.pgw.com

Cover design by Ragina Johnson.

This book was published with the generous support of Lannan Foundation
and the Wallace Global Fund.

Printed in Canada by union labor on recycled paper containing 100 percent
postconsumer waste in accordance with the guidelines of the Green Press Initiative,
www.greenpressinitiative.org.

10 9 8 7 6 5 4 3 2 1

Library of Congress Cataloging-in-Publication Data is available.

RECYCLED
Paper made from
recycled material
FSC   FSC® C103567
www.fsc.org

CONTENTS

ACKNOWLEDGEMENTS

This project was made possible through the pains and efforts of many individuals over a span of six years. An earlier iteration of the project benefitted greatly from the wisdom and perspective of Jon Shefner at the University of Tennessee, who read several drafts and suffered amicably through my many misguided attempts to articulate a clear vision of the project. Paul Barrette, Sherry Cable, Harry Dahms, and Asafa Jalata all offered tremendously helpful comments throughout. Dave Kauzlarich, Jason Stacy, and Debbie Mann at Southern Illinois University Edwardsville gave their time, support, and patience that encouraged me to continue struggling through the difficult stages of theoretical development.

Ricardo Dello Buono at Manhattan College is solely responsible for the final push to complete the project and provided invaluable guidance and friendship for the past two years. I cannot thank him enough for his help. David Fasenfest proved a patient yet demanding editor – his comments greatly improved the quality of this manuscript. I would also like to thank Rosanna Woensdregt and Peter Buschman at Brill Publishers for their advice and assistance. Special thanks to Liane Nadeau, an incredibly skilled artist and even more generous sister, for taking the time to create (and recreate) the cover art.

Financial and logistic support for fieldwork in Montréal, Ottawa, and Québec was made possible by a Canadian Studies Graduate Student Fellowship and Faculty Research Grant administered by Foreign Affairs Canada through the Canadian Embassy in Washington, D.C. Dan Abele and Emilian Papadopoulos were especially supportive of my project and scholarship. The Québec government was equally generous by providing grant support through the Québec Studies Program administered by the Ministère des Relations internationales and the tireless efforts of Yanick Godbout. Additional grant support was provided by the W.K. McClure Fund for the Study of World Affairs at the University of Tennessee and the generous support of Elizabeth Gregor. Additional support was provided by grants from Southern Illinois University Edwardsville and Manhattan College.

Several individuals must be recognized for their friendly support and exhaustive knowledge: William Floch at Heritage Canada; Katia

Bellai-Trottier and Ghislain Malette at the Canadian National Archives; Estelle Brisson at the Archives nationales du Québec; Olga Tzotis at Statistics Canada; Eleanor Read at the Social Sciences Data Services Division of the University of Tennessee Library System; Pierre Anctil, Philippe Couton, and Leslie Laczko at the University of Ottawa; Yolande Frenette at the Ministère de l'Immigration et des Communautés culturelles; Denise Plamondon at Hydro-Québec; and Stephane Pronovost at Développement économique Canada.

Finally, I would like to thank my family for their genuine support and unbelievable patience. My mother and father have always provided unquestioning support – even when they weren't quite sure they should. Thanks to my daughters Zoë and Sanna for occasionally allowing me to write and not making me feel too guilty on my research trips. Finally, thanks to my partner, Julia. Without her support, encouragement, and love nothing I have accomplished would have been remotely possible.

TABLES AND FIGURES

Tables

Figures

PART ONE

INTRODUCTION

CHAPTER ONE

GLOBALIZATION, NEOLIBERALISM, AND
THE RASPUTIN STATE

There is so little to be said about globalization that is not cliché. Globalization, apparently, has the ability to either construct world peace, or rip the world apart. It is purported to create unimaginable wealth and equally devastating poverty. In many ways, I am taking the easy road by circumventing these meta-narratives and examining an artifact of this seemingly ubiquitous and all-encompassing phenomena: The problem of so-called state decline due to globalizing political ideology and systemic liberal market integration. Obviously, "the easy way out" is a rough road as well.

State decline is regularly understood as a bit of a misnomer. State institutions are neither dead, nor on life-support. However, the form of their continued relevance has shifted somewhat leading many to argue that the global political economic structures that manipulate state capacities are a much more worthy analytical focus. The problem is that despite the theoretical appeal of a distinctly global structural level of analysis, national populations are constantly interacting with the intermediary actors and institutions of respective states. To put it very simply, states continue to play an integral social role in the lives of respective populations. More to the point, national populations play much more of a contemporary role in facilitating state authority than many perspectives recognize. In fact, it is these populations that enable (or require) the state to return from a proclaimed death time and time again.

We can take, for instance, Canada and Québec as two interesting comparative examples and notice a few contradictory elements in both. One a federal state, the other a provincial sub-state, both represent an historical tendency to build state institutions often in opposition to each other as well as relatively distinct strategies for negotiating global political economic integration. While Québec is a provincial subordinate within the Canadian confederation, it is unique among provincial states with regards to its political autonomy and its influence over federal policies. This is not to say that federal policy must pass a Québec litmus test or that other provinces are summarily ignored. Alberta, for example, engaged in a bitter dispute over the federal National Energy Program in the early 1980s, arguing that the protectionist policies would limit provincial petroleum sales to the United States and therefore restrict provincial economic growth. Alberta would soon become an essential (along with Québec) supporter of trade liberalization in the late 1980s and heavily influencing the enactment of national bilateral and multilateral trade agreements. Ontario also has an extended history of influence, particularly due to its position as the demographic and, until recently, economic capital of the country. No other province, however, enjoys Québec's level of autonomy and influence, which is primarily due to its cultural history and ability to mobilize political support/opposition along nationalistic lines – more on this later.

Canada and Québec have long been viewed as embodying a social democratic or statist attitude towards social service provision (health care and education in particular), especially when compared with its southern neighbor. Similarly, few would argue that this history of nationalization and economic protectionism reflected anything other than a particular distinction in the North American political economy. Despite these superficial observations, Canada is a uniquely divided nation with severe identity issues, constant internal calls to divest federal authority from regional interests (energy and environment in Alberta, for example), and external calls to reduce the federal states regulatory authority and provide a more liberal economic environment to promote increased growth.

Québec, on the other hand, is usually first in the line of exemplars when it comes to discussion of regional autonomy and the role of globalization in "liberating" sub-state entities from the clutches of federal, multinational states. Québec (as well as Canada) is a truly global state with substantial foreign trade relationships, foreign political relationships, and an increasingly diversifying urban population drawn from all regions of the planet. By almost all measures, Québec has utilized this globalization era to both enhance its political autonomy and its economic opportunities. Despite these impressive achievements, Québec is riddled with contradiction due to its incredibly strong statist traditions. Public pensions, health care, education, childcare, energy production and distribution (among many other services) are dominated by state management, if not outright ownership and control. The Québec state is a major institutional player in the socio-economic mechanisms of the province, which, of course, brings it into direct conflict with the dominant political ideology of globalization – neoliberalism. According to neoliberal requisites, the state should be an ancillary institution to facilitate the free and unregulated operations of the liberal capitalist market economy. The contemporary political struggle in Québec today is largely between those who would maintain the statist traditions of the provincial state and the persistent demand by neoliberal proponents and structures to reduce the role of the state.

In both Canadian and Québec political economies, the state plays a varied role in the eyes of its citizens; however, each respective citizenry plays a similar role with regard to the federal and provincial states. Each respective electorate must legitimate the authority of each state (both in terms of institutions and actors). Without such legitimacy, actors are dismissed and institutions crumble in the face of withdrawn authority. In the cases of both Canada and Québec, this legitimacy has been traditionally maintained through *economic protectionist* means. The regulation of national economic mechanisms (including markets, employment, and production) coupled with the provision of social services ensured that the health of the national economy would be protected and the commensurate adversities that accompany capitalist operations would be mitigated to a certain extent. In return for these protections, national populations granted legitimate authority to each respective state. The primary question of this book is what happens when the ability to enact economic protections is reduced? Can states maintain legitimate authority without their primary strategic mechanism for doing so?

The Problem of Economic Protections

Economic protectionism, as a form of state regulation, has long been seen as an impediment to capital accumulation by most capitalist proponents. However, it has also served as an invaluable strategic mechanism to maintain institutional state legitimacy, which is, in turn, essential to the maintenance of social stability required for capital accumulation. In this sense, the state a requisite capitalist institution, but not merely for the promotion of capital interests – it must also maintain social conditions that make economic growth (and even operation) possible. One of the more effective means of maintaining social stability is the mitigation of the negative structural effects of capitalism such as systemic inequality, labor exploitation, and national market protection. Ironically, capitalism cannot legitimate itself and requires an institution to ensure popular acceptance of a socio-economic philosophy that requires systemic inequality (see Lowi 2005). If a state demonstrates an ability to protect the economic interests of national populations (ironically, from the dangers of the same system it is attempting to manage), those respective populations will likely continue to legitimate the authority of said state institutions.

But what happens if a state's capacity to implement economic protectionist policies is weakened or eliminated? This is precisely the challenge posed by the integration of neoliberalism, which seeks to reduce the economic regulatory capacities of state institutions and privilege private capital interests. The result is, of course, a decreased capacity to meet the economic protectionist demands of respective populations and a subsequent threat to state legitimacy. This reduction of economic protectionist capacity does not change the fact that social stability is still a requisite of capitalism nor does it change the fact that capitalism in general, and global capitalism in particular, has no institutional ability to promote social stability. Thus, the state must remain an institution with legitimated authority to maintain social stability for the purposes of legitimating capitalism, itself. The question still stands, however: How can the state maintain legitimate authority while at the same time reducing economic protectionist capabilities? As I will argue throughout this essay, an emergent alternative is the move away toward the integration of existing cultural norms and definitions that can be presented as distinctly national and thus serve to legitimate both the state and its political economic goals.

In order to illustrate this shift in legitimation strategies, an analytical framework, based on the Polanyian *double movement*, is presented in the following chapter. I am specifically interested in understanding the impact of political and economic policy convergence (i.e., neoliberalism in support of global liberal market capitalism) on the strategic maintenance of state legitimacy. How has the process of state-building changed in response to shifts in political ideological orthodoxy along with the acceleration of global liberal market capitalism? How (and why) has the definition of national culture been linked to the legitimation of state institutions and policies?

The cases of Canada and Québec are instructive in this regard, particularly due to their status as core capitalist societies, long histories of economic protectionism, uneven integration of neoliberalism, and distinct challenges in defining national culture. The fact that Québec is not a traditional state is addressed below; however, it is important to note that the characteristics that define state autonomy and global market integration are found in both cases. In addition, the comparison of inter-related state-building projects allows us to not only understand the role of distinct national culture but also how sub-state autonomy is enhanced through global political economic integration.

This comparison of Canada and Québec is made much more specific by focusing on several key aspects. First, distinct historical narratives influence divergent national cultural definitions (or at least attempts to define a singular national culture) and conditions that facilitate or inhibit state protectionist capacities. Second, both Canada and Québec are fully integrated into the global market system. Both have embraced the dictates of economic liberalization; however, Québec has retained its economic protectionist capacity (and active regulatory/ownership role) to a greater degree than Canada. There are several reasons for this distinction that will be discussed in subsequent chapters; however, it is important to note the fact that this sustained state protectionist role is constantly changing and not reflective of a resistance to global economic integration.

Third, the Canadian and Québec labor markets have long-relied on immigration for labor market growth to fuel commensurate overall economic growth. Immigration is, of course, directly tied to the definition of national identity and has culturally diversified in the post-war era. The demographic diversification of Canadian and Québec immigration is a direct result of changes in global labor migration and the sustained necessity of in-migration for both Canadian and Québec labor market expansion.

Fourth, as both societies accelerate cultural diversification as a result of shifts in labor migration demographics, both states have responded with institutionalized social policies designed to foster both social integration and provide a singular national cultural definition. Canadian *multicultural* policies and Québec *intercultural* policies are presented in comparative context as reactionary policies designed to facilitate labor market stability and social integration of diverse population groups, but also as progressive attempts to articulate a singular definition of national cultural identity. This comparison helps to illustrate divergent approaches to the social effects of global labor migration as well as state capacities, particularly in the neoliberal era (roughly, the mid-1980s to the present), to maintain social stability, foster economic growth, and manage national protectionist demands.

These integrative conditions make and examination of *multicultural* and *intercultural* policies particularly relevant and illuminating. But before we address the empirical bulk of this essay, it is essential point out a few preliminary assumptions.

Conceptual Foundations

The core assumption of this project is that neoliberal globalization reduces the economic protectionist capacity of traditional states. However, this is an uneven process that is made even more unpredictable when we examine the economic protectionist capacities of increasingly autonomous sub-states. While the economic protectionist capacity of many traditional states is reduced as they integrate more and more deeply into the global economic system, many sub-state institutions are able to resist this trend, in some cases significantly. I argue that one contributing factor for this uneven maintenance of economic protectionism is the ability to integrate a singular definition of national culture. This claim rests primarily on the issue of legitimacy. State authority, and subsequently its capacity to enact social and economic protectionist policies, is based on legitimacy granted by national populations. Traditionally, this legitimacy is derived from the state meeting economic protectionist expectations on the part of national populations.

Active participation in the global economic system requires adherence to neoliberal political ideology, specifically the reduction of economic protectionist policies[1] (see Peck and Tickell 2007; 1994; Prasad

---

[1] For instance, membership in the World Trade Organization (WTO) requires adherence to the principles of liberal capitalism. According to the WTO, "The system's overriding purpose is to help trade flow as freely as possible — so long as there are no undesirable side-effects — because this is important for economic development and well-being. That partly means removing obstacles. It also means ensuring that individuals, companies and governments know what the trade rules are around the world, and giving them the confidence that there will be no sudden changes of policy" (World Trade Organization, "Understanding the World Trade Organization," http://www.wto.org/english/thewto_e/whatis_e/tif_e/fact1_e.htm, retrieved August 2, 2010). In sum, sustained membership in the organization is designed to expand global trade opportunities, but membership is contingent on the perpetual restriction of economic protectionist measures geared towards international trade. While membership in the WTO does not necessitate state decline, per se, it does illustrate how the institutionalization of the global economic system encourages the restriction of state protectionist capacities.

2006; Jessop 2002). Thus, political economic globalization reduces the ability of states to maintain economic protectionist policies, and therefore threatens sustained state legitimacy. A reduction in state legitimacy can directly impact the institutional ability to enact and maintain policy initiatives (Howlett 2000; see also Cashore 2002). State capacity to maintain protectionist policies is therefore tied directly to its ability to maintain legitimate authority. If a state's legitimate authority is contingent on economic protectionism and that protectionist capacity is reduced or eliminated as a result of global political economic integration, that state's ability to maintain policy initiatives will erode. Conversely, if a state entity is able to find an alternative means of maintaining legitimacy, it will have greater capacity to maintain policy initiatives. I argue that, due to the particular conditions created by neoliberalism and global economic integration, a particularly effective alternative legitimation strategy is the utilization of monolithic national cultural definitions to legitimize state actions and policies.

If this claim, linking neoliberal state legitimacy with the integration of monolithic national cultural definitions, is accurate it helps to explain the rise of sub-state autonomy – particularly in multinational states. This book examines the economic protectionist and social policy capacities of Canada and Québec in the hopes that it will illustrate how the proximity of state institutions to respective national cultural definitions can be instrumental in providing necessary legitimacy for state institutions and policies. If state legitimacy is increasingly reliant on national culture (*writ large*) we should expect to see both a reduction of state protectionist/regulatory capacities due to state institution acquiescing to neoliberal demands and increased efforts on the part of state institutions to define and integrate an "acceptable" or politically efficacious definition of national culture. In the case of Canada, the federal state has implemented so-called neoliberal reforms while at the same time engaging in repeated efforts to articulate a singular Canadian national cultural definition. These strategic efforts to define a singular Canadian identity reflect both larger political economic goals and larger political economic ideological realities. In short, the form of Canadian "national identity construction" shifts as global political ideology shifts to neoliberalism. The institutional history of Canadian *multiculturalism* is examined in detail as an illustration of these pressures and commensurate changes in state protectionist capacity and willful compliance with neoliberal reductionist demands.

The comparison with Québec is in historical comparative context and focuses on the gradual process of legitimating (sub) state autonomy. Rather than explain sub-state autonomy through devolution or as the product of external structural conditions, I argue that sub-state autonomy is intentional, complicit with (rather than simply a product of) the project of global economic integration, and explicitly tied to culturally-oriented legitimation strategies. Thus, as Canadian economic protectionism and social policy autonomy are predictably eroded with greater neoliberal global integration, the Québec (sub) state has a greater capacity to maintain economic protectionist and social policy initiatives due to its proximity to a singular definition of national culture – which enhances state legitimate authority in this contemporary era of neoliberal globalization.

In fact, it is this connection to a specific national cultural definition that not only facilitates sub-state development in Québec, but also differentiates the province from others within a larger federal system. Earlier, the claim was made that Québec enjoys an autonomy and influence that is great than that of other Canadian provinces. This claim is made with a holistic, rather than episodic, eye to the history of federal-provincial relations. The debate over provincial autonomy is historically derived from disagreement over legal federal authority (rooted in the British North American Act) and the assumption that centralized federal control over economic matters is detrimental to the economic health of a particular province.

The latter is exemplified by the Alberta's strident calls in the early 1980's for provincial autonomy in the area of natural resource management as well as a reduction of federal authority over trade regulations. In 1980, the federal government embarked on a policy of national energy security following the energy crises of the 1970s; the foundation of which was a reorientation of Albertan petroleum from American to Canadian markets... at lower-than-market prices set by the Canadian government. While the intent was to supply the nation with affordable petroleum, the result was a dramatic decrease in energy sector profits in a province (Alberta) that was nearly dependent on oil revenues. In response, Alberta intensified its calls for increased provincial autonomy as well as an institutionalization of liberal trade policies that would reopen American markets. Alberta would be an instrumental partner in promoting federal trade liberalization policies in the late 1980s as well as national bilateral and multilateral trade agreements that also met its (provincial) economic demands.

The point here is that provincial autonomy is not the exclusive domain of Québec. However, while most calls for provincial autonomy and accompanying efforts to expand provincial/sub-state political authority are contingent on either shifting economic conditions or a perceived federal encroachment on provincial economic matters, Québec's calls for autonomy have been rooted in a persistent demand that the distinctions of Francophone Québec be protected locally. The cultural basis of Québec's calls for provincial autonomy creates a ubiquity to its sub-state development efforts. No other province has similar cultural autonomy claims and therefore do not share Québec's persistent and nearly universal support for sub-state autonomy. The question informing this larger study is whether this persistent cultural basis supporting calls for increased sub-state autonomy is affected by global political economic integration.

Economic Globalization and the End of the State

For many, the concept of globalization functions in much the same way as a public political figure: simultaneously lionized by some as a panacea (*cf.* Friedman 2000) and vilified by others (*cf.* Falk 1999) as the primary cause of existent societal adversity. It seems obvious to many that something distinct is reshaping social interaction at multiple levels, but just what that something is commonly eludes specific description. As a result, the expansive sub-field of globalization studies cannot be called unified or consensual, which is of course antithetical to the process of understanding globalization in any singular theoretical fashion. This problem has led to the conclusion that theorizing globalization is an impossible task and one that should be abandoned in favor of other, more useful, approaches (see Rosenberg 2005; 2000).

While a generally applicable theory of globalization may, in fact, be a pipe dream, the call to move away from globalization theories is much more analytical than practical. That is, no one seriously argues that global interconnection and political economic integration are not occurring and few argue that this integrative process is not transformative. One of the more dramatic of these transformative claims is that the nation-state is being made irrelevant by global political ideologies and institutions and circumvented by global economic activity.

These claims of state decline peaked in the mid-1990s with Kenichi Omahe's *The End of the Nation State* (1995), Susan Strong's *The Retreat of the State* (1996), and Saskia Sassen's *Losing Control?* (1996) providing just a few notable examples of this seemingly ubiquitous conclusion. Of course the sheer volume of literature and its definitive tone was destined to elicit an equally strong refutation with Linda Weiss' *The Myth of the Powerless State* (1998), Robert Boyer and Daniel Drache's edited collection *States Against Markets* (1996), and Michael Mann's wonderfully titled "Has Globalization Ended the Rise and Rise of the Nation-State?" (1997) as particularly exemplary studies. An inevitable dichotomy emerged that limited theoretical development opportunities (as dichotomies are wont to do) by subsuming analyses under the "either/or" categories of state and globalization theories. As Hobson and Ramesh accurately state, "the debate tends to promote a zero-sum conception of power in which there is a trade-off between global structures and states-as-agents" (2002, 7).

Following the lead of many who have called for a more reasoned approach toward the effects of global integration, this book seeks not to articulate a grand theory of globalization, rather it attempts to begin theorizing the state in an era of globalization. Specifically, it examines the shifting strategies of state legitimation motivated by structural changes that occur as respective national states integrate into the global neoliberal political economic system. I argue that political economic globalization does work to reduce state regulatory capacities and therefore the general claim that globalization (specifically operationalized below) precipitates state decline is ostensibly accurate. However, following the lead of David Held (1995; 1999), Clyde Barrow (2005), and others, I contend that the global political economic system explicitly requires state institutions to maintain local social stability and heterogeneity of economic conditions. The result is a global political economic system based on authoritative state institutions that ensure social stability for the purpose of maintaining positive capital accumulation conditions.

Put another way, economic globalization champions liberal capitalism, which demands limited, if not non-existent, governmental regulatory power. Of course, the regulatory capacity of states is largely set by political actors and institutions; therefore, if deregulation is to be the goal, then a political ideology must be integrated into governing discourses. Neoliberalism, or the political ideology reinforcing liberal capitalism, emerged in the late 1970s as that political mechanism that gave proponents such as Augusto Pinochet, Ronald Reagan, and Margaret Thatcher the ideological platform necessary to begin dismantling state regulatory capacity and "liberate" capital accumulation from constraining state management (see Harvey 2007; Prasad 2006). Deregulation of production, labor, trade, and the evisceration of public expenditures all form primary points of neoliberal emphasis in the so-called "Washington Consensus" that led policy convergence efforts throughout the 1990s (see Williamson, 1993; Stiglitz *et al.* 2006).

This intentional weakening of state regulatory mechanisms and institutions disrupts the traditional social role of the state; specifically, the state traditionally maintains social stability through the mitigation of adverse conditions through the provision of social services and managing economic conditions such as inflation and access to market opportunities for respective national populations. For example, a state might protect national markets threatened by foreign competition such as the American steel industry. These protections might come in the form of tariffs or subsidies, but are intended to facilitate capital accumulation and employment in sectors threatened by external competition.

Similarly, states have traditionally been at the forefront of direct social service provision to mitigate the effects of systemic inequality or to facilitate integration into the labor market. From unemployment payments or subsistence and housing assistance to public education and health care, social service provision can be broad raging and cross-class. These economic protections served to maintain popular support for both capital accumulation and state authority. The former, capital accumulation, seems relatively obvious. National capital interests are met through the protection of local markets, protection from foreign competition, and through active subsidiary support from the state. The latter is less obvious, but arguably more important to overall systemic maintenance.

State authority must be legitimated. In advanced capitalist, democratic states, that legitimacy comes from national populations that continually grant and withdraw support for state institutions and actors. The purpose of the state as it pertains to national popular legitimation is as a protectionist institution (Marshall 1964; Smith 1981, 678–8). If protectionist demands are met, political leaders/institutions are granted legitimate authority. National populations demand protection from adverse conditions – in the modern era, the dominant form

of protectionism is economic, which reflects the primary social structure of capitalism that defines modernity[2]. State institutions employ
economic protectionist strategies to simultaneously encourage national
capital accumulation and address adverse economic conditions among
national populations in exchange for legitimate authority.

Given this traditional relationship between state authority and
economic protectionism, the contemporary challenge of neoliberal
economic globalization raises a curious question: If economic protectionist capacity is diminished as states integrate neoliberal ideology,
how is legitimate authority maintained? It is important to note that
legitimacy is met, in political contexts, through the provision of protection. If a particular form of protectionism (economic) is reduced or
eliminated, what other form of protection can be strategically utilized
to maintain legitimacy? That is, how are protectionist demands met if
the primary strategic alternative is incompatible with the dominant
political ideology?

Building the Neoliberal State?

The decline of state protectionist capacities has obviously encouraged
the belief that the state may be an increasingly arcane institution. The
danger, of course, is that the very concept of state decline becomes a
forgone conclusion and not a problematic condition for further study.
Some scholars have worked to overcome these tendencies and prob-
lematize the effects of so-called state decline. These efforts to look
more deeply at the effects of state decline are helpful in a methodological sense, but fall short of expanding our understanding of the state.
These analyses commonly fall into two conceptual categories that
emphasize the causal outcomes of state decline.

First, many argue that traditional states, robbed of regulatory
authority and unable to maintain social expenditures, divest themselves of these responsibilities by granting increased policy autonomy

---

[2] An interesting study of the modern nature of economic protectionism is found in
Erik Reinert's (1999) historical analysis examining the role of the state in promoting
market development. He argues that the so-called "tension" between state regulatory
protectionism and market liberation is a contemporary observation based on the fact
that state regulatory capacities were essential in the initial creation and nurturing of
national market economies. This is, of course, commensurate with a Polanyian understanding of national economic development.

to sub-state entities (see Baskaran 2009; Bullman 1996; Sharma 2005). This process of decentralization has become a common feature of the "globalization era", however, the primary point of emphasis here is that the causal explanation for this decentralization is emergent global systemic power. Sub-state autonomy is almost an accidental assumption of social protectionist responsibilities that are underfunded and often thrust upon political structures unprepared for such expansive authority and responsibilities (see Kristiansen and Santoso 2006; see also Laughlin 2000). From this perspective the development of sub-state autonomy is less the result of active efforts on the part of sub-state political entities (actors and/or institutions) and more the result of externally imposed traditional state decline.

The second conceptual category understands state decline to occur in much the same way (through neoliberal fiat), but focuses more on the political power vacuum resulting from traditional state decline. The emphasis is on the mobilization of identity-centered, culturally-oriented non-state movements (Castells 2004; Piven 1995; see also Touraine 1998; Melucci 1996). From this point of view, state decline is an embedded process that alters more than just state protectionist capacity. The encroaching ideology of neoliberalism, reinforcing the dominance of neoclassical economic theory, alters the very normative acceptance of class-oriented social action. In other words, the ideological shift to a market-oriented political economy of course results in declining state protectionist capacities, but at the same time destroys movements organized for the purpose of maximizing state economic protectionist benefits. Labor and other class-centric movements lose an ideological area in which to fight, which eventually leads to their slow demise as effective mechanisms for pressuring state institutions for increased economic protections (see Piven 1995; Waterman 1998).

As the economic protectionist capacity of the state declines, so too does its legitimate authority which both reduces the authority of economic protectionist movements (i.e., labor) and reduces the belief that state institutions could meet requisite protectionist demands. The combination encourages identity-centered mobilization – a form of organization that was linked not to (theoretically) an inclusive conceptualization of class, but toward pre-existing cultural norms. The key point of emphasis here is the movement of political power away from both state institutions and the possibility of economic protectionism toward identity-centered movements (i.e., identity politics) and the circumvention of traditional state political authority.

Both of these perspectives are predicated on the foundation of state decline as less a process to be understood and more a foregone conclusion. Global political economic structures eviscerate state responsibilities and consequently its legitimacy, which forces it to divest governance responsibilities to sub-state entities. Add to that the rise of identity-centered movements that gain power not through their adherence to an official state ideology but through their connection to normative local culture. Under attack from above and below, the state is commonly understood to be an institution in decline and therefore unworthy of sustained theorization and study. Simply put, I disagree.

This project seeks to understand state decline, strategies to maintain legitimacy, and the increased efficacy of culture in synthetic context. The basic assumptions from both aforementioned perspectives are understood to be basically accurate, but only in isolation. Taken together, the devolution of state policy responsibilities and the rise of identity mobilization are mechanical functions in a larger systemic process that occur within the context of *sustained* state authority – albeit a context that may not replicate the traditional multinational nation-state model. In this regard, this is an analysis of strategic state building in the globalization era. The contextual reality of state adaptation amid mutable political economic conditions requires a more flexible definition of the "state." If traditional states are adjusting their institutional form, what effect does this adaptive process have on sub-state entities? Does it enhance their developmental efficacy or are these sub-state entities subject to the same devolutionary pressures as traditional nation-states?

I argue state legitimacy is enhanced through the ability to link with dominant normative culture in the current neoliberal era – that is, state entities that successfully tie state institutions to singular cultural definitions can achieve a greater level of legitimate authority, which enables their active assumption of increased policy autonomy. Despite the erosion of traditional legitimation strategies, states can maintain legitimacy through increasingly cultural means. This has even more salience with respect to contemporary sub-state development. Contrary to the assumptions of some, sub-state autonomy is not an accidental artifact of a runaway global economy, nor is the increased efficacy of cultural mobilization exclusive of state institutions. Sub-states have emerged (1) as active participants in the global political economy, (2) increasingly reliant on culture/national identity for legitimation purposes, but also (3) more able to maintain economic protections than their traditional counterparts.

The empirical portions of this book are intended to compare Canada, as a traditional state, with Québec, as a sub-state, for the purpose of illustrating the following:

- Political economic globalization, specifically neoliberal political ideology and liberalized trade and financialization, create unique conditions that discourage state economic protectionist capacity, which damages state legitimacy;
- This combination of neoliberal pressures and weakened legitimate authority, decrease the capacity of state institutions to maintain social policy initiatives;
- State capacity to maintain social policy initiatives and economic protectionism, while also willfully integrating into the global political economic system, is enhanced with sustained legitimate authority;
- Legitimate authority, in the context of neoliberal globalization, is increasingly dependent on the integration of national cultural protectionist strategies

Specifically, this book attempts to show how Québec has enhanced its legitimate authority and social policy capacities, as well as sustaining its economic protectionist capacity, through the utilization of national cultural protectionist strategies. In comparison, the traditional state of Canada has undergone a process of divestment in the form of decentralization, reduced funding, and privatization. The structural motivations for these reductions in policy capacity are explicitly tied to neoliberal dictates and help to illustrate the reduced capacity for economic protectionism and social policy maintenance in the neoliberal era. Through this juxtaposition, we are able to gain greater insights into (1) how sub-state autonomy is enhanced in the contemporary era and (2) linking the increased efficacy of national identity to the necessity of maintaining legitimate authority by state and sub-state entities.

A brief note on the use of Québec as a comparative example of a nation-state is required. A cursory glance would show a methodological level of analysis problem that works to undermine any theoretical conclusions before the analysis has even taken place. This need not be a problem either on an empirical level or in terms of generating a theoretical understanding of nation-state construction and transformation. I argue that the unique history of Québec, including the cultural process of nation-building that has occurred concurrently with the Canadian nationalist project, as well as the development of autonomous governmental controls and authority make it relatively simple to show that Québec operates as a limited but functional nation-state both domestically and internationally. Castells makes a similar conceptual leap with his term "national quasi-state" to describe the experience of Québec as exemplary of "the development of nations that stop at the threshold of statehood, but force their parent state to adapt, and cede sovereignty..." (Castells 2004, 55). While this articulation of Québec as a limited nation-state is helpful, his understanding that the province "stop[ped] at the threshold of statehood" is limiting but not surprising. Castells' project is clearly focused on an understanding of the nation as a concept of increasing importance. His project is centered on the proposition that nations have increased in importance while states have simultaneously declined in their capacity as institutions of power. This proposition is supported by the established understanding that the nation is implicitly distinct from the state and thus enables the dual motions of national ascendancy and state decline in this contemporary era.

This perspective ignores the historic increase in autonomous state authority granted to Québec by the Canadian government in the fields of education, diplomacy, immigration, and trade. Granted, this autonomy is limited and any statement that understands Québec as a fully autonomous nation-state would be erroneous. Analytically, however, the increase in Québec state autonomy is undeniable and has created a situation in which the authority of Québec supersedes that of the Canadian federal government in many situations. Of course, the converse is true as Québec must defer to Canadian authority in many more instances.

As previously stated in this chapter, the selection of Québec is contingent on its ability to link to a cultural legitimation strategy. Other provinces have enhanced their provincial autonomy and developed strong sub-state institutions, but these efforts are primarily based on economic provincial self-interest. This conditional motivation is inhibiting in one very important way: Canadian provinces are not legally able to engage in bi- or multilateral trade agreements with non-Canadian states. For example, Alberta is not able to enter into a formal bilateral trade agreement with its largest export market (the United States) and is therefore subject to the trade conditions negotiated by the federal government.

Given, Alberta's strong support for federal trade liberalization has resulted in an what the provincial state sees as an improved trade climate, it is important to note that sub-state economic autonomy is limited. One interesting outcome of this limitation has been the development (indeed, proliferation) of bilateral and multilateral *provincial* trade agreements. These types of agreements were facilitated by the 1994 Agreement on Internal Trade between federal and provincial governments, which encouraged trans-provincial trade through the reduction of provincial trade protections. Recently, several interprovincial agreements, including the 2009 Ontario-Québec Trade and Cooperation Agreement and the contentious Trade, Investment, and Labour Mobility Agreement (TILMA) between British Columbia, Alberta and Saskatchewan, have been emblematic of this increased sub-state interest in maximizing economic growth opportunities.

While provincial autonomy is Canada is fairly ubiquitous (at varying levels), its limitations must be recognized. Aside from Québec, sub-state autonomy efforts are primarily centered on creating the most beneficial economics conditions based on local interests and demands. These motivations run into a ceiling due to the aforementioned institutional limitations, which essentially creates singular issue-centered motivations but no real sustainable foundation for strategic sub-state building – aside from the elimination of federal authority over national economic development. Québec, on the other hand, does not limit its strategic autonomy to economic matters and therefore has greater potential for sustained state-building efforts, which makes it unique among Canadian provinces.

I would argue that the autonomy of the Québec state, particularly with respect to immigration and culture, in conjunction with a strong nationalist project creates a situation in which the nation-state designation can be analytically applied to both Canada and Québec. As I will show in subsequent historical background chapters, both Canada and Québec have struggled to construct viable nation-states since the mid-1700s and a superficial assumption that Québec cannot be defined as a form of nation-state due to its subsumed provincial position within Canada is incorrect and belies a limited view of both nation and state.

Format of the Book

In order to address these issues and questions, I focus on the contemporary political economic histories of Canada and Québec in an embedded global context. That is, I hope to illustrate first, that both entities are integrated into the global economic system (albeit in differentiated ways) and second, how that integrative process alters the relationship between states and nations with a particular emphasis on strategies of state legitimation. The former is a necessary step that illustrates the conditional differences that emerge as a respective country moves toward deeper global integration. The latter moves beyond description and allows a more comprehensive analysis of how national populations are impacted by globalization, how states respond to these altered socio-economic conditions, and how legitimate authority is maintained in an environment of rapid change.

The structure of this book is designed to emphasize important points and conceptual relationships that are understood as essential to any comprehensive analysis of state legitimacy in the contemporary era. More to the point however, the structure is also meant to convey the cumulative effects of transformative globalization. This is not to argue that globalization is a reified concept, nor do I explicitly focus on the mechanics of global economics. Rather, I have organized this book in a way that will hopefully emphasize the nature of these changes in a more holistic, but focused, manner.

Chapters One and Two establish the conceptual and theoretical framework for the empirical comparison that comprises the bulk of the project. The current chapter provides necessary background information and establishes the analytical focus on the study. Chapter Two begins the process of conceptualizing state decline and establishing an analytical framework. The process of global political economic integration is juxtaposed with the systemic role of the state in both embedded liberal and neoliberal contexts. The importance of economic protectionism as an embedded liberal legitimation mechanism is presented and the problem of legitimation in a neoliberal ideological context is presented in more detail. Finally, a Polanyian analytical framework is presented that seeks to augment existing perspective on the neoliberal state through an understanding of the state as a mediating institution between global political economic structures and national populations.

Chapters Three and Four provide particular historical narratives for Canada and Québec, respectively. In Chapter Three, the history of Canada from First Nations settlement through the contemporary era is meant to establish a central narrative not in any monolithic or official analytical capacity, but to simply posit the existence of a central narrative. Chapter Four replicates this process with Québec – the purpose of which is to establish distinct historical narratives. While the fact that Québec is a social and political entity subsumed in the national context of Canada, both have developed in relative distinction with particular (and important) divergences (as previously stated in this chapter). The purpose of presenting both historical narratives is to reinforce the reality of an autonomous, yet inexorably connected, social history. One cannot understand national identity without an attempt to recognize the perceptual autonomy of a national historical narrative. Conversely, no national culture (or historical narrative) develops in isolation – this is even more the case in Canada and Québec, where neither national identity could emerge as they have without the other. Thus, the autonomy and interconnectedness of both national histories exist in a seemingly contradictory reality.

Chapters Five through Seven consist of a comparative-historical analysis of (1) global economic integration of Canada and Québec, (2) economic protectionist capacities in Canada and Québec, (3) demographic change resulting from shifts in labor migration, and (4) a comparative analysis of cultural pluralist policies (Canadian multiculturalism and Québec interculturalism). The purpose of these chapters is to illustrate the role state institutions play in managing and promoting global economic integration as well as how these institutional entities adapt to changing conditions motivated by increased globalization. While some chapters offer extended historical background information, the primary comparative analyses examine state activities and conditions from 1970 through the present.

Five examines the empirical claim that Canada and Québec are, in fact, increasingly integrated in global markets. This chapter illustrates the nature of global economic integration in a local context as well as identifying commensurate challenges to economic protectionist capacities in both locations. Chapter Six examines immigration policies and demographic change in both national contexts with explicit emphasis on the nature of labor migration in the contemporary era of increased global integration. Chapter Seven juxtaposes Canadian multicultural and Québec intercultural responses to shifting demographic realities resulting from global integrationist opportunities and sustained demands for labor market expansion to match capital accumulation demands. Chapter Eight offers several concluding comments including contemporary state responses to the sustained neoliberalization of Canada and Québec. The federal effort to develop an inclusive

"Brand Canada" represents a distinctly neoliberal effort to define
national culture while promoting private capital interests, while the
recent debate over "reasonable accommodation" in Québec illustrates
the challenges of presenting a pluralist national cultural definition in a
society with strong monolithic national cultural history. Both efforts
and challenges are representative of legitimation challenges in the contemporary era and point to several possible avenues for policy development as other states struggle to maintain legitimate authority in the
face of neoliberal globalization. These potential policy responses,
I argue, are increasingly dependent on the ability of a state to define a
respective national culture in order to withstand neoliberal reductionist pressures.

The primary emphasis of this concluding chapter is to point out the
potential efficacy of a reconceptualized double movement framework
for the analysis of state legitimacy and for explaining the increased role
of national culture in the rhetorical and policy making strategies of
state institutions. It also points out the need to focus on the relationship between global economic and national legitimating factors – in
the contemporary neoliberal era, economic growth through state economic protectionist decline can carry latent consequences that may
inhibit social stability and endanger integration efforts in multinational states. But before these claims can be made, we first have to
establish the theoretical foundation for this particular look at how globalization influences state policy and how this relationship enables
national cultural mobilization.

CHAPTER TWO

LEGITIMATING STATE AUTHORITY IN AN AGE OF NEOLIBERAL GLOBALIZATION

The concept of state decline has the unique honor of being both a causal outcome and a causal motivator. On the one hand, the diverse processes of globalization contribute to the decline of traditional state authority through such diverse processes as social welfare retrenchment, transnational capital mobility, international non-governmental organisation, and others. In effect, globalization processes have weakened traditional authority and policy capacities of respective state institutions. On the other hand, state decline has also been cited as the primary causal factor in motivating another phenomenon of the globalization era: the rise in national cultural conflict and mobilisation. The resurgence of religious influence in American politics is a useful exemplar that has received considerable attention: "Religion has always been a political subtext in the U.S., but in the past few decades the salience and strategic use of religion have become ascendant in a manner not seen before in modern American political history" (Domke and Coe 2007, 54). Attempts to explain the increased efficacy of local culture in political mobilisation reach the relatively common conclusion that reduced state authority, a function of increased global integration, facilitates the rise of national popular challenges centered on local cultural definitions.

There are two significant problems with these basic assumptions concerning globalization, state institutions, and national populations. First, there is substantial evidence that questions the general conclusion of state decline. While states may be adapting to shifting geopolitical and global economic conditions, they still retain considerable authority. Second, while a decline in state authoritative control may contribute to a diffusion of power – manifested through cultural means – we have yet to develop a significant methodological mechanism for examining this relationship between state institutions of sustained authority and the increased efficacy of specific national cultural definitions.

This essay examines the role of monolithic national culture as a contemporary state legitimation strategy. The predicate assumptions for this essay is as follows: (1) The contemporary era of global political economic integration encourages a market-oriented, neoliberal ideology in advanced capitalist states, which reduces state capacities to meet national protectionist demands through economic means. (2) As a result, state institutions in such situations commonly experience a decline in legitimate authority as they fail to meet the social protectionist demands of respective national populations. (3) In order to maintain legitimacy, state institutions seek alternative means to meet national protectionist demands. A common legitimation strategy in the contemporary neoliberal era involves integrating monolithic national culture into state institutional agendas and activities.

An analytical framework based on Karl Polanyi's double movement concept as a means to examine the process of neoliberal state legitimation is presented here. The double movement framework is reconceptualised to reflect changes in neoliberal state economic protectionist capacity and emphasise the phenomenon of *cultural* protectionism as a legitimation strategy. This framework is then applied to a comparative analysis of Canada and Québec policy efficacy in the areas of economic protectionist and social integration policies. This case illustrates the efficacy of monolithic national cultural definitions in legitimising state institutional entities. It also offers an excellent depiction of the relationship between neoliberal ideology and the limitations of economic protectionism.

Globalization and the Decline of the State

The concept of state decline is predicated on two empirical developments. First, the demise of the Bretton Woods system enabled the rise of global financial capital mobility which, in turn, enabled subsequent production mobility that worked to create the intersecting global commodity chains that typify global capitalism today (see Robinson 2004; Farazmand 1999; Gereffi and Korzeniewicz 1994). Second, the increasing power of transnational finance, coupled with successive fiscal crises during the 1970s in advance capitalist states, facilitated the rise of neoliberalism, a political ideology championing market forces over state regulation, in support of a shift away from Keynesian economic theory to a neoclassical/monetarist perspective.

Institutional Rise, Decline, and Fall

The Bretton Woods Agreements of 1944 revived the project of global economic integration that collapsed in 1914. Institutional control mechanisms were created in the form of the International Monetary Fund (IMF) and International Bank of Reconstruction and Development (IBRD). The latter is better known by its contemporary title, the World Bank, which was formed in 1946. In addition, a common international currency medium, the United States Dollar, was confirmed as the official currency of the revived global economic system.

A separate set of agreements liberalizing trade and subsequently facilitating international financial transfers was signed in 1947. The General Agreement on Trade and Tariffs (GATT) was created as a multilateral agreement guiding liberal trade relationships that existed in concert with, but autonomous from, the Bretton Woods institutions. For Canada, involvement in the IMF and the World Bank represented an institutional arrangement that made the country a contributing partner in the project of global economic integration. Canada, as a GATT signatory, implicitly agreed to adhere to the standards and norms of liberal trade – namely, the reduction of national trade protections such as tariffs and preferential trade relationships. One of the important aspects of GATT was the opening of financial investment opportunities among signatories in addition to its hegemonic "goal to establish a world trade regime or universal rules for the conduct of commercial policy" (Whitman 1977, cited in Gilpin 1987, 191). Though the early emphasis on global economic interaction was focused on trade, the establishment of global regulatory institutions also enabled the liberalization of financial capital that resulted in the "takeoff of financial globalization in the 1970s" (Robinson 2004, 26).

The performance of the post-war global economic system was encouraging for systemic advocates. In the words of James Foreman-Peck, the international economy "boomed...between the end of the Korean War and the oil crises of the 1970s" (Foreman-Peck 1995, 258). Industrial production and economic growth expanded significantly during this period. Immediate post-war growth was most dramatic in North America where increases in growth between 1938 and 1948 were approximately 74% in Canada and 65% in the United States (Maddison 1964, 80; Maddison 2003, 85–89). This situation, however, belied a flawed relationship with Europe that would ultimately lead to the collapse of the Bretton Woods system.

The system functioned in a unique way as the US (the producer of the official international exchange currency) was encouraged to run a budget deficit in order to maintain global dollar liquidity. The massive influx of American dollars into the global market offered an opportunity to European financial institutions. Unimpeded by the fiscal controls of

the US Federal Reserve Bank (primarily constraints on short-term interest payments), the "Eurodollar market" began to accumulate a large
investment surplus, in part from US multinational investment, but
also from other global investment interests. This situation resulted in
nearly half of the US money supply existing "outside any kind of control whatsoever by the U.S. banking authorities" (Pool and Stamos
1989, 7).

   In addition to macro-economic problems, more bilateral economic
issues emerged to prove the post-war economic boom unsustaina-
ble. The reconstruction of devastated European regions required vast
amounts of capital and manufactured materials, thus fueling this
massive increase in Canadian (and American) economic growth and
production. Once European reconstruction recovered, in terms of its
productive capacity and commensurate economic growth, the need for
capital and materials from abroad was reduced. This is reflected in subsequent drops in Canadian economic growth (declining to approximately 4% in Canada and 3% in the US) from 1950 to 1960 (Scammell
1980, 53; see also Maddison 1964).

   European recovery, coupled with the emergence of an unfettered
trade in American currency, contributed to a gradual decrease in systemic confidence throughout the 1960s. Isaak contends that the very
structure of the Bretton Woods system was flawed due to the fact that
the "constant outflow of dollars from the United States undermined
the very monetary system it serviced" (Isaak 2000, 43). He also identifies 1960 as a historical marker in the decline of the Bretton Woods
system, as "foreign dollar holdings exceeded American gold reserves
for the first time" (ibid.). While it would take another eleven years
for the institutional economic system to collapse, the foundations for
declining confidence in the disciplinary mechanism of the American
dollar had, by 1960, been laid.

   Relatively strong national economic performance in Europe and
North America coupled with this decline in global systemic efficacy
contributed to the retrenchment of national economies throughout the
late 1960s (Gilpin 1987; O'Brien and Williams 2004; Strange 1985).
This was particularly apparent in Canada as the first Trudeau government (elected in 1968) consistently cautioned against increased foreign investment and any weakening of national economic protections,
largely in response to persistent calls for liberalized trade relationships
with the United States (Canada FAIT 2005; Clement and Williams
1989; Hart 2002; Howlett et al. 1999; Randall and Thompson 2002).

In 1971, faced with a number of domestic political pressures (demands for protectionism, a trade deficit, and a pending election) and international pressures (a decline in confidence due to the expansion of an inflated dollar and the inability of the US to match its gold-convertibility responsibilities), Richard Nixon ended dollar to gold convertibility. This action effectively ended the Bretton Woods system by abandoning the primary disciplinary mechanism designed to stabilize the global currency unit (the U.S. Dollar). The effect was to confirm the suspicions within the international community that the Bretton Woods system was in decline throughout the 1960s. The effect was the wholesale embrace of nationalist Keynesian economic strategies throughout the advanced capitalist world.

While the decade of the 1970s can be safely understood as a period of economic nationalization, the Canadian experience illustrates a significant and contradictory shift in national economic policy. Canada's political economic nationalism during this period emerged in stark contrast with its "historical dependence on international trade" (Howlett *et al.* 1999, 123) that defines Canadian political economic history – with the exception of the first Trudeau Administration (1968–1979) in which nationalization of natural resource industries and a general climate of national economic protectionism reigned.

It is an unlikely coincidence that this unique period of Canadian political economic nationalism coincided with the period of global economic systemic collapse. Neither was Canadian economic nationalism unique, as this condition became the international norm due to the lack of a viable global systemic alternative. The actions of the Nixon Administration in 1971 precipitated the collapse of the Bretton Woods system and confidence in the sole currency medium was shattered. Without disciplinary mechanisms ensuring a stable global currency, the institutions of the global economic system could not enforce the system of liberal trade that was fostered in the previous twenty years. The organizational effectiveness of the established global political economic regulatory institutions was sharply reduced.

Transnational Finance

That the early 1970s through the mid-1980s represented a period of economic nationalization due to the collapse of the institutional global economic system is clear. However, the legacy of political agreements facilitating financial capital mobility, notably the persistence of GATT agreements in conditioning international financial trade, provided continued opportunities for global private capital investment. Subsequent expansion of global financial investment occurred primarily in the area of national currency speculation (a lucrative endeavor given the positive national economic conditions of the era) but also in promoting modernization/industrialization investment throughout the developing world (Gareffi 2005; Landsberg 1979; Scott and Storper 2003).

Although the regulatory institutions of the global system were left virtually powerless, global trade, particularly financial exchanges, did not cease. In the case of Canada, international financial exchanges increased dramatically in the 1970s over that of the 1960s. Canadian FDI outflows for the decade of the 1970s totaled almost $3 billion[1] – a dramatic increase over the decade of the 1960s in which FDI outflows totaled $246 million.

Table 1. Change in Canadian foreign direct investment outflow, 1950–1980

Year	FDI outflow change (in millions)
1950	18
1960	146
1970	246
1980	2,920

Source: CANSIM Table 376-0015, Balance of International Payments, FDI 1946–2004

Clearly, the collapse of the Bretton Woods system had little effect on the acceleration of transnational capital exchange and accumulation. In fact, quite the opposite occurred as private capital was functionally deregulated and increasingly autonomous from any form of state regulatory control. In other words, the collapse of the institutional global economic system gave rise to the private transnational capitalist system. States (i.e., the Canadian federal government) were forced to respond to changes motivated by transnational capital flows that were increasingly outside its governmental control.

---

[1] All dollar figures are in Canadian Dollars unless otherwise noted.

Focusing on the increasingly autonomous and mobile nature of financial capital in the post-Bretton Woods era explains the seemingly contradictory process of global institutional decline, the resultant period of national economic retrenchment, and the simultaneous expansion of transnational capital exchange[2]. As the institutional controls of the global economy declined in the late 1960s, state institutions began to increasingly protect and support national economic interests. State welfare spending, subsidies, and economic nationalization projects increased in Canada as they did throughout the advanced capitalist world. This generated desired increases in industrial production and capital accumulation in manufacturing sectors (Gilpin 1987; Howlett *et al.* 1999).

This renewed interested in *national* economic production also generated commensurate demand among private capital entities for inexpensive labor to fuel this growth in productivity. Transnational financial capital acted in the interests of the private entities in support of facilitating labor supply. The combination of liberalized trade arrangements inherent in such agreements such as GATT and the decline of regulatory institutions created an opportunity for private financial capital to be "liberated" from its traditional subordinated position with respect to state and international governmental controls. According to Robinson:

> ...globalization redefines the phase of distribution in the accumulation of capital in relation to nation-states. This means that the circulation of capital – of the wealth produced in the capitalist production process – tends to become delinked from production and removed more directly from political and institutional control in relation to earlier epochs (Robinson 2004, 40).[3]

This detachment of financial capital from state control created a condition in which private capital could influence socio-economic change *exclusive* of state oversight and control. Such economic shifts do not

---

[2] More to the point, Canadian FDI outflows increased a staggering 1087% throughout the decade of the 1970s during a period of global economic institutional degeneration.

[3] It should be noted that Robinson understands this process of capital transnationalization to be much more recent – a result of the late 1970s petro-dollar recycling phenomenon that led to a massive expansion in financial liquidity and transaction. I would argue that while this certainly led to the tremendous increases in global financial capital exchanges we are currently experiencing, the foundations for these processes were laid much earlier.

occur in a societal vacuum. Given the role the state as a mechanism of political economic regulation and protection, a political vehicle was required to empower capital while reducing the capacity of the state to regulate and manage these same capitalist activities. That vehicle came in the ideological form of neoliberalism.

Neoliberalism is defined here as a political economic ideology that prioritizes private market functions and advocates a reduced regulatory role for state institutions. Simply put, neoliberalism champions several policy-level initiatives: (1) State reduction in terms of regulatory capacity, social spending, and taxation, (2) privatization of public services, and (3) the liberalization of trade restrictions in both domestic and international contexts. Therefore, for an advocate of neoliberalism, the state is understood as an impediment to economic growth due to excessive taxation (to fund social service spending), excessive regulation (of economic activities and in other spheres including labor and environmental regulations), and restrictive of trade (traditionally understood as trade protectionism). The ideology is essentially one that places significant faith in neoclassical economic theories advocating a minimalist state that simply protects the access to and freedom of market mechanisms. Further, neoclassical economic theory (and by extension, neoliberalism) argues that the state is largely redundant due to implicit regulatory mechanisms embedded in market capitalism – this, of course, facilitates the neoliberal claim that privatization of public spending is an effective way to both enhance capital accumulation potential and reduce state spending. In sum, the focus of neoliberalism is to reduce the institutional capacities of the state (see Bourdieu 1998, Hall 1983, Harvey 2005).

Sub-State Autonomy

One of the outcomes of these processes commonly referred to as state decline is the emergence of sub-state autonomy with respect to policy and global participation. Whether we are discussing provinces in a Canadian context, states in an American context, or "constituent countries" in a Scottish context, the rise of globalization seems to also correspond with an increase in sub-state autonomy and in some cases, increased calls for political sovereignty. There seem to be both passive and active explanations for this contemporary phenomenon. Many argue that this expansion of sub-state policy responsibilities is a function of traditional state *decentralization*.

In short, the emergent dominance of neoliberal political ideology carries with it an expectation that state responsibilities will be reduced, if not withdrawn, from many traditional realms. In the words of Bulent Gedikli, an MP and member of Turkey's neoliberal Justice and Development Party (*Adalet ve Kalkinma Partisi*), "The state's role should be to provide basic services, and the word 'basic' is important here." (BBC 2010). The combination of reduced tax revenues and ideological demand to reduce services at the national level is driven by the belief that such social services should be either privatized or provided by local political institutions (Peck and Tickell 2002; see also Lobao 2005). The result is a shift of service provision responsibility and subsequent policy autonomy to sub-state institutions. In this way, sub-state institutions are granted increased autonomy, but through imposition from external processes (see Heller 2001).

A more active explanation of sub-state autonomy is found in the work those who link the rise of sub-state autonomy with a connection to a specific national identity. That is, linking sub-state political activities to a particular local cultural identity can facilitate sub-state autonomy. Béland and Lecours put it simply: "Substate nationalism can impact social policy making in at least two ways: by reshaping the policy agenda at both the state and the substate levels and by reinforcing regional policy autonomy, which is developed as an alternative to centralist schemes" (2005, 676). In this sense, sub-state autonomy is a result of circumventing centralized state authority. For example, let us assume that a sub-state institution (Québec) existing within a larger federal entity (Canada) continually argued that its distinct and unique subnational culture was threatened by a more dominant nationalist milieu. One could argue that the most effective way to ensure the survival and health of a distinctive national culture is to maintain control over the political affairs of that said national population (so goes the *indépendantiste* argument) – thus, national identity can only be enhanced with less centralized control and more local/sub-state autonomy.

Globalization processes assist this trend in several ways. First, the embrace of neoliberalism at the federal level encourages decentralization of state service provisions. The caveat with this is that neoliberalism is also embraced at the local level – so it could be easily argued that neoliberalism as a singular causal explanation is weak at best. The second opportunity for sub-state autonomy is in relation to the expansion of trade liberalization in the past few decades. If the trade regulatory and economic protectionist capacity of federal states is reduced with global market integration, opportunities for bilateral trade relationships emerge. Québec, for instance, could circumvent Canadian regulatory authority in a free market and develop trade relationships with the United States as an equal partner. This is one of the primary reasons why the *Parti Québécois* and other advocates of Québec sovereignty actively supported the North American Free Trade Agreement (NAFTA) and even suggested their support for a North American monetary union (see Keating and McGarry 2001).

While the work of Béland and Lecours is representative of an active explanation of sub-state autonomy, other discussions of this link between national culture and sub-state autonomy maintain the prominent conceptual role of traditional state decline. Nicola McEwen (and Parry 2005) makes it clear that the maintenance of state services with respect to social welfare provision is highly contingent on a perceived connection to national identity. National popular support is more likely if citizens feel they are supporting a larger national community. She does, however, not simply view sub-state autonomy as an artifact of active promotion: "When such rights are denied and services withdrawn in the face of neoliberalism and globalization, social and national solidarity is weakened, contributing in some cases to increased demands for territorial autonomy at the sub-state level" (McEwen 2005, 111). Similarly, Michael Keating argues that it was the initial success of the global economic system from the mid-1950s through the late-1960s that enabled Québec nationalism to thrive. Increasing global economic integration led to a loss in Canada's "capacity for territorial management" (1995, 217) thus weakening the dependence inherent in the relationship between Canada and Québec (see also Keating 2001).

State decline is therefore understood as the result of reduced economic regulatory capacities and the integration of neoliberal ideological reforms reducing institutional resources and protectionist capacities. While the effects of both global economic integration and neoliberalism are broad, this essay examines the concerted effort to reduce economic protectionism. As previously stated, I argue that the decline of economic protectionist capacity can have a corrosive effect on state authority; however, it also encourages states to increasingly rely on alternative means to ensure sustained legitimacy. One such strategy is the increased efficacy of singular definitions of national culture as a means to sustain legitimate authority. Put simply, global economic integration and political ideology, commonly referred to as elements of globalization, motivates state integration of monolithic national culture. Understanding how this process occurs and how it influences state policy outcomes is the primary goal of this project.

The Rise of National Culture

The causal impact of globalization on local cultural mobilisation is generally recognised, but not comprehensively studied. David Held and Henrietta Moore recently published an edited collection encouraging greater attention to the role of culture (generally termed) as a mechanism for both promoting and maintaining global political economic transition as well as an increasingly efficacious mechanism for resistive mobilisation. Moore focuses on the struggle over cultural definitions as a primary conflict of the globalization era: "The irony is that culture has become the idiom through which capitalists, anti-globalization supporters, nation states and the communities who seek self-determination within them, corporations and the guardians of traditional lifeways all make their claims to uniqueness and authenticity" (Moore 2008, 28).

While Moore includes "nation states" as entities integrated in this cultural resurgence, the traditional analytical focus on the relationship between state and culture is centered on the promotion of an "official" state ideology (Held and Moore 2008). If we are to assume that globalization processes reduce state authoritative capacities, it stands to reason that the ability of state institutions to promote a singular *national* ideology has also decayed. The perspective offered in this essay is consistent with this causal assumption; however, I do not agree that the state is removed from the process of utilising national cultural definitions. The decline of state legitimate authority also reduces state capacity to promote a singular ideology, which facilitates the rise of competing definitions of national identity and culture (see Abu-Lughod 1997; Gorz 1994). This does not, however, signify the demise of state authoritative capacity or the withdrawal of the state from the promotion of similar monolithic national definitions. Due to the necessity for strategic adaptations (that will be discussed below), state institutions must seek legitimating support through the integration of broadly amenable definitions of national culture, which encourages a similarly monolithic conceptualisation of national cultural identity.

The major difference from the "age of ideology" (to borrow a melodramatic phrase) to the globalization era is the role of national populations. State institutions are decreasingly able to dictate ideological definitions and must utilise popular cultural definitions, which both empowers certain cultural movements and exacerbates conflict between movements and other groups over the ability to influence state institutional legitimation. In other words, this apparent weakening of state ideological capacity has led not to a universal decline of state authority, but has enabled a strategic shift in legitimation – empowering monolithic national cultural definitions.

That local culture has become more effective as a political mobilisation strategy is well established. While David Harvey (2005) specifically identifies the effect of neoliberalism as generating social change which promotes local cultural strategies to mediate such change, most scholars focus on general globalization processes and the subsequent decline in state authoritative capacity as a primary causal factor facilitating the "rise of postmodern nationalism" (Castells 2004, 34). Anthony Giddens, for instance, links the rise of sub-state nationalism to the corrosive tendencies of global political economic integration:

> Globalisation is the reason for the revival of local cultural identities in different parts of the world. If one asks, for example, why the Scots want more independence in the UK, or why there is a strong separatist movement in Québec, the answer is not to be found only in their cultural history. Local nationalisms spring up as a response to globalising tendencies, as the hold of older nation-states weakens (Giddens 2003, 13).

His integrative focus should encourage readers not to overemphasise the role of either "cultural history" or state decline, but rather that globalization, combined with local cultural historical conditions, can motivate mobilisation centered on a monolithic national cultural definition.

Jürgen Habermas argues that the integrative requirements of globalization have adversely impacted the ability of state institutions to fulfil necessary redistributive responsibilities. The mediated relationships between nation and state that supported the Keynesian welfare state have been eliminated by neoliberalism and global economic integration (Habermas 2001, 51). More than simply describing an emaciated neoliberal state, Habermas argues that neoliberal globalization "fundamentally challenges the relevance of the nation-state as a continued political model" (*Ibid., xiii.*). The danger is that once the economic protectionist power of the state is eliminated[4] the stability maintained by the exchange of economic protectionism for legitimate authority is also destroyed. He develops the link between state decline (or, the decay of state economic protectionism and legitimate authority) and the rise of culturally-centered nationalist mobilisation:

> ...there is the further question of whether globalization also affects the cultural substrate of civil solidarity that developed in the context of the nation-state...Our own prosperous societies are witnessing a rise of ethno-centric reactions against anything foreign...The loss of solidarity touched off by issues of redistribution can lead to political fragmentation (*Ibid.*, 71–72).

In sum, the decline of the state is the primary motivating factor for the rise of national cultural mobilisation, or in Habermas' view, fragmentation. Or, as Paul Gilroy observes, there is a sense of cultural decline associated with the experience of dominant populations in the contemporary era: "That concern has fed new anxieties that have been expressed about the ebbing of a "core culture" which could anchor national identity as the country completes a large transition towards new circumstances in which its whites will have to adjust to the new experience of being a minority" (Gilroy 2008, 196).

George Yúdice's exploration of globalization and the use of culture identifies several similar connections. He mirrors Habermas in directly ascribing state decline with the collapse of the Bretton Woods system (i.e., Keynesian welfare states) in favor of neoliberalism (see Yúdice 2005, 11–12, 94, 215, and 284). Yúdice is perhaps more explicit in developing the linkage between state decline and the rise of national culture. For instance, he agrees that state decline, motivated by neoliberal globalization, is a primarily political economic process:

> Economic integration into the world economy meant reduced state power to shield citizens from the ups and down of the world market, the disciplining of labor by the criterion of competitiveness, and the unprecedented dissemination of the ideology of the free market (*Ibid.*, 94).

However, he continues to argue that a significant latent effect of state decline has been the reduced capacity for state institutions to promote

---

[4] Habermas clearly argues that the state, in the neoliberal era is unable to enact economic protectionist measures. In his words: "The nation-state has fewer and fewer options open to it. Two of these options are now completely ruled out: protectionism, and the return to a demand-oriented economic policy." (*Ibid.*, 51).

a singular state ideology, or official nationalism. This point is illustrated in cases throughout his text but dramatically described in cases centered on the development of counter-ideological "urban youth cultures" in Brazil and the indigenous Zapatista movement in Mexico (See *ibid.*, pp. 93, 96–108, and 109–132.).

Yúdice argues that the declining power of the state to manage and control a singular national cultural ideology has facilitated the rise of competing conceptualisations of respective national culture. In citing the case of the United States, he makes the observation that: "The culture wars were in part the result of the receding compromise between sociocultural and economic modernisation struck in the U.S. version of Keynesianism. In other words, globalization and commensurate state decline "...certainly sharpened the contradictions that were already auguring a reconfiguration of national culture" (*Ibid.*, 227).

Clearly, state decline, prompted by increasing neoliberal pressures for entry into the global economic system, is identified as the causal link between globalization and the rise of national cultural mobilisation/conflict. The problem, however, is that many state theorists offer substantial evidence that the state has maintained its socio-political authority. Most of these analyses[5] acknowledge that global economic integration has altered the capacities of state institution; although the broadly accepted conclusion is that general proclamations of "state decline" must be contextualised and tempered (see Evans 1997; Scholte 1997; Weiss 2003). Two perspectives prove helpful with respect to explaining the increased integration of national cultural definitions in state institutions.

The first conceptualises state decline without simply proclaiming the end of the Keynesian welfare state and the Bretton Woods period of embedded autonomy. Bob Jessop's work is exemplary; he argues that the state has not universally declined, but has adapted to the realities of an increasingly neoliberal global system. His primary thesis agrees with Habermas and others that globalization has drastically limited state capacity to protect national populations through economic means, although he contends that this process represents a substantial

---

[5] Some state theorists have marshaled the majority of their efforts toward defending the conceptual utility of the state from what they perceive to be erroneous claims of global systemic dominance. Such studies primarily center on areas in which "globalists" argue have been eroded by transnational/global processes; examples include; economic nationalism (see Pickel 2003); state sovereignty (see Smith, Solinger, and Topik 1999); and welfare state decline (see Swank 2002).

restructuring from 'Keynesian welfare national states' (KWNS) to 'Schumpeterian workfare postnational regimes' (SWPR) and not necessarily wholesale decline (Jessop 2002; 1993). That is, as states embrace the logic of "Post-Fordism[6]" and summarily reduce economic protectionist capacities alter the relationship between national populations and state authority: "The changes in economic and social policy associated with the shift from the KWNS to the SWPR serve to undermine the primacy of the national state as the site on which particular techno-economic, narrowly political, and ideological functions are undertaken in the interests of capital accumulation" (Jessop 2002, 205).

State adoption of neoliberal/Post-Fordist economic strategies empowers transnational and domestic economic elites; more so, states wilfully withdraw from economic protectionist responsibilities once the norm in Keynesian state models. This does not eliminate the role of the state as an institution of local authority, rather the state fulfils a social regulatory function necessary for the success of the global economic system, according to Jessop:

> Indeed, the state retains an important role precisely because of the development of such [Schumpeterian workfare postnational] regimes; for it is not only an important actor in many individual governance mechanisms, but also retains responsibility for their oversight in the light of the overall balance of class forces and the maintenance of cohesion (*Ibid.*, 208).

In sum, Jessop argues that legitimacy is retained, in part, through the partial fulfilment of limited economic protectionist strategies that facilitate neoliberal/Post-Fordist economic goals (for example, flexible labor market integration and a withdrawal of state social service responsibilities); however, the limitations of these protectionist strategies result in a decentralisation of state authority (in favor of sub-state regionalisation) and a decline in the central authority of state institutions to maintain "the distinctive unity and identity of the state" (*ibid*, 211). The result is a decentralised[7], neoliberal state that has

---

[6] For all intents and purposes, "Post-Fordism" is a concept that describes the globalization of a political economic ideology relatively complementary to the basic requisites of neoliberalism. The transition to a "post" form of Fordism was the result of a shift among advanced capitalist countries to move away from Keynesian economics and Fordist production in favor of more flexible labor and production strategies (see Ash 1994; Koch 2006).

[7] Conceptualised as "denationalization," or the distribution of state authority to regional, sub-state entities and as "destatization," or the shift from active political

limited capacities to temper struggles over competing national cultural mobilisation.

The second perspective is relatively similar with Jessop's in that it seeks to develop a more clear understanding of the role of the state with respect to *both* national populations *and* global systemic structures. Derived from the work of Immanuel Wallerstein (1974), Robert Cox (1997; 1987), and Leo Panitch (1994), this perspective understands the state to be a mediating institution that ensures systemic stability through the pacification of domestic (national) and global structural demands. As Pantich states: "...the role of states remains one not only of internationalising but also of mediating adherence to the untrammelled logic of international capitalist competition within its own domain, even if only to ensure that it can effectively meet its commitments to act globally by policing the new world order in the local terrain" (Panitch 1994, 71–72).

A recent essay by Clyde Barrow serves as a primary exemplar of this perspective. Barrow agrees with the contention that states are "principle agents of globalization" (Barrow 2005, 123) and continues to argue that without the support of state institutions globalization would be unable to sustain itself. Barrow identifies a similar problem in that, "...within the new global political economy, state elites must still manage the contradictory pressures of (global) accumulation and (national) legitimation" (*Ibid.*, 125). For Barrow, like Jessop, the state meets the challenges of neoliberal globalization through a decentralisation of authority – in effect reducing traditional state-centered authority by reallocating traditional responsibilities to local, sub-state, agents/ institutions:

> As the state becomes overloaded with demands on its national and local administrative capacities, it continues to delegate and disperse regulatory and distributive powers to quasi-public corporations, trade associations, professional organization, social service corporations, labor ᴜnions, chambers of commerce, scientific associations, and many other private non-profit organizations. These actors are being delegated quasi-sovereign functions (or usurp these functions) and thereby relieve the national state of a number of responsibilities (*Ibid.*, 144).

More to the point, Held and Moore identify a significant connection between neoliberalism and national cultural efficacy: "The current

---

leadership to the management of national and transnational relationships (see Jessop 1994).

phase of globalization – contrary to the views of many critics – does much to promote nationalism because of the manner in which neoliberal discourses underpinning strategies for economic growth figure the nation as a competitive player in a world market, seeking to establish the best possible climate for doing business" (Held and Moore 2008, 9).

These analyses offer several key insights. First, we can understand that the rise of national culture as an efficacious political mobilisation strategy is the result of state decline. Second, we can understand state decline to refer to the withdrawal of state institutions from the traditional economic protectionism inherent in Keynesian welfare state models. The problem is that we are left with a limited monocausal explanation for the rise of cultural nationalism/national cultural conflict and even less of an analytical method of explaining the *integration* of monolithic, essentialized national cultural into state institutions. We may be able to generally attribute the rise of culturally-based national conflict to state withdrawal, but we cannot move toward an integrative theory of the state if we simply assume that it is reducing itself through some sort of bureaucratic attrition – state institutions remain central as Barrow, Jessop, and others have shown; I argue states maintain their authoritative centrality through an increasing reliance on national cultural definitions to maintain legitimate authority. The question at hand is how to analytically examine this adaptive change.

A Polanyian Analytical Framework

I argue that it is possible to examine the increased efficacy of national culture in state-level political actions through the rearticulation of Karl Polanyi's notable *double movement* concept. This section is presented in three succinct parts: the first describes Polanyi's embedded theory of the state; the second explicates the classical double movement as originally presented in *The Great Transformation* (Polanyi 2001); and third, justifying a reconceptualisation of the double movement to facilitate the inclusion of national culture.

The State

The double movement is, put simply, a description of the relationship between systemic economic forces and national populations. As liberal ideology pervades local economic practice, the unfettered and unregulated version of capitalism creates hardship conditions that elicit a national popular reaction through the development of a "protectionist counter-movement." This process will be explicated below, but is important to mention here due to the fact that it illustrates the central function of the state in the Polanyian perspective. The state exists, in part, to mediate the dynamics of the double movement.

For Polanyi, the ideology of liberal (laissez-faire) market economics is a fallacy in practice. That is, there has never existed any condition in which the "laws of the market" have structured any respective social order. As liberal market economics emerged as hegemonic in the 19th century, liberal proponents consistently relied upon the state to support and protect nascent and established economic interests (*Ibid.*, 147). Conversely, as liberal markets created adverse conditions for local populations, demands for protection from these circumstances increased in frequency and volume. In his critique of (liberal) economic isolationism, Polanyi comments on the centrality of the state: "...no purely monetary definition of interests can leave room for that vital need for social protection, the representation of which commonly falls to the persons in charge of the general interests of the community – under modern conditions, the governments of the day" (*Ibid.*, 162).

The state, from this perspective, is responsible for facilitating hegemonic demands to deregulate national markets and liberalise trade, yet it is also responsible for ensuring that these actions do not decimate national populations. Block and Somers clearly articulate the mediating position of the state: "...the state acted in the interests of society as a whole when it passed protective legislation, and yet the same was true when it passed premarket laws; it clearly did not 'belong' to either of these forces" (Block and Somers 1984, 68).

The Classical Double Movement

As previously stated, the double movement concept illustrates the adversarial relationship between liberal market structures and national populations. The contemporary relevance of this perspective has been recognised by those seeking to understand the simultaneous process of global market predation and local popular resistance (see Birchfield 1999; Mittelman 1997) and many have pointed to the importance of Polanyi's mediating role for the state in managing systemic performance and national stability (see Bernard 1997; Mosley 2007); however, attempts to develop an analytical strategy centered on Polanyi's understanding of the state have been few and far between (see Block 2007; Block and Somers 1984).

Polanyi's original conceptualisation of the double movement emphasises (as the title would suggest) the *dual* pressures of global market integration and national popular resistance (Polanyi 2001, 79–80). Yet what is often lost in studies of globalization and movement mobilisation/resistance is Polanyi's emphasis on state mediation capacity. The state is responsible for the historical rise of liberal market hegemony (*Ibid.*, 145–148, 162) and is thus reliant upon the satisfaction of liberal market economic demands. However, the conditions created by unregulated liberal capitalism create conditions of adversity for large portions of respective national populations. From agrarian production to nascent industrial production to threats to labor, the integration of a national economy into unregulated global markets creates adversity as competition and price fluctuations destabilise national economic relationships.

The role of the state was then to mediate and manage the integration of national market liberalisation (*Ibid.*, 147, 216). The mechanisms available for the state to meet these mediation requirements were largely economic in nature. The primary mechanism was control over monetary policy, which allowed states to adjust local prices in times of increased foreign competition or scarcity (*Ibid.*, 214). The two other forms of economic protectionism, "land and labor," are linked to the regulatory influence of states in managing labor laws and enabling social protections that ensured at least a minimal level of survival as well as agricultural subsidies that remain in force to this day. In sum, the role of the state in tempering the effects of the dually-supported liberal market system was essential and took the form of restricted economic protectionism. This classical relationship is illustrated in Figure 1.

This model results in the development of the advanced capitalist state form representative of the Bretton Woods period of "embedded liberalism" – in which state institutions maintained local monetary control and emphasised the development of "demand-side" economic strategies. The Bretton Woods agreements facilitated national economic autonomy under the aegis of American dollar hegemony, while the development of social welfare expenditures demonstrated a dedication to class-compromise. In short, it appeared that Polanyi's

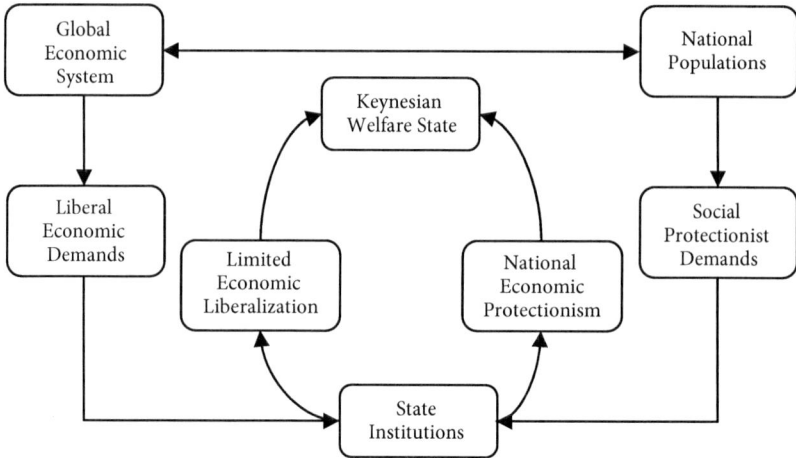

Figure 1. Classical double movement in the era of embedded liberalism
Source: Author

prediction of a "New World" in the post-war era was coming to fruition:

> Out of the ruins of the Old World, cornerstones of the New can be seen to emerge: economic collaboration of governments and the liberty to organise national life at will…the end of market economy may well mean effective cooperation with domestic freedom (*Ibid.*, 262).

The collapse of the Bretton Woods system in 1971, however, ushered in a new era that would alter the strategic capacities of the state within the double movement.

The Reconceptualised Double Movement

While the protection of national economic interests served as the foundation for the classical double movement, contemporary neoliberal hegemony weakens this alternative. David Harvey succinctly summarises these changes: "As the state withdraws from welfare provision and diminishes its role in arenas such as health care, public education, and social services, which were once so fundamental to embedded liberalism, it leaves larger and larger segments of the population exposed to impoverishment" (Harvey 2005, 76).

The decline of the Keynesian welfare state is a well-known story, as previously mentioned in this essay. Less prevalent are investigations of the collapse of the Bretton Woods monetary system in 1971, which effectively ended monetary policy control by respective states. In short, the decision by the Nixon Administration to take the US Dollar off of its standardised gold valuation of $35 per ounce facilitated the emergence of a floating currency exchange system in which private currency markets determined national currency value. As the FOREX system of floating exchange rates matured, a transnational trade in currency speculation and foreign direct investment emerged that reduced state efficacy in managing economic policy – particularly monetary policy (see Cerny 1994; Robinson 2004; Sklair 2001).

In effect, state institutions could influence currency values through the enacting of market-friendly policies and the minimisation of state regulatory control, taxation and subsequent expenditures, and other demand-side strategies available during the period of Keynesian embedded liberalism. The commensurate reduction in state control over financial capital and national currency valuation would be disastrous for embedded liberalism. William Robinson comments on this shift:

> Newly liberated global financial markets began to determine currency values, to destabilise national finances, and to undermine the national macroeconomic management of the earlier Keynesian regime of capitalism…The dramatic loss of currency control by governments meant that state managers could no longer regulate the value of their national currency (Robinson 2004, 112).

The crisis years of the 1970s ultimately resulted in a condition in which state socio-economic spending became increasingly expensive and decreasingly viable due to increased capital mobility and inflation. With sustained popular expectations that state institutions would protect national economic interests but decreased ability to manage domestic capital flows, state institutions were increasingly unable to meet national social protectionist demands through economic means.

This decline in economic protectionist capacity resulted in a broad "crisis of legitimacy" with respect to state institutions in advanced capitalist nation-states (see Castells 2004; Habermas 1975; O'Connor 1973). As previously shown, however, state institutions continue to serve requisite roles in support of global capitalism – therefore, state institutions are required to utilise alternative strategic means for maintaining legitimate authority from national populations.

While the economic protectionist strategy of the embedded liberal period, and the classic double movement model, is diminished, the necessity to maintain social stability through double movement mediation remains. Therefore, adaptive strategies to meet national

protectionist demands must be considered. One such strategy is
the integration of monolithic national cultural definitions to meet
short-term protectionist demands and maintain state legitimacy. This
adaptive strategy is reflected in Figure 2.

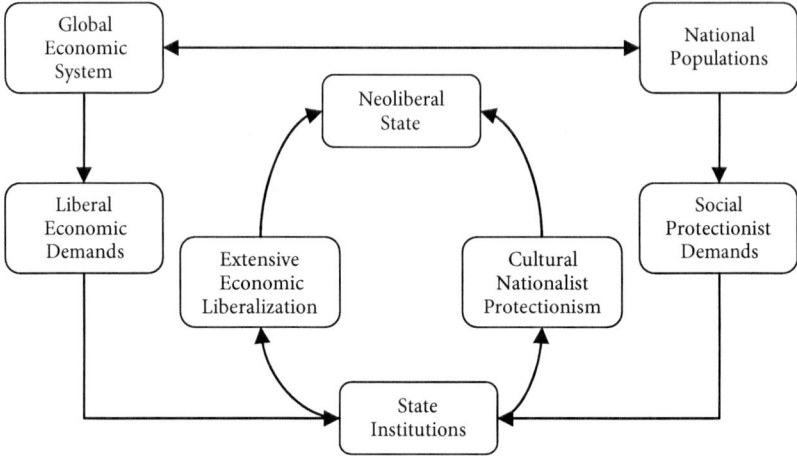

Figure 2. Reconceptualised double movement in the era of neoliberal
globalization
Source: Author

The increased efficacy of national culture in state-level political
action can therefore be conceptualised as an integrative process on the
part of the state to maintain legitimate authority. That is, national culture is not merely mobilised in civil societal sectors, but is also integrated into state institutions and political structures and summarily
utilised as a strategic means for meeting the sustained protectionist
demands from national populations increasingly affected by neoliberal
market hegemony.

Conclusion

The purpose of this extended comparative study is to illustrate the
increasingly efficacious role of national culture in state legitimation.
The very nature of this project requires a more detailed examination of
the assumption of state decline and a focus on not only the contemporary function of state institutions, but also the mechanisms employed
by states to maintain institutional authority. This latter point is an

essential focus on the process of state-building in a neoliberal era seemingly designed to reduce the authority of state institutions and the need for state-building emphases.

As previously stated, the global political economic system has no mechanisms to maintain local social stability and relies heavily (as it always has) on the established national state authority to ensure market and labor stability (if not outright compliance). The democratic state must maintain its legitimacy if it is to ensure this requisite stability, which is granted by satisfying (to some degree) the demands of both liberal capitalists and national populations. The former has remained a central feature of state economic policies in advanced capitalism since the 19th century; while the latter appears more episodic with regards to state efforts to protection national populations from the caustic effects of unrestrained liberal capitalism. The result is a seemingly cyclical process of liberal ebb and flow – with the state serving as a governor waiting to impose mitigating restrictions in order to avoid a reduction in popular support for both the state and capitalism, itself. This balancing act is not a novel observation, Marx, Smith, and countless others have pointed out the inequalities inherent in systemic capitalism and commented on the strategies employed to circumvent this serious structural flaw. Put simply, the state has long functioned as an institutional mechanism to regulate the destabilizing potential of systemic inequality. Economic protectionism, therefore, has existed as a primary strategic means for states to achieve this end.

The primary question becomes, how can a state maintain legitimate authority over national populations in an era where the dominant political economic ideology excoriates economic protectionism? The remainder of this book is a comparative examination of exactly that question in a deep historical comparative context. The cases of Canada and Québec offer a unique opportunity to examine the development of state-building strategies and the specific effects of state decline on state institutional capacities. More to the point, the inclusion of Québec will illustrate how sub-state entities can engage in effective state-building projects and in many cases, have more success in maintaining legitimate authority and institutional support for policy initiatives. Québec, in particular, has been successful in linking a national cultural definition with state-building efforts. The comparison of Canada with Québec raises several intriguing questions, not the least of which is whether neoliberal state-building requires a strong national cultural definition to legitimate state authority?

PART TWO

HISTORICAL BACKGROUND

INTRODUCTION

This section, comprising Chapters Three and Four, is designed to provide a cursory introduction to the general histories of both Canada and Québec. There are several issues that require initial contextualization prior to the presentation of these comparative background chapters. First, these are limited histories that can claim neither universality nor particularity. This is, of course, a weak disclaimer but one that is necessary nonetheless. The purpose of these chapters is to provide appropriate historical context for the more contemporary discussions of economic globalization, immigration, and cultural integration that will take place in subsequent chapters.

The generality inherent in these brief historical depictions should allow for a rudimentary understanding of Québec and Canadian national histories and many of the significant events and challenges faced by both in the effort to build nation-states during a colonial and later, post-colonial context. The first condition that should be apparent from these chapters is that Canada, as a unified political entity, is a binational country with both French and English socio-linguistic roots. This binational legacy is essential to any understanding of Canadian state-building; however, the reality of Québec as a national entity within a larger Canadian national context requires comparative analysis. Put another way, Canada cannot be understood without attention to the influence of Québec and Québec cannot be understood without sensitivity to the reality of the Canadian federation and state. However, as Chapters Three and Four will show, the emergence of Canada and the persistence of the "French Fact" in Québec are both products of deliberate nation-building efforts and supported, at various times and to varying degrees, by institutional state-building. One cannot argue, as both Québécois and Canadian nationalists will, that the history of Canada is the history of Québec. The converse is also readily apparent. The existence of dual national projects obviously requires dual national histories – the reflection of which is the inspiration for bifurcating Canada and Québec into separate historical chapters.

The immediate concern that emerges from such a dichotomization is that the nation-state of Canada emerges from a distinct colonial singularity. The existence of New France gave way to Upper and Lower

Canada under British colonial rule (1791), which eventually morphed into the Union of Canada in 1840 (with the confederation of Canada in 1861). The point is that the binational roots of Canada emerged from an amorphous, yet singular, primordial political creature. As such, the histories of both Canada and Québec are initially indistinguishable and gradually develop distinction as the Anglo- and Francophone populations develop and become entrenched as Canadians/*canadiens*. There are times in both Chapters Three and Four where the reader will sense a redundancy within the juxtaposed historical narratives. This is unavoidable at times and certainly diminishes as both nations age; however, it should be noted that this repetition is understood as being reflective of the shared colonial histories of Canada and Québec.

More to the point, the structural condition of Québec's sub-state role requires a constant reflexivity with respect to its historical narrative (as is also the case with Canada, albeit to a less reactionary degree). In a sense, Québec's national status is largely defined in relation to Canada's political economic dominance. Therefore, any historical narrative emerging from such a subordinated condition must be developed in reaction to the institutional power of the Canadian state.

The second issue that must be reiterated is the nature of the Canada/Québec comparison, itself. These two chapters are designed to provide an historical juxtaposition that supports the larger methodological comparison of Canada and Québec that underscores the entirety of this project. This is a relatively unique juxtaposition and requires an additional discussion with respect to the methodological nature and intent of this comparison. The primary issue is, of course, the comparability of Canada and Québec; however, the goal here is to illustrate state-building strategies in the globalization era. Canada, as a traditional nation-state, and Québec, as a national sub-state, provide a unique opportunity to examine how historical and contemporary conditions converge to create strategic state-building challenges and opportunities.

Put simply, Canada and Québec are incomparable if taken as independent state entities. The reality is, however, that they cannot be understood as independent. Canadian national economic, social, and cultural policies are contingent on and reflective of global ideological and structural conditions. More telling, few federal initiatives are undertaken without addressing provincial impact. As will be illustrated in the forthcoming section, Canadian federal policies and even institutional composition is regularly challenged by the reality of a binational history. Despite the dominance of an English/Anglophone government and economy, French/Francophone cultural and political checks persist. While federal policies have, of course, been enacted without the support of Québec, but few have come into existence without being influenced by the cultural and political demands of the province.

Québec, on the other hand, is a sub-state entity with the larger Canadian federation. It can make no claims to *complete* economic, political, social, or even cultural sovereignty. Its autonomy in these areas is significant, however, as is its ability to maintain a national cultural identity following centuries of subordination. While this national autonomy is significant (and, in fact, provides the root of this comparative analysis), Québec cannot claim to be an independent nation-state. It relies heavily on financial support from the federal government and has parlayed its position as a "distinct society" into beneficial arrangements that enhance both its autonomy and policy capacities; however, this autonomy is rooted in structural dependence on this unique federal-provincial arrangement. In sum, Québec's contemporary sub-state autonomy is significantly depended on its sustained relationship with the federal Canadian state.

As such, this comparison is not one that juxtaposes like units; rather, it compares a nation-state with a sub-state within its federal sphere. More specifically, the comparison is focused on how sub-state autonomy emerges and is enhanced through global political economic integration (globalization). In this sense, the comparison of divergent national historical narratives belies larger nation- and state-building projects that require further analysis if our contemporary understanding of the state is to evolve and progress in response to global political economic structural developments.

CHAPTER THREE

CANADA: HISTORY AND THE QUEST FOR NATIONAL IDENTITY

The history of Canada tells both a unique and common story. It is unique in that its history of conquest, expansion, and legislative management are centered on the reality of bilingualism and the presence of at least three (broadly defined) founding peoples: those of English, French, and Aboriginal ancestry. Canadian history is common with respect to its story as a British colonial possession. One can find common experiences, patterns of action, and strains of governance in British post-colonial societies such as Australia and New Zealand to name a few.

This chapter chronicles the general history of Canada with specific attention to the project of creating a singular Canadian nation-state. With at least three ethno-cultural groups claiming status as "founding peoples" defining a distinct nationalism is essential in the fight for political capital (not to mention the social and economic benefits of cultural dominance). The history of Canada, from a Canadian nationalist perspective, is distinct from indigenous, Québec, or any other ethno-cultural national history. The purpose of this chapter is to tell this national story, but also to illustrate the struggles to promote a singular Canadian nationalism, particularly from a singularly English-Canadian perspective.

Prehistory, First Contact, and the Colonization of New France[1]

The archeological evidence of Canadian pre-history has identified two migrations of native peoples. The first migration is believed to have occurred in successive waves from anywhere between 20,000 and 10,000 BCE. Archeological evidence supports the "land bridge theory" of Asiatic migration of Native American peoples. This theory

---

[1] This section was compiled from several narrative historical sources including Dickason (1997), Eccles (1972; 1969), Parkman (1983; 1962), and See (2001).

and evidence is, in turn, supported by recent genetic evidence that links Native Americans with Asian (particularly Siberian) ancestry (Lell *et al.* 2002; Santos *et al.* 1999; Bonatto and Salzano 1997). A second migration is thought to have taken place between 8,000 and 3,000 BCE and explains the linguistic differences apparent between Inuit and Aleut arctic cultures and southern native peoples (Brace et al. 2001; McGhee 1978, 1996; See 2001)[2].

These Native Canadians comprised a population that arguably reached 500,000 or more prior to European contact. Geography and linguistics traditionally separated these peoples into several distinct groups from the Chinook and Salish of the Pacific Northwest to the Blackfoot and Chipewyan of the Plains to the James Bay Cree and Huron of the Eastern Woodlands to the Beothuk and Penobscot of the Atlantic Maritimes to the Inuit and Dene of the Arctic. Prehistoric Canada was clearly a land of great demographic diversity. The European "Age of Discovery," as was the case in the entirety of the hemisphere, brought about the end of indigenous predominance in North America. The continued (to this day) centrality of native peoples to the history and culture of Canada cannot be discounted. Politically, however, the establishment of New France would sound the beginning of European dominance over the region.

Norse sagas make mention of contact with Native Canadians at or before 1000 CE, but sustained contact between Native Canadians and Europeans was not to occur until the 16th century. Explorations by John Cabot (1497) and Giovanni de Verrazano (1524–1528) were two of the many who began to explore the Atlantic coast of what would become Canada. Verrazano was of particular importance as he sailed under the French flag (commission by King François I) and proclaimed the land *Nova Francia*. The common story of exploration was told again in "New France" as commercial opportunity drove the first settlements. Fishermen eager to take advantage of fishing stocks off the shallows near Nova Scotia and Newfoundland established the first temporary settlements, while Basque fishermen and whalers did the same.

---

[2] It should be noted that traditional Native Canadian beliefs reject these scientific theories of migration on the basis that they contradict First Nations religious beliefs that respective tribes have lived on what is now Canadian soil from the beginning of time. These scientific theories are viewed as being political tools to discount First Nations claims of sovereignty and autonomy.

Jacques Cartier's three voyages in the early 16th century did little to encourage French settlement but did develop an improved cartographic knowledge of the St. Lawrence River including visits to what would be Québec and Montréal. For years, informal fishing settlements constituted the European population of New France. These settlements established trading relationships between European groups (French, English, Portuguese, and Basque) and Native Canadian groups.

French interest in Canada rose in conjunction with demand for beaver furs in Europe. Samuel de Champlain succeeded in establishing the colony of Québec in 1608 after a failed attempt in Nova Scotia four years earlier. Champlain's retention of the Algonquin name *Québec* reflects a relationship with the local Algonquin peoples that would enable the settlement to survive. This was a relatively reciprocal relationship as the French engaged in Algonquin-Iroquois conflicts on behalf of their allies for years. Of course, disease and sporadic French-Algonquin conflict would ultimately decimate the once populous group.

As the settlement of Québec began to show that a permanent French settlement was possible and as the trade in beaver fur remained lucrative, more settlers began to arrive to settle the St. Lawrence region. However, tenuous support from the French government and the failure to discover alternative sources of income (other than furs) ensured that the colony would remain small in comparison with English, Dutch, and Spanish possessions to the south.

New France did succeed in cultivating enough land in the St. Lawrence region to stabilize their population. The French settlers had another series of advantages over larger colonies; the geography of the region was especially conducive to the fur trade as well as providing transportation infrastructure for future commercial endeavors. The St. Lawrence River System provided a series of inland ports and protected harbors that served the French well. The fur trade provided ample financial incentive to invest and travel to New France, if only as a temporary resident. The consequence of this expansion of the fur trade and settlement in the Mississippi River Valley as well as in the Great Lakes region was that conflict with the also expanding British colonies would be inevitable.

King William's War (1690–1697) represented the first of many violent conflicts between the French-Algonquin alliance and the British colonials. These conflicts ebbed and flowed with the currents of war blowing from Europe, but the conflicts in New France and the American colonies took on a regular pattern of coordinated raids on towns and ports from the late 1600s through 1763. A series of European treaties (Utrecht in 1713 and Aix-la-Chapelle in 1748) ensured that the political map of North America was in constant flux. Both the British and French used colonial possessions as bargaining chips throughout the treaty process. Settlers seemed to be constantly in a state of raid-preparedness and uncertainty over claims to forts, lands, and strategic geography. This state of constant contact and conflict culminated in the Seven Years' War (1756–1763) and effectively ended French political and economic participation in the settlement of North America.

The Seven Years' War and the Conquest of French Canada

The Seven Years' War began as prior colonial conflicts had – as both extensions of European continental conflict and local conflict between groups seeking the same material resources. In 1754 colonial British and French forces met near Fort Duquesne at what would become the city of Pittsburgh. This relatively minor conflict illustrated the fact that French dominance of the Mississippi River Valley was increasingly challenged by British-American colonists crossing west over the Appalachian Mountains. As colonial settlers battled for territory and resources, their European masters continued the long history of French and British warfare. The colonial conflict soon escalated from frontier skirmishes to a full-scale war culminating with British victories at Québec and Montréal. The particulars of the protracted War have been chronicled to the point of mythology, especially the battle at the Plains of Abraham in which both Generals Montcalm and Wolfe died[3]. The eventual defeat of French forces in North America effectively ensured British and American control of the northeastern portion of the continent.

With the fall of Québec in 1759 and Montréal in 1760, New France was officially captured territory in the hands of the British. The 1763 Treaty of Paris officially granted the lands of New France to the British ensuring that, for the time being, territory stretching from the Atlantic

---

[3] Full and detailed accounts of both the Seven Years' War as well as the legendary status of the battle for Québec on the Plains of Abraham have been eloquently written by Fred Anderson (2001), Francis Parkman (1962), and Francis Jennings (1988).

seaboard to the Mississippi River Valley and from Georgia to the Arctic Circle was British. In the same year a Royal Proclamation created the colony of Québec and set the conditions for French assimilation. The Catholic Church was ignored by the new colonial administration, as was the feudal land-grant system of *seigneurial* control. English criminal and civil law replaced the dominant authority of both the French colonial administration and the Catholic Church. Clearly, the goal of the 1763 Proclamation was to assimilate the French population as quickly as possible. The British colonial authorities underestimated the desire of French-Canadians to retain their language and culture. In addition, the dominance of the Catholic Church in the life of the average *Canadien*[4] was unquestionable. English efforts to eliminate Catholicism from Québec were met with staunch resistance. The population and culture of French Canada was too entrenched for any comprehensive assimilationist policy to be effective.

Anglophone immigration was limited to "mostly administrators, merchants, and military leaders" (Conrad, Finkel, and Jaenen 1993, 249) and could not counter the population and solidarity of the Francophone *Canadiens*. The British responded to the failed policy (1763 Royal Proclamation) with the Québec Act in 1774. This act restored French civil law, including recognition of the Catholic Church, while maintaining British criminal law and political authority. This Act served the dual purpose of pacifying *Canadien* dissent and bolstering British colonial authority on the eve of the American Revolution. Unlike the Royal Proclamation of 1763, the Québec Act was successful in quelling any potential Francophone revolt and keeping Québec out of the American Revolution.

The issue of the American Revolution is significant in its impact on Canadian history. British loyalists (Tories) migrated en masse during the War as a result of American discriminatory measures and their desire to maintain ties to the British Empire. A first migration of Tories moved to Nova Scotia and petitioned the British to create a new colony that would become New Brunswick. There was also a later movement

---

[4] The term *Canadien* refers to Francophone citizens of Canada. This is a cultural distinction made by French-Canadians that implies a distinct history and lineage of a colonial founding people. The term can be compared to *habitant*, which is an original French-Canadian farmer that worked under the seigneiurial system of land tenure in early Québec history. The *habitants* are a specific rural group with strong ties to the rural, agricultural history of Québec, while *Canadien* is a term that can be applied to Francophone citizens of the larger Canadian nation-state.

to the border region between the St. Lawrence River and Detroit
(Lanctôt 1967). This second migration of English-speaking British loyalists would also petition the British government for political autonomy due to the conditions of the Québec Act, which denied them the
right to British civil law. The British responded to this request with the
1791 Constitutional Act that divided Québec into two: Upper (English)
and Lower (French) Canada. The Act allowed respective legal, religious, and civil systems to exist in each region while maintaining
British political control.

The division of Canada allowed local cultural and civic institutions
to function. To say that this was a concession to the Francophone
Canadiens would be an overstatement. The British instituted a mercantile trade relationship with Canada thus facilitating Anglophone control of trade. Trade and merchant relationships with Britain were of
supreme importance and thus much of the fur trade commercial management fell into the hands of the English, particularly in Montréal.
This shift in control of commercial centers would create an historical
condition of economic stratification that will be discussed in the next
chapter. By the beginning of the Nineteenth Century, the political and
economic face of Canada was increasingly English.

Post-conquest and Confederation, 1800–1870[5]

Canada in the first half of the Nineteenth Century would be defined by
intermittent rebellious sentiment, an evolving relationship with the
United States to the south, and the persistent problem of the "French
Fact." Each of these conditions contributed to the environment that
spawned the first of Canada's multi-act constitutional documents: the
Constitution Act of 1867.

A series of rebellions against British colonial authorities began in
1837 due to the effects of an economic downturn earlier in the decade
caused by poor harvest and political reform in Britain that did not
extend to the Canadian colonies. These conditions created a certain
level of anti-authoritarian sentiment on the part of both French and
English Canadians and were directed squarely at the British colonial
authorities, including their local representatives in both Upper and
Lower Canada. The ideological influence of the United States on

---

[5] The chapter was compiled from several historical narrative sources including
Buckner (1985); Conrad, Finkel, and Jaenen (1997); Hallowell (2005); and See (2001).

Canada during this period cannot be ignored. The combination of lethargic British colonial administrative reforms and the example of liberal capitalist governance to the south created quite a strong desire among Canadians for change.

These rebellions were poorly organized and relatively sporadic in both Upper and Lower Canada. The level of British colonial control and the languid pace of political and economic reforms provided ample motivation for reform oriented leaders whose message of change was eagerly absorbed by impoverished farmers. In terms of generating large scale change or even wide-spread revolutionary action, these rebellions were failures. The outbreak of violent insurrection in Canada so soon after the American Revolution greatly alarmed both conservative (Tory) Canadians and the British government.

The motivations for these rebellions in Lower Canada and Upper Canada were reflective of the larger transitions from a mercantilist to liberal economic relationship with the United Kingdom. The British government was resistant to reforms, particularly in its established colonies that provided the bulk of England's raw material resources. While the rebellions could easily be classified as a "middle-class" reaction to the British refusal to reform economic structures, the rebellions in Lower Canada also contained a level of ethnic mobilization and included many lower-class farmers. This difference is entirely consistent with the economic inequalities present between Upper and Lower Canada at this time. The free-holding agricultural system of Upper Canada was more amenable to capital accumulation and thus a greater middle-class agricultural population. In Lower Canada, the *seigneurial* system was based on a quasi-feudal relationship between a landed *seigneur* and a tenant farmer. The lack of property ownership and the rent requirements of this relationship ensured that the *habitants* remained landless and poor.

While these resistive activities did little to affect immediate administrative change, they did pressure the British to establish an inquiry led by Lord Durham in 1838. The subsequent Durham Report suggested establishing a unique level of Canadian governmental autonomy while remaining within the British Commonwealth. The intent was to effectively address the causes of the rebellions but also maintain supreme authority in matters of political and economic relations between Canada and Great Britain.

The Durham Report is significant for two historical reasons. The first was the promotion of a confederation model of governance that would shape the future of Canadian federal-provincial relationships for years to come. The second issue of significance was the resurgence of anti-French sentiment through the Report's insistence on French assimilation in Canada. The legislative importance of the Durham Report is of primary importance in this chapter. The cultural legacy of the Durham Report will be revisited in the following chapter.

The emergence of an autonomous government in Canada began with the 1841 Act of Union that united Upper and Lower Canada into the single colonial entity of Canada, while maintaining the legislative distinction of Canada West and Canada East, respectively. Both entities were allowed legislatures of equal numbers but firm executive power resided with the Governor who was the Crown's official representative in Canada, thus maintaining British political authority. These political organizational changes were reflective of the larger economic shifts away from mercantilist empires to a more open liberal market economy. Domestically, the colonial divisions of Canada were view by colonial authorities as an impediment to civic improvements projects and economic development, particularly westward expansion. Liberal economic reforms were viewed as the solution to economic stagnation, particularly agrarian reforms that allowed both land ownership and the ability to accumulate reinvestable capital by Canadian farmers with the goal of expanding the agricultural production capacities of the colony.

These reform impulses motivated the Confederation Debates between all British-Canadian colonial entities at the 1864 Québec Conference. The most contentious and historically persistent issue of federal and provincial relations was that of autonomy under the aegis of a confederated Canada. In short, the proposed federalist system of governance included a level of centralized control that was disconcerting for some colonies. These issues were enough to keep Prince Edward Island and Newfoundland from participating in the confederation project. The novel concept of an autonomous state within the British colonial system became a reality with the British North America Act (BNAA) in 1867.

The British North America Act

The BNAA reflected the conflicts and conditions that originally motivated the Durham Report. International relationships, with the United States and the United Kingdom played a significant role in the shaping of the BNAA with respect to federalism and national identity construction. In the case of federalism, the recent American Civil War motivated the Canadian framers to attribute more power to the federal government of Canada than to individual provinces. The mechanics of the document promoted the three ideals of "peace, order, and good government" in an obvious departure from the language of the American Declaration of Independence. This attempt to differentiate Canadian and American histories, societies, cultures, and identities is the first legislative effort to create a unique Canadian national identity. This would be a difficult and prolonged effort that continues to this day and serves as one of the single most important challenges to Canadian government as will be shown in subsequent chapters.

The Act established a House of Commons and a Senate with legislative powers. The British monarchy retained executive powers with the appointed Governor-General serving as the Crown's proxy. The BNAA did allow room for legislative interpretation with respect to authority granted to the central Canadian government and that of provincial authorities. This ambiguity concerning federal and provincial authority was largely responsible for nonparticipation by Prince Edward Island and Newfoundland in 1867 and continued to color Canadian history with respect to the numerous debates concerning federal and provincial authority. The federal government was granted powers of taxation and veto with respect to provincial legislation, while the provinces were granted autonomy over educational policies and issues of civil rights.

The BNAA also granted the legal status of two official languages in the country: French and English. This provision again shows the persistence of the "French Fact" in the face of considerable English pressure for the assimilation of the *Canadiens*. The legislative recognition of linguistic equality in conjunction with the federal-provincial balance of powers that was established by the BNAA would create significant platforms for issues of political autonomy and control. The issue of federal-provincial relations undergirds the previously mentioned issues of culture and national identity in Canada. These relationships will be discussed at length but bear mention here for the fact that their origins lie with the British North America Act. It should be noted that the BNAA, while providing the necessary political autonomy for a national-state foundation, was motivated in large part by the British government. The BNAA was instrumental in providing a framework on which a Canadian national project could be built, but should not be understood as a distinctly Canadian product. Rather the BNAA reflects the growing political economic potential of a British colony in a time of declining empire.

Westward Expansion and the Beginning of the Canadian Nation-State

With the (partial) unification of Canada completed, the newly elected federal government under the leadership of Canada's first Prime Minister, Sir John A. Macdonald, undertook the massive project of westward expansion. This was seen as an economic imperative as the vast plains of Manitoba and Saskatchewan presented vast agricultural potential and the newly established province of British Columbia (1871) offered a Pacific port for future trade with Asia.

Two substantial, yet conjoined conditions stood in the way of Canadian federal expansion. While the marshland of western Ontario posed a subtle geographic barrier, the legacy of the *Canadien* fur trade would prove much more difficult. Since 1670, much of the land targeted by the Canadian government for the development of an agricultural hinterland was owned by the Hudson's Bay Company (HBC). The significant profits from fur in the Hudson Bay drainage basin sustained private interest in the region and "discouraged [settlement] in the region because of its threat to the fur trade" (Francis 1993, 238). The decline of the HBC in the 1850s, resulting from challenges to its trading monopoly by the independent Red River Settlement and American westward expansion, allowed the Canadian government an opportunity to begin its national expansionist project. The Rupert's Land Act of 1868 transferred control of the drainage basin to the Canadian government for a sum of 300,000 pounds. The Act effectively ended the private control over a huge land area, but more importantly it allowed the newly autonomous Canadian government control over massive agricultural and other natural resource potential.

The federal government began to encourage expansion through the development of the Canadian Pacific Railway and a concerted effort to promote migration both domestically and internationally to the newly acquired prairies. The legacy of the Hudson Bay Company monopoly meant the acreage appeared relatively "empty" from Ottawa's perspective; however, the government soon realized its nation-building goals would be met with substantial skepticism on the part of those already living in the region. Specifically, national integration and land appropriation resulted in resistance, rebellion, and conflict in the Red and Saskatchewan River regions. The combination of the encroaching railroad (which was more reflective of Eastern migration and a lasting federal interest) and a massive government effort to settle and exploit the interior plains pressured the indigenous peoples and Métis[6] to respond. The Red River conflict of 1869 saw a period of sporadic violence between settlers and the Métis provisional government. This provisional government was designed to protect the culture and land of indigenous and Métis inhabitants of the region in response to Canadian encroachment. The conflict and outcry over the actions of these Catholic, Francophone, and mixed-race Métis pressured the Macdonald government to diffuse the situation. The federal response was to establish the province of Manitoba in 1870 while maintaining many of the local protectionist policies of the provisional government.

This compromise was not to last as rapid settlement and frequent treaty violations, commonly in the form of land acquisition pushed many Métis west to the Saskatchewan River region. Conditions continued to deteriorate as several treaties claimed former Native Canadian land for federal government use. The 1876 Indian Act, designed to encourage assimilation of Native Canadians, also inflamed already tenuous relations between the Métis and settlers. The resulting North-West Rebellion resulted in the execution of several indigenous combatants including the leader of both the Red River and Northwest rebellious actions, Louis Riel. This was the last organized resistance to Canadian westward expansion.

The repression of indigenous and Métis resistance in the West allowed the nationalist expansion project to continue. Under the Macdonald "National Policy" the shape of Canada drastically changed.

---

[6] The Métis are the children of French and English fur traders and members of the Cree, Ojibway, and Saulteaux tribes. The Métis played a significant leadership role in the history and governance of Manitoba. In fact, the entrance of Manitoba into the Canadian confederation in 1870 illustrates the influence of the Métis. The Manitoba Act (1870) ensured separate educational institutions based on linguistic preference as well as recognizing English and French as official provincial languages. The 1873 "Half Breed Land Grant Protection Act" was only partly successful in protecting the land claims of the Métis settlers of the province, but it does serve an historical purpose in exposing the power of the Métis people to motivate provincial protectionist legislation on their behalf.

British Columbia became a province in 1871, the Canadian Pacific Railway was completed in 1881, and the late Nineteenth Century saw Canada's first massive recruitment effort to populate and exploit the vast natural resources of the country. It was clear very early in the colonial Canadian project that the resources and land-spaces of Canada were far too vast for the small population of French and English settlers to productively exploit. New sources of labor were needed if westward expansion was to be successful. The federal government actively promoted the Canadian interior as a place of amazing agricultural potential.

The National Policy of 1879

The push westward incurred tremendous cost both financially and politically. Added to these early national growing pains was an economic depression (the Panic of 1873) that engendered federal deficits and limited financing for federal expansionist efforts. The standing Liberal government of Alexander Mackenzie (1873–1878) was saddled with the expansionist mantle albeit with decreasing abilities to finance such ambition. The Liberals attempted to address the economic downturn through an expansion of liberalized trade with the United States, which had been in decline since the end of the Reciprocity Treaty[7] in 1866. The inability of the Liberals to negotiate a favorable free trade agreement with the United States opened an opportunity for the Conservative opposition to propose a protectionist economic policy designed to limit international trade in favor of expanded Canadian manufacturing and national economic (protected) development.

The return of John Macdonald and the Conservative Party to power in 1878 allowed implementation of the National Policy the following year. The economic policies were extensively based on a singular

---

[7] The Canadian-American Reciprocity (Elgin-Marcy) Treaty was brokered by the British government in an attempt to stem growing protectionism in the United States. The Treaty itself permitted tariff-free trade of Canadian agricultural products and natural resources to the United States in exchange for expanded fishing rights in the North Atlantic. The Treaty was signed in 1854 and significantly expanded Canadian exports into the United States. American political and business interests resisted the liberalization of trade and following the Civil War ended the Reciprocity Treaty in favor of more insular economic development policies.

ideological foundation: Canadian nation-building. From Macdonald's perspective, the prospect of liberalized trade entailed nothing less than a reorienation away from Canada's British roots and a shift toward an American sphere of influence. As would be repeated in the next hundred plus years, Macdonald warned against the subsumation of Canada under the dominance of an emergent United States. The National Policy was an attempt to both address the mires of economic depression and enable a truly independent Canada to emerge.

The foundation of the policy was a strategic raising of import tariffs on manufactured goods and a decrease in raw material tariffs. The goal of these twin approaches was to encourage industrial production in Ontario and Québec, which would theoretically create a domestic supply of manufactured goods that would meet demand throughout the rest of the country. This form of economic nationalism was not unique in terms of domestic economic policy; however, it allowed the Conservative government to promote westward expansion as a national economic project. Eastern manufacturing would supply Western agricultural development and ensure national (east-west) economic growth. However, the two significant problems of transportation and population limited the exploitation of the prairie – both would be addressed in the National Policy as Macdonald linked national economic development (and, rhetorically, the nation of Canada, itself) to the completion of the Canadian Pacific Railway and a massive expansion of immigration.

The former would be completed shortly after the suppression of Real's second rebellion in 1885. The existing railway allowed federal troops to move into Saskatchewan with unprecedented speed and facilitated the government's claims that that railway was central to national stability and growth. The latter, a substantial need to increase the agrarian population in the West was addressed through a halting, yet ultimately effective, shift in immigration policies that will be addressed in the following section and in Chapter Six. Of importance here is the three-fold approach of the National Policy, the seemingly disparate goals of national economic protection, railway development, and immigration reform find consensus when viewed through the lens of nationalism. This was a contemporary recognition that was certainly less than consensual throughout the new nation.

The National Policy was hugely unpopular among already existing agricultural producers in the West. It made needed manufactured goods from the United States (and elsewhere) more expensive by effectively forcing Western consumers to purchase goods manufactured in Eastern Canada and eliminating lower cost imports as well as minimizing lucrative export opportunities. The value-added cost of these Eastern manufactures was increased by higher railroad freight charges for westward shipments – given the decreased competition from American manufacturers, the Canadian West was basically subject to the will of Ontario and Québec. This perceived exploitation of Western populations would fuel the Northwest Rebellion (1885) and contribute to the future development of "Western Alienation." However egregious the sense of exploitation in the West, Eastern population centers benefitted economically from increased manufacturing and relatively guaranteed national markets. That being the case, Québec was suspicious of this expansion of federal authority. Although an economic beneficiary, the capital spoils were largely restricted to the Anglophone business class and the sustained sense of Anglo dominance – particularly from a newly emergent federal government in Ottawa – would encourage Québec support for increased provincial autonomy. This response will be further elaborated in the following chapter.

Despite existent opposition, the National Policy would become hegemonic due in part to Conservative nationalism but also to persistent economic recession. The twin challenges of economic recession and American economic expansion led many to argue that economic liberalism was both a failed strategic approach as well as a danger to Canadian autonomy. Canadian economic development was couched in specifically nationalist terms, which was a distinct shift from the mercantilism of the colonial period (ending in 1867) and the latter "free trade" liberalism reflected in both the Reciprocity Treaty and Liberal party platforms. From Macdonald's perspective, Canadian national health would be ensured through an insular, nationalist economic system running on reliable infrastructure. This "defensive expansionist" (cf. Aitken 1959; Eden and Molot 1993) economic strategy for nation-building could not, much like its American exemplar, rely entirely on insularity if the Policy was to be successful. The expansion of labor migration was absolutely necessary for the development of a practically national economic system to function. The successful expansion of Eastern manufacturing and the desire to people the West to expand agricultural production was contingent on the recruitment of new Canadians.

Immigration and the Peopling of Canada[8]

The organizational and deliberate promotion of selective immigration in order to encourage agricultural growth in Canada was led by the Minister of the Department of the Interior, Clifford Sifton[9]. The Department's Immigration Branch began to distribute promotional materials in strategic locations such as the United States and Great Britain. The emphasis on recruitment in the United States was quite successful with an estimated 750,000 Americans emigrating between 1901 and 1914 (Citizenship and Immigration Canada 2000). The provincial creation of Saskatchewan and Alberta in 1905 further emphasized the managed growth and dominion claims of the Canadian government. Encouraged by the success of the American and British recruitment efforts.

Sifton continued to expand his efforts into Central and Eastern Europe. His goals for peopling the interior of the country were colored by desires for a specific type of immigrant, the "stalwart peasants" (Citizenship and Immigration Canada 2000). The most numerous of these people agreeing to Canada's offer of settlement were from the Ukraine. The Ukrainian example is an historically important one as this was an ethnic group that actively strove to maintain its cultural and linguistic heritage in an adopted land. In 1905 the province of Manitoba financed a teacher education program in the Ukrainian language, enacting arguably Canada's first multicultural policy outside of the traditional triad of Indigenous, French and English peoples. The years preceding the First World War were characterized by massive recruitment and immigration to Canada. Ukrainian settlers were followed by Germans and Italians who settled both in urban and rural areas. An example of this massive growth is Saskatchewan, which saw its population explode from approximately 91,000 in 1901 to 500,000 in 1911 (Bitner and Newman 2005).

---

[8] The section was compiled from several historical narrative sources including Brown and Cook (1974), Cameron (2004), Halli and Driedger (1999), Owram (1992), See (2001), and Waite (1971).

[9] Sifton served as Minister for the Department of the Interior from 1896 to 1905 under the Liberal government of Wilfrid Laurier. Information pertaining to his ministerial career and policies was obtained from Citizenship and Immigration Canada's *Forging Our Legacy* project, http://www.cic.gc.ca/english/department/legacy/.

The active recruitment of immigrants led to a populist political backlash. Public sentiment against non-Northern and Western European immigration was palpable, particularly against the expansion of Chinese immigration in British Columbia. As early as 1885 (and again in 1900 and 1903), financial disincentives were established to reduce Chinese immigration into the country. When Sifton resigned his post in 1905 he was replaced by Frank Oliver, whose approach to immigration was focused much more on public sentiment and political opinion. One year later the federal government passed the first of several laws regulating immigration into Canada. The Immigration Act of 1906 established definitions for "immigrant" and established restrictions on acceptable individuals (denying the mentally disabled and incompetent, criminals, those "afflicted with a loathsome disease" and the very poor) and occupations (criminals and prostitutes). The real impact of this Act, however, was in the federal codification of immigration regulations with standardized procedures and penalties for non-compliance[10].

The 1906 Act provided the legislative precedent for further restrictions in 1910. The Immigration Act of 1910 was much more explicit in its prohibitions (adding the blind, deaf, and dumb to its existing list of physical and mental maladies) and allowing more subjective leeway for immigration officers, particularly with respect to race and ethnicity. For example, Section 38 of the Act states that immigrants of "any race deemed unsuited to the climate and requirements of Canada, or of immigrants of any specified class, occupation, or character[11]". Clearly, the welcome for non-Western European immigration had been rescinded in Canada. These measures would serve to pacify public outcry against increasing ethnic diversification due to liberal immigration policies – a common theme in North America at the turn of the century.

---

[10] The Immigration Act of 1906 is a watershed legislative moment in Canadian history. In just one year the official stance of the federal government went from promoting Canada as an opportunity to restricting landings and legislating discriminatory policies. The text of the Act can be found at the Canadian National Library at http://www.canadiana.org/ECO/ItemRecord/9_07188. Of particular note are the stated restricted peoples listed and defined in sections 26–29.

[11] The Immigration Act of 1910 is viewed as the logical outcome of its 1906 predecessor. While racially-specific immigration policies regulating Asian migration had been in effect since the 1860s, this was the first federal regulatory measure applied to immigrants with *general* racist criteria. The text of the Act can be found at the Canadian National Library at http://www.canadiana.org/ECO/ItemRecord/9_07184.

World Wars and Political Autonomy[12]

By the time of the First World War, Canada had expanded its industrial capacities, thanks in part to protective tariffs and a concerted effort to expand the pool of available labor through immigration. The coming of the First World War brought the realization that Canadian isolation, or at least its status as a subordinate British colonial possession, had come to an end. Prior to 1914 many Canadian economists and business leaders began calling for the commencement of reciprocal trade with the United States and the removal of nationalist trade protections. Their reasoning was reflective of the growing sense of Canadian autonomy and a desire to realign economically from a fading global power to a more geographically convenient emergent power. The defeat of the Liberal party platform of trade reciprocity with the U.S. in 1911 quelled this argument for a time, but Canadian involvement in World War I would usher in an era of greater political economic autonomy for Canada and shift the dominant international economic relationship from the United Kingdom to the United States.

In a sense, Canada was drawn into World War I at the behest of the British. General public support for England and France in Canada was not in serious question; however it was Canada's position within the British Empire that created a de facto position of military support. Ironically, this support and Canadian political actions after 1918 would further distance the country from its colonial past and work to create a modern nation apart from the constraints of the British Empire.

Canadian contributions to the war effort included increased industrial production, support services (including medical and transportation services), and a significant military contribution. These military contributions, specifically conscription which was instituted by the Military Service Act of 1917, served as the most contentious issue on the Canadian home-front. Resistance to conscription was widespread throughout the country but remained a minority position outside of Québec. This popular position (in Québec) was indicative of the French-Canadian argument against European imperialism. Why, it was argued, should French-Canadians support a war on the grounds of saving the British Empire when Québec was a victim of

---

[12] The chapter was compiled from several historical narrative sources including Bothwell, Drummond, and English (1989; 1987); Brown and Cook (1974); Granatstein (1975); See (2001); and Thompson and Seager (1985).

British imperialism? The fact that France was under attack was of little consequence as many French-Canadians viewed France as having abandoned their kin to the British. Both the military effort in general and the Military Service Act went unsupported in Québec and resulted in anti-conscription riots throughout the province. These events further illustrated the divergent attitudes and opinions that belied a Canadian national identity. For the federal government however, these domestic conflicts and disagreements were secondary to the process of building a sovereign nation-state. Independent participation in the war effort was an important step in this nation-building process.

The level of Canadian participation in World War I accelerated its emancipation from Britain. The inter-war period illustrates the level of this emancipation on both positive and negative tracks. Immediately following the war, Canada participated in the short-lived League of Nations as an independent member. This political autonomy was further exemplified with the negotiation of the 1923 Halibut Treaty that codified Pacific Northwest fisheries. This treaty was negotiated and enacted between the United States and Canada without participation of the British government. In 1926 Lord Balfour advocated a level of political sovereignty of countries within the British Commonwealth. This support from Balfour was essential in promoting the 1931 Westminster Statute that officially created the British Commonwealth including the recognition of independence with respect to domestic and foreign policy but retaining British legislative authority.

Economic Interdependence

In terms of trade and economic issues, the decade of the 1920s saw the emergence of the United States as Canada's single greatest trading partner. This economic relationship would motivate a decrease in national protective tariffs, particularly on the part of Canada and drastically increase the level of economic interdependence between the two North American countries. No experience is more telling of this relationship than the nearly identical experiences of Canadians and Americans during the Great Depression.

The expansion of liberal market economics in the latter half of the 1800s pushed individual nations toward increasing their export capabilities. This reorientation would prove disastrous for most Western countries during the Depression Era. The immediate and persisting effects of economic depression ensured that foreign orders would decrease – in most cases drastically. In turn, decreased domestic income due to the collapse of export income would allow no viable avenues for short-term recovery. These conditions were exacerbated in a situation of massive economic interdependence like that of Canada and the United States. The resulting "Dirty Thirties" saw matching industrial and urban poverty levels rise dramatically. Agricultural regions and sectors were heavily impacted as drought and a decline in market demand combined to create conditions of abject destitution. The "Dust Bowl" conditions so passionately captured in photographs ran from Mexico to the northern reaches of agricultural production in Saskatchewan and Manitoba.

Political responses to the Depression era were also quite similar. The Conservative government of Richard Bennett attempted to replicate the relative successes of Roosevelt's "New Deal" by providing programs such as unemployment insurance, industrial oversight, and permanent economic planning. These efforts were unsuccessful and resulted in the defeat of the Conservative government in 1935. The result of these collective experiences was a nearly universal belief that the federal Canadian government was not doing nearly enough for its citizens, particularly in times of crisis. The post-Depression period would see a desire to establish clear social responsibilities of the federal government. This desire to strengthen the state was reflected in the 1940 Rowell-Sirois commission report. The Rowell-Sirois Commission pointed to the increase in provincial power due to judicial decisions as a serious problem for welfare provision. The report advocated a resumption of the federal authority established by the 1867 British North America Act. Much of the Rowell-Sirois report was supported by the inability of provincial governments to address the massive social and economic welfare crisis of the Great Depression. This era would see the legitimation and practical expansion of the Canadian state that would play an essential role in the post-World War II history of the nation.

The Expansion of the Canadian Welfare State

The Second World War again saw Canada enter a major international conflict and provide significant human and material resources on behalf of the Allied powers. The typical Canadian story during World

War II told of support for the Allied effort, particularly on behalf of a besieged Britain. There were exceptions particularly in Québec where the resurgent criticism of British support ensured that the Canadian effort would not be universally supported. Conscription again emerged as a contentious issue with Québec in opposition to a reestablished draft. The majority of Canada, however, supported conscription and welcomed the massive increase in industrial production that accompanied the war years.

The post-war devastation of Europe created a significant opportunity for Canada. The industrial and economic infrastructures that supported the war effort remained intact and Canada's position as a growing power to the north of the Western Superpower of the United States ensured increased international visibility. The country was a major participant in the founding of the United Nations in 1945 and an early leader in humanitarian efforts within the organization.

Domestically the post-war period continued massive increases in industrial production and economic growth. This period of economic growth was extended by Canada's participation in the Korean War, but would come to an end in 1957, as the global trends of economic growth would slide into recession. The classic Canadian problem of manpower again served as a significant post-war problem. Increases in immigration provided essential labor to fuel Canada's economic boom. This situation of economic growth hampered by persistent labor demand would play a significant role in the development of contemporary Canada and will be addressed in subsequent chapters. In brief, the period from 1945 through 1960 saw increases in state responsibility for social welfare, a massive rise in immigration through the late 1950s, and a growth in Canada's international status as a central political and economic power. The major outcome of this period would be centered on an old but intensifying Canadian problem: national unity.

The Diefenbaker government of 1957–1963 offers several illustrations of these dynamic yet ominous times. First, Diefenbaker clearly understood the dangers and threats to national unity posed by rapid economic growth and accompanying increases immigration. His government promoted two efforts to stem the liberal notion of individual ethnic identity and encourage an assimilationist Canadian nationalism. The first was a general emphasis on national unity called "One Canada." This policy was designed to deemphasize racial, ethnic, and cultural identification and promote a singular nationalistic ideal of personal identity. The second effort was the 1960 Bill of Rights that provided legislative justification for the ideological positions of the "One Canada" policy. This was the first of many legislative efforts to promote and define Canadian nationalism as a singularity. Diefenbaker should be credited as one of the first to legislate a definition of "Canadian."

Both the ideological and legislative nationalism of the Diefenbaker government seemed the final straw for Québec. In 1960, the long-standing conservative provincial government of Maurice Duplessis (1936–1939 and 1944–1959) was defeated by Jean Lesage's Liberals who immediately began a project of Keynesian economic and governmental reforms intended to modernize the province. These reforms would evolve into a political and cultural period of empowering change known as *La Révolution tranquille* (Quiet Revolution). The consequence of this period in Québec would be the motivation of a more inclusive nationalism and the strengthening of the Canadian nation-state.

The Quiet Revolution and Ethnic Challenges to Pan-Canadian Nationalism[13]

In brief, the Quiet Revolution was a period of political and economic modernization in conjunction with an urban cultural nationalism centered on the uniqueness of Québec. The "revolutionary" aspects of this period describe the incredible speed with which the province shifted from an agrarian rural society that was largely defined by its Catholic faith and social institutions. Following the Quiet Revolution, we find a Québec that is urban, industrial, and increasingly secular in its worldview. For English Canada, the Quiet Revolution represented a significant acceleration of the demands and volume of French-Canadian nationalism. The emergence of an articulated Québécois identity in conjunction with the persistent call for Québec sovereignty led many in English Canada to begin to question whether Canada could, in fact, survive this challenge to its national-state framework.

Briefly, the Quiet Revolution was a period of political change that instituted liberal economic reforms (within a socially democratic

---

[13] The chapter was compiled from several historical narrative sources including Bashevkin (1991); Bothwell, Drummond, and English (1989); Fitzmaurice (1985); See (2001); and Thomson (1985).

context) and ethno-nationalist social and cultural reforms. The "Revolution" formally ended traditional structures of socio-political control in the form of the Catholic Church and Anglophone economic dominance in Québec commercial centers. The provincial state quickly replaced the Church in providing social services to the Québec population through the expansion of state control over education, health care, and other social services. The state also increased its role in economic sectors with the nationalization of power and water utilities (Hydro-Québec) and gaining control over a provincial pension plan that also had the ability to protect specifically Francophone businesses. The goals, and in fact the actual outcomes, of the Quiet Revolution were to reassert the Francophone, Québécois nature of Québec society while at the same time expanding economic sectors and productive capacities to harness the growth potential of liberal (economic) market integration.

The full impact of the Quiet Revolution will be discussed in the following chapter. Its importance to the development of a French-Canadian identity and culture that was neither Canadian nor French but *Québécois* cannot be understated; however its role in the history of Canada is of primary importance here. The "revolutionary" aspects of this period are debatable and will be further discussed. The extended nature of this process of change does connote some level of significant change; however the sentiment of French-Canadian or *Québécois* nationalism was neither new nor revolutionary. The significance of this change was the provision of a secular state support structure that allowed *Québécois* nationalism the opportunity to thrive as a progressive alternative to stagnant isolationism. The Quiet Revolution period was complex with divergent attitudes and directions yet served as a focal point for a people who generally felt repressed by the power of Anglophone Canada.

During the same period, Canada was faced with yet another problem – that of a resurgent economy (following the recession years of 1957–1961) and a dwindling source of labor migrants. As Europe began to recover and promote intra-continental labor migration, Canada saw a precipitous decline in its traditional sources of immigration. Labor from alternative source countries was needed if Canada was to continue its long-term project of economic growth. As a result Canada passed a series of legislative acts designed to reduce racial and ethnic restrictions on possible immigrants. In 1962 the Minister of Citizenship and Immigration announced the de-racialization of

Canadian immigration by emphasizing educational attainment and vocational skills as entry criteria. In 1966 the Assisted Passage Loan Scheme (a program of loans to desired immigrants) ended its European-only policy and was amended to include migrants from the Caribbean. Finally, in 1967 Canadian immigration policy completely eliminated race and country of origin from its selection criteria with the implementation of the Points System, which evaluated vocational and language skills, education, and other aspects of potential immigrants.

The result of this economically driven shift in immigration policy was the rapid diversification of Canadian immigration and the increasing diversification of Canadian urban areas. For example, prior to 1962 the top three origins of Canadian immigrants were the United Kingdom, Italy, and Germany. By the year 2000, the top three origins were China, India, and Pakistan (Citizenship and Immigration Canada 2000). Changes in Canadian immigration policy in the 1960s would forever change the face of metropolitan Canada and pose additional challenges to the idea of a pan-Canadian nationalism.

Managing Ethnic Diversity

The pressures of the Quiet Revolution on Canadian federalism prompted the Royal Commission on Bilingualism and Biculturalism in 1963. Their work was intended to solidify Canadian nationalism through the recognition and inclusion of Francophones as "founding peoples." The ethno-cultural dichotomy assumed by the Commission led to discontent and protest from Canadians of neither English nor French ancestry. This so-called "Third Force" rejected any bicultural definition of the country and motivated the addition of Book IV to the Commission's final report chronicling the "The Cultural Contributions of Other Ethnic Groups" in 1970. The Commission on Bilingualism and Biculturalism Report (B&B Report) would serve as an important tool for one of the most controversial Prime Ministers in Canadian history, Pierre Eliot Trudeau.

Trudeau came to power in 1968 and immediately resumed Diefenbaker's project of creating pan-Canadian nationalism. It is unclear whether Trudeau originally agreed with Diefenbaker's singular or mono-cultural view of Canada, but a resurgent Québec and a labor migrant population that was increasingly ethnically diverse motivated a shift in the federal position in defending and defining Canadian nationalism. The B&B Report allowed Trudeau to sponsor a series of cultural policies designed to define Canadian nationalism and acknowledge the changing face of the Canadian nation. The 1969 Official Languages Act recognized both English and French as national languages and in 1971 Trudeau laid the groundwork for a federal multicultural policy. These actions countered the ethnic nationalist message of the Quiet Revolution in Québec through their message of inclusion and the recognition of diversity throughout the country. In other words, through the official embrace of ethno-cultural diversity, the multiculturalism of the Trudeau administration effectively recognized the distinctive *Québécois* culture while recognizing this diversity as being of equal status to that of other non-Anglo groups in Canada. Québec was, in the eyes of the federal government, distinct but equal, and above all a *Canadian* province like all the others.

The Multicultural Policy of 1971 had yet another nationalistic purpose in its ability to distinguish Canadian diversity policy from that of the United States, thus further distinguishing a distinctly Canadian national culture. By promoting the "cultural mosaic" model over the American "melting pot" strategy, Canada could distinguish itself internationally as an increasingly distinct and independent society. This was further exemplified by the federal government's continuing concern over foreign economic investment and ownership of Canadian production facilities. Trudeau's lack of support for increased "free-trade" between the United States and Canada, as well as his unwillingness to fully support US actions in Vietnam and the Cuba trade embargo, further distanced the two countries politically while maintaining the status of mutual primary trading partners.

The question of national unity, which was a continuing priority for the Trudeau government, suffered a significant blow in 1976 with the election of René Lévesque and the Parti Québécois (PQ) in the province of Québec. The PQ wrested provincial power from the traditional liberal party (Parti libéral du Québec) on the platform of sovereignty through a renegotiated relationship with the Canadian federal government. The PQ was successful in bringing about cultural policies intended to codify the cultural goals of the Quiet Revolution. Among the most significant legislative achievements of the Levesque administration was the passage of Bill 101 (Charter of the French Language) that officially enforced French as the language of major business and government as well as requiring that new immigrants to Québec send their children to French-language schools. In 1980, the PQ brought about a public referendum on that they termed "sovereignty-association." If successful the referendum would grant authority to the provincial government to negotiate the extent and level of provincial autonomy leading toward increased sovereignty. The referendum failed as sixty percent of provincial voters rejected the proposal. The failure of the 1980 Québec referendum was a significant victory for the Trudeau administration that had dedicated tremendous resources to the defeat of the referendum. This failure for the Parti Québécois led Levesque to approach an emboldened Trudeau and work with him on a standing promise to revise the relationship between federal and provincial authorities.

Constitutional Repatriation and an Autonomous Canada[14]

These promised revisions to the British North America Act prompted Trudeau to bring provincial leaders together in the hopes that a new constitutional agreement could be reached that would replace the British North America Act. This process would grant Canada a domestic tradition of self-governance and officially remove the British legislative legacy from a political system that was practically free of British influence by this time. In November 1981 all but one of the provincial ministers signed the revised constitution (Constitution Act), which was passed as the Canada Act by the British Parliament in 1982. Québec abstained from signing the document and joined with several Native Canadian nations in rejecting the language and process of constitutional repatriation.

The Constitution Act is a significant document that articulates Canada's final entry into sovereign statehood, however also reflects the tradition of compromise in Canadian politics. The most significant point of ambiguity was the "notwithstanding clause" that allows provinces to ignore certain aspects of the Constitution that infringe on local authority. The potential invocation of this clause is particularly problematic when the Charter of Rights and Freedoms is taken into account. The Charter is an inclusive legal statement defining and

---

[14] The chapter was compiled from several historical narrative sources including Bothwell, Drummond, and English (1989); Clarkson and McCall (1994; 1990); Hart, Dymond, and Robertson (1994); and See (2001).

protecting liberal equality making the Charter "one of the most progressive constitutional documents in the world..." (See 2001, 178). Section 15 clearly exemplifies the inclusive nature of the document:

> Every individual is equal before and under the law and has the right to the equal protection and equal benefit of the law without discrimination and, in particular, without discrimination based on race, national or ethnic origin, colour, religion, sex, age or mental or physical disability[15].

The Constitution Act finally defined Canada as a fully autonomous country with a functioning constitutional foundation. Many have pointed to this document as an ultimate success for Trudeau and his projects of nation-building and pan-Canadian nationalism. However the persisting domestic thorn in Trudeau's side was Québec. Despite his tireless efforts to include the province within a unique nation-state, the province continued to be dissatisfied with the lack of recognition and authority granted by the federal government on a number of issues.

The Constitution Act is a significant illustration of this disparity due to the continuing absence of a Québec signature. To date, the province of Québec has not signed the Constitution Act yet functions within the federal Canadian system as if it had. Again, the legislative ambiguity of federal-provincial relationships serves as a double-edged sword in the quest for a united Canadian nation-state. Although the challenges posed by the Quiet Revolution and the 1980 Québec Referendum resulted in a stronger federal Canadian state, the nation continued to be increasingly fragmented.

The Meech Lake and Charlottetown Accords

The problems of national fragmentation and unequal state participation were addressed by Prime Minister Brian Mulroney and Québec

---

[15] This statement is a general definition of equality rights. The entirety of the Charter of Rights and Freedoms continues to include groups as protected Canadians on the basis of race, ethnicity, language, culture, sex, religion, and disabilities with significant legal protections for all Canadians. The document also shows the imprint of provincial negotiations in its specific language. For example, in Section 16 on Official Languages, subsection two clearly identifies New Brunswick as the only officially bilingual province in a bilingual Canada. The entire Charter of Rights and Freedoms is included in the 1982 Constitution Act, which can be found at http://laws.justice.gc.ca/en/const/annex_e.html#I.

Premier Robert Bourassa in the 1987 Meech Lake Accords. Provincial ministers agreed to modify the existing Constitution Act to recognize Québec as a uniquely distinctive society within Canada, reinforce the federal commitment to bilingualism, allow provinces additional authority in matters of immigration, and give greater authority to provincial constitutional veto powers. Clearly, the federal government was willing to give Québec and other provinces increased authority in exchange for national unity. The Manitoba Legislative Assembly, however, did not agree and refused to sign the Accord. Newfoundland then followed the Manitoban example and rejected the Accord as well. Objections were raised over the significance of Québec society and federal recognition of uniqueness over all other Canadian provinces, cultures, and concerns. The First Nations also objected that their concerns were not addressed and that their level of participation was not acceptable. With passage in only eight of the required ten provinces, the Meech Lake Accord failed to resolve the lingering constitutional non-participation of Québec.

The 1992 Charlottetown Accord again attempted to reconcile Québec's concerns with the 1982 Constitution Act. A group of provincial, federal, First Nations, and Métis representatives reached an agreement designed to encourage national unity and promote a singular Canadian nation-state. The Accord limited federal powers over provincial statues; guaranteed federal funding of social services such as health care and education while limiting provisional requirements for funding; included a "Canada Clause" that recognized certain values as being officially "Canadian" such as equality, diversity, and again recognizing the distinct nature of the Québec province, culture, and society; and interestingly included a statement on liberalizing trade through the abolition of protective tariffs between provinces. The Charlottetown Accord, unlike the failed Meech Lake Accord, was to be put to a national vote through the referendum process, although unanimous approval was again required for ratification. Only five of the twelve Canadian provinces approved the Accord with Québec rejecting the proposal 57 to 43 percent.

The failure of the Charlottetown Accord to resolve Québec constitutional non-participation led to the defeat of Bourassa's Liberal government in Québec. The Parti Québécois again gained power in 1994 led by Jacques Parizeau and held another referendum the following year. The 1995 referendum was supported by the PQ, a new federal separatist party, the Bloc Québécois, led by Lucien Bouchard, and popular dissatisfaction with federal efforts to resolve Québec's objections to the Constitution Act. The 1995 referendum was only narrowly defeated (50.6 percent to 49.4 percent) and continued the legacy of ambiguous cooperation in a Canada that continues to struggle with issues of domestic unity.

Economic Growth and the Shift to "Free-Trade"

The 1970s saw a continual rise in Canadian economic growth as well as international political status. The federal government further clarified immigration definitions through the 1978 Immigration Act that created categories for refugees and other humanitarian immigration cases as well as further reducing discriminatory measures targeting medical problems and sexual orientation. The process of urbanization and ethnic diversification continued throughout Canada creating a country that could be defined as primarily urban with 76 percent of all Canadians living in urban areas in 1980 (Statistics Canada 1996). Canadian economic growth and geographic proximity to the United States led to inclusion in the 1976 G7 economic summit and subsequent participation in the group's meetings and operational agreements. Some have pointed to this inclusion as being somewhat artificial as mid-1970s Canadian economic performance was not necessarily on par with that of other G7 countries and perhaps promoted Canada to international prominence before the state was prepared to assume such a role (Hawkins 1988, 12). This premature promotion to the global political economic elite continued Canadian global market integration, particularly with respect to liberal "free trade."

The election of the Conservative Mulroney government in 1984 ushered in the end of large-scale trade protectionism, even though the official Conservative party platform was against expanding Canadian "free trade" agreements. In fact, the issue of "free-trade" was, by this time, already in practice between Canada and the United States with the most notable liberal trade policy being the Canada-United State Automotive Agreement (Auto Pact) of 1965. There were significant trade protections remaining that were effectively demolished by the Canada-United State Free Trade Agreement (CUFTA) in 1987. Political opposition to this liberal trade agreement and the fears that this would usher in the fall of Canadian economic and cultural independence made CUFTA the central issue of the 1988 federal elections.

Mulroney's Conservatives won, but the two parties (New Democratic Party and the Liberal Party) in opposition to CUFTA received the majority of total votes. Liberal opposition was short-lived as the 1993 election of Jean Chretien's Liberal government saw the expansion of CUFTA to include Mexico with the enactment of the North American Free Trade Agreement (NAFTA) in 1994.

Liberal trade agreements remain an issue in Canadian politics, but opposition to liberal trade and globalization has been marginalized. The only remaining political party in opposition to "free-trade" agreements remains the New Democratic Party. However public opposition to NAFTA has been resurgent in the past few years largely due to the United States' failure to adhere to the trade agreements[16].

Present-day Canada is by most accounts a successful nation-state despite the failure to resolve several key national problems. Canadian economic growth has out performed its fellow G8 countries for the past several years and fiscal solvency projects have resulted in federal surplus revenues for the past six years. This economic growth has not been without cost. The federally funded health care system (Health Canada) is facing increased financial difficulty after years of reduced funding. Education and cultural programs, including the vaunted Multicultural Program have experienced years of reduced funding. In addition, increased regional dissatisfaction with federal appropriations and intrusion on perceived provincial matters has continued to mar federal and provincial relationships. The ever-increasingly close economic relationship with the United States continues to serve as a thorn in the side of Canadian nationalists as they often lament the loss of distinctive Canadian culture to American symbols and affinities. The combined threat of external influence and internal dissatisfaction poses a major problem for future Canadian leaders, particularly with respect to promoting an acceptable national identity. The recent "Adscam[17]" scandal illustrates the immediacy and problematic nature

---

[16] The continuing dispute over softwood lumber sales to the United States has been a significant obstacle. The US position on applying tariffs to Canadian softwood timber was ruled illegal by the NAFTA adjudication body on several occasions. A recent World Trade Organization ruling was more amenable to the US position, but the situation has yet to be resolved.

[17] "Adscam" is the informal moniker given to the scandal that has brought about the recent fall of the Martin Liberal government. Briefly, the Chretien Administration authorized the payment of millions of dollars to several Québec marketing firms for the purpose of promoting Canadian nationalism in the province. The intent was

of promoting a pan-Canadian national identity. For the Canadian government, this is a necessary project if Canada is to survive.

Despite these simultaneous successes and failures, the issue of most significance is the persistence of the "French Fact." The solidification of Québec as an autonomous and culturally distinct province within Canada continues to be problematic for the federal government and its project of pan-Canadian nationalism. The following chapter adds more detail to the history of this "French Fact" and juxtaposes Québec history and nationalism with that of Canada.

The goal of Chapter Three, however, is to establish a clear, yet problematic, nationalist project in Canada. Economic under-population, dual European colonial heritage, indigenous autonomy and sovereignty claims, and increasing ethno-cultural diversification are just a sample of the challenges to articulating a singular Canadian nationalism. This has not stopped the federal government and other supporting groups from attempting to define what in fact a Canadian actually is. This challenge is increasingly important as the national population of Canada becomes more diverse as a result of shifting immigration sources. This project argues that culture is becoming increasingly important in maintaining nation-state stability. The history of Canada implies that culture is a continually problematic notion, but also that the state has continually worked to define Canadian nationalism in various attempts to maintain a singular national cultural ideal. The remainder of the monograph examines the changes that have occurred in the post-World War II era and argues that the challenges facing the Canadian state with respect to defining a national culture and maintaining national stability are increasingly complex and problematic. The essay also argues that control over cultural definitions and symbols is increasingly important and necessary for core states such as Canada. Chapter Four will examine the same process of Québec national cultural definition in historical context.

the encourage Québécois voters to support Canada as opposed to the PQ and its project of sovereignty. In reality, this support of Canadian nationalism took the form of illegal financial contributions to the Québec provincial wing of the Liberal party (the PLQ). The money meant for marketing purposes was, in effect, laundered through these marketing firms and used for political purposes in support of the PLQ and defeat of the PQ.

CHAPTER FOUR

QUÉBEC: HISTORY AND THE CENTRALITY OF
NATIONAL IDENTITY

This chapter illustrates the interdependent history of Québec as a Canadian province. It also tells the story of Québec national cultural development as a process and project independent of Canadian nationalism. In this way the history of Québec is the history of Canada; however, the nationalist history of Québec retains significant autonomy from that of Canadian nationalist history. The persistence of this duality, a shared yet distinct history, is problematic for both Canadian and Québec nationalist projects. Chapter Four examines this shared history with particular attention to distinctive events, conditions, and occurrences that have defined Québécois nationalism and enabled a distinct Québec national history to develop alongside Canadian national history. The existence of dual nationalist histories is important in support of methodological comparative efforts as well as understanding divergent approaches to global market integration that will be shown in Part III.

The persistence of this duality is has historically provided the most significant obstacle for a singular Canadian nationalism. The "French Fact[1]" of a Francophone founding people is a reality that Canada is continually forced to reconcile. Any discussion of one must include a substantial discussion of the other. However, the unique and relatively insular creation of culture in both Québec and in Anglophone Canada raises serious questions concerning the development of a homogenous historical narrative[2]. The question of autonomy is very real when

---

[1] The "French Fact" is a term describing the reality of bilingualism in Canada. This is a phrase that is used mainly in an Anglophone and federalist context. The 1774 Québec Act was the first official recognition of the "French Fact" in an otherwise Anglo colony. This attitude of resignation has given way to the official incorporation of the "French Fact" into state policies of bilingualism. As stated by the Canadian Heritage Department, "Recognizing the importance of the French fact at home, as well as its international dimension, the Canadian government joined *La Francophonie* [this refers to the international cooperative entity consisting of Francophone countries] very early on and was involved in establishing and developing its many institutions."

[2] The issue of cultural diversity by region and settlement patterns has always been present in Canadian history. The unique history of the Acadian (New Brunswick)

discussing both Canadian and Québec histories. The reality of history necessitates a dual telling of the Canadian story. The historical reality of the "French Fact" in Canada is that Québec has created a culture and society that is national in its actions and composition. This chapter will also show that the relative successes of Québécois nationalism present equally challenging conditions as Québec integrates into the global market economy.

As previously stated, this chapter takes the position that it is not only possible, but also historically necessary to understand Québec as a semi-autonomous nation-state in a political, economic, and cultural sense. In support of this methodological definition, a brief telling of the Québec provincial story is necessary.

Settlement to Conquest[3]

The French were the first European group to actively colonize what would become Canada. Of course this was a project of appropriation as many Native Canadians occupied the land desired by encroaching Europeans. The French experience in Canada was typical in the sense that disease and warfare worked to decimate a once populous general Native Canadian population. The experience was unique, however, in the sense that there was a level of cooperation and cohabitation with indigenous groups that existed on a scale not often seen in the history of American colonization.

The first claim of French sovereignty over the lands of Eastern Canada was made by Giovanni da Verrazano whose voyages were funded by the French monarch François I between 1524 and 1528. The French began their colonial endeavor by joining Portuguese, Basque, British, and Irish fishing expeditions off the Newfoundland and Nova Scotia coasts. François also sponsored Jacques Cartier's three explora-tory voyages between 1534 and 1542. Cartier's mission was to find the mythical Northwest Passage to China but instead "discovered" the

region differs from that of Québec, from that of Alberta, from that of Vancouver. To say that there is even a clear homogenous narrative in Francophone or Anglophone Canada would be incorrect. The growth of Canadians of neither French nor British origins further complicates the project of constructing a singular Canadian historical narrative.

[3] The chapter was compiled from several historical narrative sources including Dickason (1997), Eccles (1972; 1969), Mathieu (1991), Parkman (1983; 1962), and See (2001).

Native Canadian settlements of Stadacona and Hochelaga, which would be renamed Québec and Montréal respectively as the French settled and took control of the region. Successive voyages saw Cartier and a French nobleman by the name of Roberval attempt settlements at Stadacona (Québec) with no success. It seemed that no passage to the Orient would be found nor would the land produce the mineral wealth found by Spanish expeditionary forces in Central and South America. Cartier's voyages yielded little in terms of material wealth but did produce considerable information concerning geography and natural resource potential. Contact with Native Canadians was simultaneously negative and cooperative. Cartier's kidnapping of several Iroquois who died under his care set the stage for centuries of French-Iroquois conflict. Conversely, Cartier was able to gain information and negotiate limited trade with several Iroquois and Algonquin groups. Perhaps Cartier's most lasting contribution was his use of the Iroquois place name *Canada* to identify the region.

More than half a century passed before sustained French efforts to settle Canada were resumed. Samuel de Champlain, with the financial backing of the Sieur de Monts, first attempted a permanent settlement near the present-day border of New Brunswick and Maine on the St. Croix River. This was a short-lived experiment as the settlers, including Champlain, were forced to abandon the location in 1607 and return to France. Undaunted, Champlain led another settlement expedition in 1608, this time in the more protected St. Lawrence River region. Champlain's desire to facilitate trade between the French and Native Canadians promoted a fairly successful cooperative effort to coexist. A benefit to such a cooperative agreement on the part of the Algonquin was the acquisition of a powerful ally in their persistent conflicts with the now southern tribes of the Iroquois Confederation. This agreement created local security as well as an ally for the new settlement of Québec on the former Iroquois site of Stadacona. It also would create a European-Indigenous alliance that would serve to allow French settlement and the nascent fur trade to succeed.

The settlement of Québec, and later Montréal, succeeded and became important trade centers for the single most important commodity being exported to Europe from Canada: furs and pelts. The relationship between Québec and France was strictly mercantilist. The colony had a monopolistic trade relationship with the French Company of Hundred Associates and barred Protestants from settling in what was then called New France. This dominance of Roman Catholicism would shape the history and destiny of New France and later Québec until the latter half of the Twentieth Century.

As the colony began to grow, agriculture became a more sustained project. Clearing of the St. Lawrence River Valley became a priority and was seen as essential to the sustained growth of New France. The model of land appropriation was modeled on the feudal French seigneurial system. The crown would grant land to *seigneurs*, direct representatives of the French monarchy, who then divided the land grant among tenant farmers who became known as *habitants* (although officially termed *censitaires* by the French authorities). Most of these agricultural communities remained in the St. Lawrence Valley and served as the central grain-producing region of New France. Life in colonial New France was rural, religious, and feudal in its structure. But, as Scott See states, "ample evidence suggests that *habitants* enjoyed some freedoms, aggressively asserted an independent streak, and regularly ignored state regulations or church edicts. In short, the peasants of the Old World were swiftly becoming the *Canadiens* of the New World" (2001, 45).

New France began to grow as a result of an agricultural base that supported the semi-urban settlements of Québec and Montréal, which in turn supported the flourishing fur trade that created the urban center of Montréal and solidified its place as the commercial capital of New France. This demographic and economic growth, in addition to the strategic transportation value of the St. Lawrence River system, ensured that the colony of New France would soon come into conflict with the burgeoning British American colonies to the south. A series of European continental conflicts (King William's War, 1689–1697; the War of Spanish Succession, 1701–1714; and King George's War, 1744–1748) instigated tensions between colonial rivals that resulted in nearly continual military and paramilitary conflict in North America from the mid-Seventeenth to the late Eighteenth centuries. These conflicts culminated in the Seven Years' War in which the British gained complete control over all former French colonial possessions in North America.

As stated in the previous chapter, the short period of British assimilationist efforts in the newly named colony of Québec failed miserably. The recognition that Québec would always be a French culture was recognized by then-Governor James Murray. The 1763 Royal Proclamation that removed legislative support for the seigneurial system as well as support for the Catholic Church, made it illegal for Catholics to hold public office, and imposed both British criminal and civil law upon an unwilling populace created an impossible position from which to govern. Murray and his successor Guy Carleton supported ending this assimilationist project and partially succeed with the enactment of the Québec Act in 1774.

Post-conquest and a Bicultural Existence[4]

The Québec Act was designed to reinstate French civil controls in the hopes that those reinstated elites would support the larger British colonial project. This was increasingly important to British colonial authorities due to growing rebellious sentiment in its American colonies. As Conrad, Finkel, and Jaenen (1993) state:

> Designed to strengthen the traditional elites in the colony, the act was based on the mistaken belief that those elites would ensure the loyalty of the masses in time of war (P. 254).

The austere provisions of the 1763 Proclamation were reversed to allow Catholics to worship, hold office, and ensure that the traditional system of religious authority would continue. In addition, the seigneurial system of land ownership and administration was officially recognized by the British colonial authorities. British criminal law and, of course, colonial authority remained entrenched. The result was a colony extending from the Labrador coast to the Ohio River Valley that was uniquely French, Catholic, and governed by the anti-democratic cooperation of priest and seigneur that pleased few outside of the local power structures in British North America, including American colonists and many *habitants*.

As previously stated, the Québec Act was as much of a British protective measure as it was a policy designed to control the French-Canadian population. The hope that Québec colonials would support the British was initially dashed as invading American contingents under Richard Montgomery met little or no resistance in their march to Montréal. The city was taken without a struggle in September 1775 with Governor Carleton escaping to Québec. The mobilization of resistance to the American invasion was less a result of the Québec Act

---

[4] This section was compiled from several narrative historical sources including Conrad, Finkel, and Jaenen (1993); Fitzmaurice (1985); Plourde (2000); Rioux (1974); and See (2001).

and more the actions of the occupying American forces. Antagonistic actions against the Catholic Church and the illegal acquisition of property and supplies by Montgomery's men led to a rapid increase in local support for the British defensive forces. By the time Montgomery joined with Benedict Arnold (who had marched from what is now Maine) at Québec they met heavy resistance in defense of the city. On December 31 the combined American forces saw Montgomery killed and Arnold wounded in a last major attempt at taking Québec. The siege was ended in May of 1776 when ten thousand British troops sailed down the St. Lawrence to reinforce the besieged colonial forces (numbering fewer than 600) at Québec.

The lack of local *habitant* support for the British war effort troubled British colonial authorities. Elite control over the local "peasant" populations envisioned in the Québec Act never materialized. The position of the British political hierarchy was soon to be reinforced through the immigration of large numbers of British migrants. After the 1783 Versailles Treaty that ended the American Revolution, thousands of British Loyalists (Tories) escaped to the colony of Québec. This massive population shift significantly altered the demographic composition of the colony and prompted British authorities to take action.

The newly arrived Tories demanded an elimination of the French system of civil law and a return to the monopolistic British controls inherent in the 1763 Royal Proclamation. French-Canadian elites were not sympathetic to the demands of the Tories for obvious reasons. A compromise was found as the 1791 Canada Act officially divided Canada into Upper (English) and Lower (French) halves. Upper Canada, roughly present-day Ontario, was home to approximately 20,000 Anglophone Canadians and Tories and maintained British criminal and civil systems of governance. Lower Canada, roughly present-day Québec, included the metropolitan areas of Montréal and Québec with a population of approximately 110,000 and maintained the French civil/British criminal system established by the Québec Act (Conrad, Finkel, and Jaenen 1993). In comparison, the Canadian population near the turn of the century is estimated at 250,000 (Klein, Goldewijk, and Battjes 1997). The French-Canadian population constituted a significant portion of the total national population and was able to resist assimilationist efforts on the part of British colonial authorities. The British government grew increasingly aware of its inability to assimilate such a large population and sought a compromise solution. The Canada Act effectively created a bifurcated colonial nation-state by creating legislative and administrative divisions between English and French Canada.

Growth and Rebellion under British Rule

Lower Canada in the beginning of the Nineteenth Century was a colony governed by an odd mix of Anglophone commercial and political elites supported by the Francophone seigneurs and clerical elites. This relationship, and the centrality of English control over the commercial activities in Montréal and Québec, would create a condition of stratification. The sustainable farming tradition of the habitants created a condition of poverty that was much more extreme when compared to English wage-earning farmers in Upper Canada. The lack of land ownership coupled with a relatively feudal system of social and commercial interaction for Lower Canadian, Francophone farmers allowed the consolidation of wealth in urban areas and primarily in the hands of the Anglophone commercial merchants and political elites. Of course a significant amount of wealth was distributed to Francophone seigneurs and to the Church, which resulted in limited elite motivation to alter the status quo. The situation of urban (particularly in Montréal) Anglophone control over wealth and commercial resources would couple with the strong social service (health care, education, moral guidance, etc…) structure of the Catholic Church to create an unfortunate disparity in wealth and resources that largely followed cultural lines.

Despite the socio-economic stagnation engendered by the British colonial power structure in Lower Canada, economic expansion was occurring. The decline of the fur trade that had largely created the commercial center of Montréal was replaced by timber extraction. Lower Canada became the primary supplier of timber to the British Navy further reinforcing the commercial power of the Montréal Anglophone elite. The desire to increase the English presence throughout the colony led to the granting of land to Anglophone farmers (mainly expatriate American Tories) willing to move to Lower Canada. Approximately 20,000 agricultural migrants settled in what is now known as the Eastern Townships to the South and East of Montréal following the 1791 Constitutional Act. The Townships remain to this day one of the few examples of a rural Anglophone presence in Québec.

The dominance of the English-Catholic alliance in Lower Canada was dealt a blow by the French Revolution, but a blow that would only be felt years later. With the conservative French-Canadian Catholic Church aghast at the liberalism and independence of French Revolutionary ideals new sources of educated priests (not immediately influenced by the liberalism of France) was required. The Church established Francophone colleges throughout Lower Canada to train future clerical leaders. Many of these graduates would choose a secular path and created a limited but important Francophone middle class. These were mainly civil servants and lawyers who were ultimately subject to the ethnocentric controls of the British that kept many in this increasingly populous professional class unemployed. This educated and skilled Francophone group began to advocate a Francophone nationalism that embraced political democracy while retaining the feudal economic and cultural controls embodied in the seigneurial system and the Catholic Church. This uniquely conservative nationalism would speak on behalf of Québec sovereigntists until 1960. This rise of a Francophone intellectual elite was coupled with a growing population that was impoverished by the proto-feudal seigneurial system[5].

The persistence of poverty in Québec promoted anger and frustration particularly among the Francophone *habitants* who viewed the accumulation of wealth and power by the Anglophone minority in Montréal, as well as increased agricultural prosperity in Upper Canada, as signs of English oppression. In fact, it was the combination of arcane economic controls and the cultural promotion of high birth rates that contributed most greatly to the agricultural (read: economic) crisis of the early Nineteenth Century. This fact was not lost on the British colonial authorities who did little to assist Québec in alleviating nearly universal rural poverty among the Francophone population. In fact, the acquisition and distribution of land in the Eastern Townships added to the sense of abandonment on the part of the habitants as these acquisitions were based on the liberal capitalist notion of land-granting and thus outside the patronage of the seigneurs. Thus the only individuals and groups able to acquire these newly created agricultural plots were

---

[5] As population increased in the early Nineteenth Century, there were not enough *seigneurs* to supply land appropriations in order to meet demands. The seigneurial system was based solely on patronage and thus did not allow the *habitants* an opportunity to accumulate capital in the same manner as their English peers. The Roman Catholic Church culturally promoted large families and the inevitable condition of a large population with little to no capital and an agricultural system that was ill designed to deal with the reality of capitalism led to massive poverty. Add this to poor crop yields in the post-1812 era and a picture of dire poverty is painted of the Québec rural landscape.

those with disposable capital, which excluded nearly the entirety of the habitant population.

The newly emergent Francophone intellectual elite seized this opportunity and created the *Parti canadien* (PC), a nationalist political party designed to gain power through legislative means in the Québec House of Assembly. The conservative nationalism of the political party was welcomed by the traditional Francophone elites (seigneurs and Catholic clergy) due to the fact that it allowed the retention of their social station and power. In 1822, the *Parti canadien*, with the support of the Catholic Church, defeated a British proposal to unite Lower and Upper Canada. In 1827, the PC won nearly ninety percent of the available seats in the House elections due to habitant support for a policy of increased seigneurial holdings that meant greater agricultural opportunities for a desperate rural population. These demands persisted and created a significant level of tension between Anglophone merchants and their allies in both Upper and Lower Canada who viewed this "obstructionism" (through their promotion of an *expanded* seigneurial system) as being anti-commercial and thus a threat to economic growth in Canada (Conrad, Finkel, and Jaenen 1993, 414). As a result, steps were taken in 1837 to circumvent Assembly control and increase privately held land outside of the seigneurial system. Funds were appropriated by the British colonial government for the sale of millions of hectares of land to the British American Land Company; these holdings were then sold to the highest bidder – effectively excluding most Francophones. These actions allowed the PC and its leader Louis-Joseph Papineau to legitimate their claims that the British government cared little for improving the lives and democratic rights of its Francophone citizens.

A series of economic and civic disobedience tactics ensued that were intended to subvert British political and economic controls. Sporadic violence broke out between Anglophones and Francophone *patriotes* in Montréal and the Governor of Lower Canada, Lord Gosford, called for the immediate use of British troops to quell any Francophone nationalist sentiment and violence. Papineau and other *patriote* leaders were ordered arrested and many, including Papineau, fled to the United States. Organized resistance in the form of organized *habitant* militias defeated a British colonial force at St-Denis in November 1837. The days following this initial victory saw a deflated (after Papineau's escape to the United States) rebellion crushed by British troops. A brief attempt at rekindling the rebellion occurred the following year when approximately four thousand patriots, led by leaders who had escaped to the US in 1837, attacked British positions in Lower Canada. They were quickly defeated and the British sought to quell any future rebellion through the execution, deportation, and exile of *patriote* leaders.

These relatively minor armed rebellions were important examples of the development of *Canadien* nationalism; however their defeat illustrates a conflict of interest between political, economic, and cultural spheres of Québec society. Prior to 1837, the *Parti canadien* transformed into the *Parti patriote* which succeeded in promoting a reduction in the socio-political power of the Church in Québec society. The obvious outcome was that the Church refused to support the rebellion and thus an opportunity for legitimation was lost. The continuing affirmation of the seigneurial system by the *Parti patriote* was also a source of consternation for many *habitants*. Why should they risk their lives to maintain a traditional system of land allocation that denied them ownership and profits? These points did little to engender universal support for the *patriote* rebellions and possibly contributed to their ultimate failure.

As stated in the previous chapter, the political outcome of the Lower (and Upper) Canadian rebellions was the compilation of the Durham Report that advocated assimilation of all Francophone *Canadiens* through a process of colonial unification. The Durham Report prompted the 1841 Act of Union that promptly infuriated nationalist *Candiens*, but offered a unique opportunity for compromise between English and French parliamentarians. The Act of Union occurred simultaneously with a British move away from mercantilist trade and toward a liberal "free-trade" model. This created increased trade opportunities between Canada and the United States, resulting in the 1854 Treaty of Reciprocity. The result was a situation that encouraged modernization of political economic systems of control in a traditional Lower Canadian society.

Encroaching Liberalism and Confederation[6]

As Canadiens struggled for executive governmental inclusion (achieved through an Anglo-Franco Executive Committee in 1842, rescinded by

---

[6] This section was compiled from several narrative historical sources including Conrad, Finkel, and Jaenen (1992); Linteau, Durocher, and Robert (1983); Mann (1982); Morton (1964); Plourde (2000); and See (2001).

the subsequent Governor General Metcalf, and reinstated in 1848) an alliance between economic and political liberals crossed ethnic lines. An unintended parliamentary majority emerged that advocated reforming the existing socio-economic structure of Canada in order to facilitate increased trade. The result was the dissolution of the seigneurial land-patronage system in 1854, increased spending on public (secular) education, and massive transportation projects (railways and canals) intended to encourage expanded trade with the United States. Thus, the Durham Report and the subsequent Act of Union succeeded in achieving a measure of assimilation through the destruction of the unique land-holding system and monopolistic control over education held by the Catholic Church that created the differences upheld as "distinct" by the conservative nationalists of the 1830s. Cooperative multiethnic governments showed that the common political economic goals of liberalism and "free-trade" could overcome linguistic and cultural differences. This serene picture of cooperative economic development hid the continued stratification of economic conditions between Upper and Lower Canada.

The political alliance of Anglo and Francophones based on a common desire for liberal economic reforms was an elite alliance. Popular support for such reform-centered cooperation was limited by the persistence of economic stratification based on ethno-linguistic lines. These economic divisions created the opportunity for political dissent on the part of conservative opponents of liberal reforms in Québec. These conservative nationalists relied on cultural definitions of Québec traditions and norms and provided the basis for a unique Québec nationalism that was based on cultural affinity and traditionalism.

The Canadian response to the American Civil War and a decline in trade volume with both the United States (who refused to renew the Treaty of Reciprocity in 1866) and Britain was to promote a more politically sovereign union. The result was the Confederation of Canada under the British North America Act of 1867. Within Lower Canada, liberals and the conservative clergy celebrated the prospect of Confederation as an opportunity to alleviate pressures of American annexation and to establish political control over a provincial government. There was significant opposition to Confederation in the form of the *Rouges* who advocated a nationalistic and democratic ideal that mirrored that of their *Patriote* founders. The *Rouges*-led opposition could not overcome the liberal-clerical alliance and Confederation became a reality in 1867. The new parliamentary system established minimum rates of representation for provincial Members of Parliament (MP) and consolidated strong central federal control over political and economic matters. Fitzmaurice provides a useful example of this renegotiated trade reality:

> The Provinces of course lost their customs revenue, but the Dominion of Canada assumed their debt and paid them an annual subsidy (Fitzmaurice 1985, 20).

This exemplifies the series of compromises made on the part of Provincial representatives in the hopes of creating a strong union to expand economic production and political protections (largely from encroaching American capital investment and population in the West). What it does not show is any legislative evidence of continual *Canadien* nationalism that was embodied by the *Rouges* opposition to Confederation.

Westward Expansion and the National Policy Reaction

One of the primary goals of the post-confederation federal government was national economic development. As discussed in Chapter Three, the philosophical difference between the liberalism of the Liberal Party and the protectionism of the Conservative Party would compete until the late 1870s when Macdonald's third term as Prime Minister would usher in a dominant era of economic protectionism through the National Policy of 1879.

Reaction in Québec to the National Policy and its economic goals of insular national trade was generally favorable. In fact, the expansion of manufacturing and other materials production would significantly enhance the capital base of the province. However, the nationalism inherent in this economic was limited by its inability to transcend historical cultural disparities. This oversight was significant at both provincial and national levels. Provincially, Québec was governed by a cultural code that lionized the Francophone ideal as rural, agrarian, and Catholic, which facilitated an urban, industrial space for the Anglophone population in and around Montreal. Put simply, the ideological promotion of a Québec national identity outside of urban wealth centers ensured both relative Francophone poverty and Anglophone economic dominance.

Despite the fact that Montreal was approximately 60% Francophone in 1871, the overall percentage of Francophones in the province living in an urban area was under 9% (Levine 1990, 10). This demographic majority did not, however, translate into economic power. Post-conquest control over the fur trade shifted to the English as the Hudson Bay Company both institutionalized its control over the trade and utilized Montreal as the financial and distribution terminus. The capital centered in and around Montreal was firmly in the hands of Anglophones and would perpetuate an economic inequality along linguistic lines until the 1980s (see Fenwick 1982; Vaillancourt 1996; see also Albouy 2006). Wealth, particularly urban capital, was distinctly English.

While the promotion of a Francophone cultural nationalism discouraging urban capital accumulation certainly contributed to this disparity, structural conditions – historical and cultural – created an urban inequality that placed Anglophone financiers and industrialists in a position to take advantage of the industrial development and market protections encouraged by the National Policy. Francophones, either rural farmers or urban laborers, may have benefitted through increased job creation, but certainly not through expanded wealth creation or a resolution to the culturally-based income inequality in the Montreal area. Broad Francophone support for this level of national economic protectionism was tepid, at best.

Culturally, however, provincial support for nation-building was much more problematic. The danger in the minds of many Francophones was that the emergent nation of Canada would eventually coalesce around Anglo or British cultural-historical norms – the effect of which would minimize Francophone Canada through cultural attrition. Given Macdonald's emphasis on the British roots of any Canadian national future, it seems that these Francophone fears were based in substantial ideological fact.

The newly formed Dominion of Canada was reminded of the persistent "French Fact" when Louis Riel led his fellow Métis[7] in an open revolt against the westward expansion and the inattention of the new federal government to several land greivences made by indigenous and Métis populations. Riel was born in the Red River region

---

[7] As stated in Chapter Three, the Métis were a distinct population born of intermarriage between English and French fur trappers and indigenous peoples in the interior of Canada. The Métis are historically known for their mixed ethnicity and the fact that they are predominantly Francophone. The linguistic nature of this Canadian population is of primary importance in this chapter and in the relationship between the *Canadien* population of Québec and the resistance actions of Riel and other Métis in what is now Manitoba and Saskatchewan.

of what is now Manitoba but received a clerical education in Montréal. Educated, Francophone, and Métis, Riel personified Canadian diversity and became an important symbol for many Francophones in Eastern Canada.

During the Red River and Northwest rebellions of 1869–70 and 1885 respectively, Riel and his followers were largely objecting to the acquisition of land and resources by the federal government and to what they perceived as the development of a monopolistic power of the federal government over these resources. While both rebellions were ultimately repressed, the fundamental issues resonated in Québec. Although the actions of Riel and the Métis were antithetical to the liberal project of westward expansion, his resistance to an oppressive federal force that was attacking yet another Francophone claim of sovereignty and uniqueness generated public support for the man throughout Québec. The sentiment was just as strong in the opposite direction throughout English-speaking Ontario, as they viewed Riel as a traitor and enemy of Canadian economic growth (Siggins 1994). Bowing to strong Anglophone pressure, Macdonald ordered Real's execution on November 16, 1885. This decision solidified popular opposition in Québec to both the universality project of Confederation and to Macdonald's Conservative party (which was then in power in Québec at the time of real's death).

The political and economic union of the Confederation-era clearly did not reflect the cultural differences still evident between French and English Canada. While Riel's actions did little to stem expansion, they did illustrate persisting frustration and a sense of repression on the part of French-Canadians, particularly in Québec. The Dominion of Canada was a political and economic compromise of the day, and not indicative of any cultural unification on the part of the citizens of Québec in support of a pan-Canadian nation. A tangible manifestation of this dissatisfaction was the 1887 Interprovincial Conference, organized by then-Premier Honré Mercier.

Mercier's ascendency was the first electoral reaction to Real's execution. As leader of the opposition Liberals, Mercier was able to capitalize on provincial anger and promote a coalition alternative, briefly allying with the reactionary and nationalist *Parti Nationale*[8], to the ruling Conservatives. His election in 1886 allowed him to extend his

---

[8] The Liberal-*Parti National* alliance lasted was approximately one year – after the 1886 provincial election it was obvious that the moniker was merely windowdressing

goals of provincial autonomy beyond Québec as he organized the first Interprovincial Conference in Québec City. While provincial attendance was not complete (British Columbia and Prince Edward Island were not in attendance) and its resolutions non-binding, Mercier's leadership illustrated that the provinces were not quiescent members of the Canadian federation, nor would Québec simply protest in isolation.

Industrialization and Urbanization

The mid-Nineteenth Century in Québec was a time of rapid change. Modernization and urbanization began to weaken the traditional controls of the Catholic Church and the patrimonial seigneurial system of land appropriation had been abolished allowing individual farmers at least the opportunity to own their own land. The post-Confederation period was also a time of massive expansion in industrial and demographic growth. The Macdonald National Policy necessitated expanded migration – and Québec's location as a primary European gateway meant that Québec City and Montreal would be initial ports of call for many European migrants[9]. European immigration served to augment the limited Canadian labor force and engender the expansion of manufacturing so desired by Canadian capitalists. Québec's role in this process was significantly determined by geography. The most logical ports of call for European immigrants were Halifax, Québec, and

---

as the vast majority of Mercier supporters remained Liberals. Mercier soon reassumed the title of *Parti Libéral du Québec* soon after becoming Premier in 1886.

[9] By the mid-Nineteenth Century urban Canada was fairly limited. Two of the four major metropolitan areas were in Québec and both located along the major transportation throughway of the St. Lawrence River. Montréal (100,000) and Québec (50,000) continued to serve as trade ports and centers for Canadian commerce during this period. Québec could eventually lose much of its metropolitan and commercial power nationally due to the reorientation of trade patterns from the United Kingdom to the United States. Trans-Atlantic trade was facilitated by the protected ports on the St. Lawrence, but as trading patterns shifted southward the river system declined in relative economic importance. This shift in predominant trading partners is also reflected in the rise of both Montréal and Toronto as commercial urban centers. The rise of Toronto (60,000) would continue unabated and ultimately become the desired destination for many labor migrants. Halifax (20,000) continued to be Canada's main maritime trading center, but the fragile economic conditions of the Maritime Provinces as well as the transportation costs associated with domestic Canadian trade would ensure Halifax's eventual decline in commercial importance.

Montréal. Halifax, as Canada's primary Atlantic seaport, offered a simple first-stop for European migrants on the road to Canadian economic opportunity. The relative isolation of Halifax and the Maritime Provinces in general discouraged many from settling in Halifax. The major urban centers of Québec and Montréal provided much more in terms of employment and transportation opportunities. As the only opportunity to travel from Europe to North America was by seagoing vessel the St. Lawrence once again provided a maritime highway for facilitating economic growth in Canada.

The increase in railway and canal construction in the 1850s made Québec and especially Montréal very attractive ports of call for European migrants. There were significant economic opportunities for Europeans in both cities, but the shifting trade relationship to the United States was already making Montréal the singular commercial center of the province due to its proximity to New England and New York commercial centers. For this reason many immigrant chose to continue down the St. Lawrence to Montréal. As Montreal increased in economic importance, further efforts to link to the interior of the continent. The emergence of Chicago as a western terminus for huge volumes of agricultural products made rail and waterway connections to interior Canadian and American markets essential for future growth. This is an important historical and contemporary condition with respect to Montreal – its proximity to American markets in the northeast and as an eastern distribution and trade center would limit its support for national economic protectionism. In fact, calls for trade liberalization would find consistent support in the province, which continues to the present day.

The other major factor contributing to Montréal's importance to Canadian immigration was that the Grand Trunk Railway provided transportation opportunities to Canada's other growing metropolitan center, Toronto, as well as to points west. Until well into the Twentieth Century, many immigrants to Canada used urban centers as stopover points on their way to the land and agricultural opportunities of the West. Many though stayed in Québec, with most settling in the Montréal metropolitan area. Much more will be said on these points of ethnic diversification later in Chapter Six The period of massive immigration promotion on the part of the Canadian government did much to provide Montréal with a base of labor that would allow the city to continue its growth and economic viability in both Canadian and international economic contexts.

The geographic position of Montréal as an island at the intersection of two major transportation throughways (the St. Lawrence River and the Grand Trunk Railway) ultimately created a multiethnic urban center in the mid to late 1800s – well before the well-known multicultural perception of Canada in the 1970s. Italian, German, Ukrainian, and Irish communities began to grow and participate in the economic and cultural life of the city. This did not, however, have a significant impact of the political and economic power structures in place in either the city of Montréal or the province of Québec. The shift of major trading patterns from England to the United States did little to disrupt the Anglophone control over commercial institutions. It also did little to alleviate persistent rural poverty and the inability of many poor Francophone framers to own their own land. This led to a massive exodus of rural (and some urban) French-Canadians to New England towns such as Manchester, New Hampshire; Fall River, Massachusetts, and Woonsocket, Rhode Island in search of employment. The reality of Francophone life in Québec was still a picture of income inequality and monopolistic control of wealth and political power by the Anglophone minority in Montréal supported by an Anglophone federal government in Ottawa. The sustained inequalities and rural impoverishment of Québec did little to reduce ethnic nationalist sentiment although little was done formally to protest the situation.

The War Era and the End of Traditional Québec[10]

The first half of the Twentieth Century was transformative in Québec in several ways. The onset of imperial war in 1914 illuminated what most in Québec, but few in English Canada understood: The country was substantially divided and the issue of cultural autonomy was at the heart of this division. Canadian and Québec nationalists came into direct contact and the simmering tensions of divergent expectations exploded repeatedly. From 1914 on, Québec nationalism would move beyond a lingering political norm and ascend to a strident cultural articulation during this period.

---

[10] This section was compiled from several narrative historical sources including Bothwell, Drummond, and English (1989; 1987); Brown and Cook (1974), Lacoursière (1997); Roby (1976); See (2001); and Thompson and Seager (1985).

The Conscription Crisis and Beyond

The onset of the First World War in 1914 shattered any superficial perceptions that Québec had been pacified. At first, active opposition to
Canadian involvement, and thus Québec's involvement, in the War
effort was limited to a minority of pacifist individuals and organizations. However, there was a distinct passive undercurrent in Québec
that viewed involvement in this European conflict as misguided, at
best. Francophones, unlike many Anglophones who had been raised
on the nationalistic link to the United Kingdom, felt no particular alle-
giance or debt to the UK. Similarly, there was no particular rush to
support France, as the conventional wisdom had long been that France
basically abandonded Québec and left it to the whim and will of the
English in the 18th Century. Apathy would perhaps be the best word to
describe the initial Francophone view of World War I.

This was to change in 1917 with the passage of the Military Service
Act that instituted conscription for Canadian military service. Québec
vehemently rejected being forced to fight for a federal government that
was perceived as being, at best, discriminatory. In fact, the stage for
Québec opposition to conscription had been set in 1913 when Ontario
passed provincial legislation severely limiting French language instruc-
tion from its public schools. For Francophones, Regulation 17 (as the
Ontario measure was known) reflected an explicit discrimination
against Francophones and Québec. Put all too simply, the federal
government and many Anglophone pundits viewed the paucity of
Francophone military volunteers as a sign that Québec was not contributing its "fair share" to the war effort (see Auger 2008). In response,
Francophone opposition cited the discriminatory treatment of Francophone volunteers as well as the refusal to expand Francophone units in
the Canadian Army. The federal government wanted volunteers, so
went the Francophone complaint, but refused to recognize that an
English-language military was not a *Canadian* military. This abandonment of the bilingual ideals of the country inflamed anger and resent-
ment at English Canada in general. The federal demand that
French-Canadians serve in the national military was, in many ways,
the last straw.

Riots and protest marches occurred in Québec and Montréal from
1917 though 1918, culminating with the Easter Riots in which gunfire
between anti-conscription protestors and military reservists from
Ontario resulted in at least five deaths. That the military was present in

Québec at all was the result of the federal invocation of the War Measures Act that allowed federal authorities to ensure social stability. Added to this condition of perceived oppression at the hands of English Canada, a federal political alliance of Conservatives and pro-war Liberals engineered[11] an election in 1917 that would put a new Union government in power. This government was rejected in Québec and added to the belief that the federal government was doing all it could to not only dismiss, but repress the provincial population. In addition to the violence of anti-draft riots, legislative efforts toward sovereignty were unsuccessfully promoted in the Québec National Assembly. It became increasingly clear that the cooperative political successes of economic partnership were both falling into ruin and exacerbated by a federal government that was increasingly hostile to the public sentiment and demands of Québec.

The effect of both the Military Service Act and the extraordinary use of the War Measures Act to instill a temporary martial law in Québec had a dramatic and lasting effect. Provincial support for both federal initatives and the national Conservative party evaporated. More to the point, the nationalist reaction to both the federal authorities and the ideal of monolithic Canadian ideals and institutions would elicit a political and cultural discursive nationalism that would first reinforce then dramatically collapse the traditionalism that had underscored Québec cultural nationalism for generations.

Duplessisme: Urbanization and Conservative Nationalism

Questions of culture and national identity were put on tentative hold as the global capitalist economy collapsed in the 1930s. Québec's urban regions suffered severe unemployment, but the collapse in grain prices decimated the rural population. Montreal and Québec both saw population increases as impoverished Francophones sought employment or, more long-term, a future outside of traditional agrarian occupations.

---

[11] Robert Borden, the Conservative Prime Minister, sought to crush opposition to his government and war opposition by allying with selected Liberals. In 1917 he passed a series of electoral measures that allowed voting rights only to women who were serving in the military or who were related to male service members and prohibited war-opponents (broadly defined as "conscientious objectors") from voting. The result was a large victory for this Conservative-Liberal Union government.

The post-Depression recovery period in Québec was assisted by the resumption of demand for Québec raw materials such as timber, asbestos, and refined materials such as aluminum and paper products as well as the resumption of manufacturing in Montreal.

Politically, the rise of Maurice Duplessis and his *Union nationale* (UN) political party in 1936 embodied both the realities of a transnational economic crisis as well as the nationalist cultural politics of Québec. Duplessis worked to expand both the liberalization of trade and expansion of manufacturing primarily through the recruitment of foreign (and Anglophone) capital as well as attempting to create the most business-friendly climate possible by viciously attacking unions throughout the province. In a sense, Duplessis' efforts to combat the effects of the Depression was to give carte-blache to business interests in urban Québec; however, this also entailed a further empowerment of Anglophone business elites in Montreal. This created a bit of a political issue given the requisite nature of Québec nationalism – Duplessis resolved this "problem" through the reinforcement of the traditional definition of that nationalism. For Duplessis and the UN, the true epitome of the Québec national identity was found in the rural, agrarian, and above all, Catholic *canadien*.

The platform of the UN was conservative in that it advocated a return to the Catholic, traditional nationalism reminiscent of the *Parti canadien* but augmented with a liberal economic strategy that actively repressed union activities and persecuted socialist and communist organizations throughout the province. Duplessis' popularity throughout the province was due, however, to his nationalistic (albeit within a Canadian framework) rhetoric that reflected French-Canadian frustration with continual minority Anglophone control over economic institutions in Montréal and throughout the province.

The onset of the Second World War in 1939 brought about a familiar disagreement. The Liberal federal government of Mackenzie King promoted active Canadian involvement in the war effort, while Duplessis questioned the necessity of Québec's involvement. The resurgence of these positions led to the federal government's involvement in the 1939 Québec provincial elections in which the Québec Liberal Party defeated the UN[12]. Duplessis and the UN would return to power in 1945 but not after a less-dramatic return to the conscription crisis of 1917–18.

---

[12] The federal government actively promoted and financed the provincial branch (PLQ) of the Liberal ruling party. The high level of support and participation in this provincial election is significant and bears mention due to the importance King and

King won the 1939 elections by pledging not to reinstitute conscription. By 1942 it became obvious that volunteer military contributions would not be enough to sustain the Canadian war effort. King called a national plebiscite to release the government from its non-conscription pledge. Eight provinces voted to release the government from its promise, while over three quarters of Québec voters held the government to its anti-draft promise. The government reestablished the draft in 1944. The street violence and sovereignty initiatives that characterized the 1917–18 era were not replicated, however the popular understanding in Québec continued to center on the belief that the federal government was ignorant of Québec concerns, desires, and will. The continued public statements of King on Québec were commonly antagonistic, particularly his use of the anti-nationalist phrase "*Québec est une province comme les autres.*[13]"

The post-war period of Québec history was, again relatively similar to that of Canada. Increased immigration, industrialization, and overall economic growth characterized the post-war years. Politically, the return of Duplessis continued the socially conservative project of clerical social and educational service provision coupled with liberal economic policies. These conservative policies did little to elevate the status of Québec within Canada as the reference to the province as "priest-ridden" was common in the post-war era. Clearly, the socially conservative nature of the Duplessis regime was responsible for this perception but also for pushing the *Duplessisme* agenda[14] so far that it generated one of the most significant cultural reactions in Western history: *la Révolution tranquille.*

La Révolution tranquille and the Birth of les Québécois[15]

La Révolution tranquille (the Quiet Revolution) describes the period of the early 1960s that saw the dramatic transition of Québec political

---

his administration placed on national unification and a singular Canadian national-state.

[13] "Québec is a province like the others."

[14] *Duplessisme* is largely defined as having authoritarian governmental tendencies, anti-statist with respect to the provision of social services or economic controls, and incorporating a romanticized or lionized view of rural, Catholic Québec as symbolic of true French-Canadians – all tenets of the *Parti canadien* and thus staunchly conservative and nationalist.

[15] The chapter was compiled from several historical narrative sources including Bashevkin (1991); Bothwell, Drummond, and English (1989); Fitzmaurice (1985); Godin (1991); Pelletier (1983); See (2001); and Thomson (1985).

and cultural institutions shift from traditional norms to more state-centered proactive views of Québec nationalism. In short, the long dominant Catholic Church was literally removed from its position as the primary social service provider and replaced by the Québec state. Hinderences to nationalized economic institutions were removed and the state became a primary motivator for liberal economic reforms. Culturally, the integrative idea of a French-Canadian was replaced by a more autonomous and independent *Québécois* national identity: neither French nor Canadian, les Québécois were a culturally distinct population.

La Révolution tranquille was more of a cumulative effect than any sort of temporally distinct or spontaneous action. The evolution of this 'cumulative revolution' occurred in economic, political, and cultural facets of Québec society. Economically, the continued dominance of Anglophone commercial and business centers in Montréal were a source of constant French-Canadian ire. The traditional Anglophone monopoly was in decline however, as the process of economic modernization continued to unfold in the province. What started with the clerical expansion of educational opportunities to fill the demands of a growing priesthood and was secularly advanced by the political cooperative efforts of English and French liberals in the mid 1800s resulted in a population that was predominantly urban, educated, and oriented toward industrial production. In addition, the expansion of educational and economic opportunities for Francophone citizens in Québec ensured that the status quo could not be maintained. Francophone intellectual and economic (largely small business) elites began to attack traditional economic and social structures, namely Anglophone business entities and the Catholic Church, as retarding Francophone social and economic progress.

The political foundations of *la Révolution tranquille* clearly lay in the early Nineteenth Century divide between traditionalists and liberals within Québec society. The early attempts by the *Parti canadien* to bridge the divide by maintaining traditional ties to the existing power structures of the seigneurs and the clergy were partly successful in winning some liberal reforms, however the efforts of the *Parti patriote* to secularize Québec society and liberalize its quasi-feudal agricultural system were met by reactionary forces that worked to retrench the conservative structures of authority. The Duplessis regime in the first half of the Twentieth Century is an excellent example of this reactionary change.

The post-World War II period of expanded global economics further stressed the traditional isolationism of the Duplessis and conservative political elite in Québec. Duplessis did invite massive foreign investment, however the expanded economic opportunities brought about by this liberal urbanization project reduced the traditional rural political base of the *Union nationale* and allowed for a new *urban* Francophone political consciousness to emerge. It became increasingly clear that an emphasis on export-orientation in terms of trade, which motivated urbanization and industrialization, could not be supported by rural Québec. In fact, Duplessis did sense the impending changes that were shifting the entire nature of the province from a rural-agrarian to urban-industrial society. He enacted several reformative measures intended to reduce the religious control over education and some social services. The problem for Duplessis was in finding replacements for these services as the *Union nationale* rejected a large-scale expansion of state-provided social services.

The cultural organization of Québec underwent significant change in conjunction with the structural changes of the period. Statistically the province was one of the most religious in the Western world with upwards of 85 percent of the population regularly attending Catholic Mass. This superficial description belied a continual conflict between those who promoted a progressive modernization of Québec society and those who maintained that traditional social institutions should be maintained and strengthened. The process of cultural change is difficult to articulate and can only be viewed through the persistent instances of conflict between liberal and traditional groups that has been briefly presented in this chapter. Perhaps the most striking statistic is that active Catholics in Québec dropped from the aforementioned 85 percent prior World War II to less than 30 percent by 1970 (Fitzmaurice 1985, 60). This massive and rapid cultural shift cannot be simply attributed to rapid, short-term action. The decline of Catholic hegemony in Québec was a process that simply required an alternative support structure in order to complete the project of secularization that had begun in the early 1800s.

That Catholic controls over social and educational services were gradually eroded cannot be disputed. Even the staunch traditionalist Duplessis and the UN were resigned to continue these liberal reforms. Their political decision to replace these clerical social and educational services with state-sponsored services opened the door to the possibility of Keynesian state-centered strategies for economic modernization.

The confluence of economic, political, and cultural history in
Québec created an industrial infrastructure while maintaining political and economic restrictions on its expansion, a political structure
that attempted to maintain legitimate authority through a dubious mix
of traditionalist ideology and tacit liberal reforms, and a cultural system in the Catholic Church that had been declining with respect to its
cultural authority for decades. The stage was set for large-scale social
change. All that was required was a stagehand to raise the curtain on a
new Québec.

Lesage and the Institutionalization of Change

Jean Lesage and the Parti Liberal du Québec (PLQ) were elected to
power in the 1960 provincial elections. Lesage's message was liberal
and progressive in both rhetoric and action. The PLQ leadership began
to implement the state-centered strategies of social service provision
and an expansion of nationalized controls over utilities and transportation that were avoided by the Duplessis administration. Hydro-
Québec[16], the state-owned electricity producer, represents the most
successful example of this process of nationalizing the utility infrastructure. It is doubly significant in that was also entirely Francophone
in its leadership and, most importantly, considered French its language
of business.

The provincial educational system was significantly reformed with
the opening of tuition-free secondary education and the expansion of
a Francophone university system with the founding of the Université
de Québec system with campuses in Montréal (1969), Chicoutimi
(1969), Trois-Rivières (1969), and Rimouski (1973). This expansion
of a state-sponsored educational system is merely an example of the
massive increase in state spending that characterized the Lesage
government. Civil service employment in the provincial government
increased from 32,000 in 1960 to over 70,000 in 1966 (Pelletier 1983).
The purposes of these political economic reforms were first, the modernization of the Québec economy and its liberation from a stagnating
traditionalism and secondly, to create state control and protections

---

[16] Hydro-Québec is the primary provider of electricity to Québec and a significant
power source for the Northeastern United States. For a more detailed description of
Hydro-Québec please see Chapter Five.

that would enable and facilitate Francophone economic participation and correct the economic inequalities that had colored urban Québec society for centuries.

The promotion of secular government as responsible for the social welfare of Québec citizens occurred in conjunction with a rearticulation of French-Canadian nationalism. Gone was nationalistic promotion of tradition and a romantic past inherent in *Duplessisme*. This nostalgic affirmation of the status quo was replaced by a renewed sense of autonomy that embraced Québec as a unique nation that was neither French nor Canadian but *Québécois*. Lesage's oft-repeated slogan, "*matres chez nous*[17]" clearly differentiated this new era of political leadership from the inclusive association position of the Duplessis conservatives. He was not, however, an advocate of Québec sovereignty. In fact there was a distinct minority of Québec citizens who advocated an *independantiste* position of Québec state-hood.

This cultural distinction from *Canadien* to *Québécois* was not simply a political promotion of an official nationalism. Literary journals such as *Cité Libre* and *Maintenant* created a public discourse and motivated debate concerning the nature and scope of social change in Québec. One significant articulation of this public discourse was the emergence of *Joual*[18] as a class-centered dialectical alternative to orthodox French that became symbolic of this new Québécois identity. This dialect was the clear understanding that being Québécois also had political and economic components. The history and experience of Francophone poverty and subordinated status was reinforced by English Canadian authority and could not be divorced from a mere shift in linguistic and cultural identification.

Nation and State Development

The relationship between the federal government and Québec provincial government after 1960 was culturally and politically contentious

---

[17] "Masters of our own house."

[18] The title *Joual* describes a unique dialect that is French with truncated phrases and partially incorporated English terminology. The term is derived from the Montréal working-class use of the word "joual" in place of the French word "cheval," which means "horse." Malcolm Reid's *The Shouting Signpainters* (1972) offers a colorful and expressive discussion of the emergence and importance of *Joual* to the emergence of a Québécois identity.

at best. One of the most interesting points of compromise came with Québec's insistence on controlling its own immigration. In 1968 the provincial government established a Department of Immigration that had little real power, but clearly exemplified the ability and the desire of the Québécois to control their own foreign policy. In 1974, the Liberal Premier Henri Bourassa demanded "cultural sovereignty" for Québec if relations between the federal and provincial governments were to be reconciled. This "sovereignty" included final veto power over all federal laws pertaining to language, culture, and communications technologies as well as expanded control over immigration decisions.

The 1975 Ottawa-Québec agreement on immigration began the process of allowing provincial control over matters of migrant entry into the province, which ultimately led to the Cullen-Couture Agreement codifying provincial immigration controls. While the Cullen-Couture Agreement is fairly limited in the scope of federal-provincial relations it does establish the important precedent of autonomy for Québec over matters of provincial culture. This is a point that will be revisited many times throughout this monograph, although its historical importance can only be touched on at this point. While the nationalist sentiment of Québec can be clearly viewed through symbols and language it is the political codification of relationships and positions that gives us a greater view of the power to control and shape culture. The Cullen-Couture Agreement (1979) granted Québec a level of international diplomatic autonomy – a position normally reserved for nation-states. In a limited sense, this act is the beginning of legitimated Québécois statehood.

The mixed-economic mission of the PLQ found a ready audience in a Québec population seeking a replacement for the weakened social protections offered by the Catholic Church. In many ways the state became the new Church in the lives of many Québécois. Social services, education, and cultural authority quickly moved from the private to public spheres as the provincial government mobilized Québec society under its leadership. That the Québec population so quickly turned its back on the Catholic Church should come as little surprise when the history of anti-statism in Québec conservative political leadership is taken into account. With the removal of this political barrier and the implementation of a state "safety-net," the Québécois were given the freedom to choose their own paths. The result was a secular nationalism centered on the government of Québec to lead their cultural shift to a national Québécois identity.

The importance of the Quiet Revolution to the modern articulation of Québec nationalism is clear. The outcomes of the political economic changes under the Lesage government were varied. The UN wrested power back from the PLQ in 1966, but did little to reverse the state-centered modernization implemented under Lesage. In fact, the UN leadership oversaw the most internationally visible articulation of Québécois nationalism during a state visit of French President Charles de Gaulle in 1967. Speaking to a large crowd from the balcony of the Montréal City Hall he emotionally proclaimed "*Vive le Québec libre!*[19]" The remainder of his visit to Canada was cancelled when federal authorities reacted negatively to his support for additional sovereignty for Québec.

This *independantiste* sentiment was clearly growing in the latter half of the 1960s. One of the architects of the PLQ's nationalization project, René Lévesque, decided that the Québec liberals were not sufficiently pursuing sovereignty for the province. He left the party in 1967 to form the *Mouvement Sovereignté-Association* then the *Parti Québécois* (PQ) in 1968. The emergence of the PQ gave Québec citizens a political party that was clearly advocating the political sovereignty of Québec (albeit thorough continued political and economic association with Canada) for the first time. Lévesque's frustration with the PLQ's lack of action of sovereignty was not isolated. In 1969 a radical movement known as the Front de libération du Québec (FLQ) embarked on a course of bombings and political kidnappings that culminated in the assassination of the provincial Minister of Labor Pierre Laporte in 1970.

The actions of the FLQ and other radical groups prompted Prime Minister Pierre Trudeau, with the support of the Québec government, to invoke the War Measures Act and declare martial law in Montréal. Citizens suspected of communist or other radical affiliations were summarily arrested and questioned. The declaration of martial law and the presence of federal troops in the streets of Montréal resulted in a mixed reaction. While many radical student groups supported the FLQ, the majority of Québécois did not support their actions, although the presence of federal troops in the province was even less popular. Trudeau's invocation of the War Measures Act, even though supported by provincial political leaders (including the PQ), directly resulted in a loss of votes in Québec and his minority government of 1972.

---

[19] "Long live free Québec!"

The Parti Québécois and Sovereignty[20]

The violence of the FLQ suppressed any revolutionary urges that may have existed within the majority of the Québécois, however it did little to stem the tide of *independantiste* sentiment. Growing frustration with the UN and PLQ on the subject of federal intrusion (with respect to the 1970 crisis and successive legislative attempts by the Trudeau government to promote pan-Canadian nationalism) brought the Parti Québécois to power in 1976[21]. The PQ was elected on a platform supporting provincial sovereignty that greatly worried the Trudeau government in Ottawa.

> The new government that settled into control in Québec City sent shivers down the spines of Canadians, essentially because the PQ had been elected with a promise to negotiate a new relationship with Canada. The PQ believed that Québec was already a nation. What it lacked was the sovereignty to pursue its own destiny (See 2001, 172–73).

The PQ government, led by René Lévesque, continued the provincial project of modernization and state-sponsorship of social services. It was in this economic arena that the contending political parties of Québec agreed. This is not surprising, as the desire to promote liberal capitalism has long provided grounds for political cooperation, as evidenced by the Anglo-Franco cooperative organizations of the mid-1800s. Throughout the Quiet Revolution and to the present day there is little disagreement over issues of provincial economic development.

A useful example of this common economic project between the PLQ and PQ in spite of divergent political and cultural goals is the massive James Bay Hydroelectric project. This project was begun in 1971 under the watch of the PLQ and has been of central concern for subsequent liberal and sovereigntists governments. Massive political and social pressure was put on the provincial government by the local James Bay Cree who received little to no compensation for the loss of land or disruption of traditional ways of life. In 1975, Hydro-Québec

---

[20] The chapter was compiled from several historical narrative sources including Bernard (2000); Fitzmaurice (1985); Linteau, Durocher, Robert, and Ricard (1991); and See (2001).

[21] This frustration existed despite the PLQ's passage of Bill 22, which established French as the language of government and business in Québec. Bill 22 would be the precursor to better-known language legislation in Québec, but this was the first time that the linguistic culture of Québec was codified.

and the James Bay Cree signed an agreement that could compensate the Cree but left other ownerships claims unresolved. Successive provincial governments to this day have dealt with continual construction, legal, and commercial problems with the James Bay Project. For instance, in 1992 the State of New York withdrew a $17 billion purchasing contract with Hydro-Québec, largely due to the efforts of Cree leaders who embarked on an informational tour that showed the negative social effects on the local Cree due to the massive project. This setback led to a cooperative effort on the part of the Québec government that enabled Hydro-Québec to sell to the entire North American electricity market in 1997. Agreements in 2002 and 2004 between Hydro-Québec and the James Bay Cree resolved many of the legal issues surrounding the project and provided substantial compensation for the local Cree. This continual support of the James Bay Project serves as a cursory illustration of the common liberal attitudes and economic orientation of the ruling provincial parties or Québec.

Also common among Québec political parties was a desire to see French nationalism codified. The PLQ and the PQ differed significantly on the issue of sovereignty, but were in agreement with respect to the position of Québécois supremacy in the province. Bill 101 (Charter of the French Language) was passed in 1977 that allowed English language public education only if both parents were educated in English in Québec. Basically, all new arrivals to the province would be forced to send their children to French-language schools. The Charter also required that French be the language of business in Québec. The implementation of Bill 101 was a victory for Québécois nationalism as it protected the culture and language of the province and ensured that the children of immigrants would be able to linguistically integrate into Québec society. Conversely, Anglophone citizens of the province rejected both the platform of the PQ and the intent of Bill 101. Many left Québec for Ontario and other English speaking provinces in the late 1970s as a result of these political actions.

The PQ decided to press their political hand in 1980 with the first referendum on political sovereignty. While the referendum would not declare independence for Québec, it would give the PQ authority to negotiate for full control over taxation, legal institutions, and foreign relations. The federal response of the Trudeau administration was immediate and aggressive. The federal government attacked the wisdom of the PQ leadership in advocating increased sovereignty and offered Québec the opportunity renegotiate the British North America

Act and develop a new constitutional agreement. The result was a resounding 60 to 40 percent defeat of the referendum. Despite this sound defeat on sovereignty Lévesque and the PQ were returned to power in the 1981 provincial elections.

With national sentiment against Québec, Trudeau pressed ahead with his plan for constitutional repatriation. This was a referendum promise to the citizens of Québec but the process of writing a new constitutional agreement met with disapproval by the Québec delegation. In November 1981, Trudeau reached an agreement with nine other provinces on a Canadian Constitution that circumvented Québec's objections to the document. Known as the "*La Nuit des Longs Couteaux*,[22]" the resultant Constitution Act of 1982 remains unsigned by Québec despite the resumption of constitutional negotiations between Lévesque and Prime Minister Brian Mulroney in 1984. These "beau risques" negotiations resulted in a split within the PQ and Lévesque's resignation the following year.

The PLQ regained power in 1985 and attempted to restart constitutional negotiations with the Meech Lake Accords in 1987. The failure of Meech Lake to be ratified in 1990 further convinced many Québécois that Canada was comfortable in their refusal to accept Québec's unique history and place in the country. The continuation of these age-old frustrations led Lucien Bouchard to found the Bloc Québécois, a federal level political party intended to bring about Québec sovereignty. The following year Bill 150 was passed by the PLQ-led National Assembly that asserted Québec's right to secede from Canada and called for another referendum on sovereignty in 1992. This was highly significant as it represented the level of frustration and discontent in Québec. If the PLQ, who had opposed the PQ in their calls for sovereignty, was endorsing Québec right of secession then it can be safely assumed that federal-provincial relations in the early 1990s were, at best, strained. The federal government quickly responded with calls for another round of constitutional negotiations in Charlottetown on Prince Edward Island. The call for a sovereignty referendum was shelved to allow for the national referendum on the Charlottetown Accords, which failed in the fall of 1992.

The failure of both the Meech Lake and Charlottetown Accords illustrates the persisting divide between English and French Canada.

---

[22] "Night of the Long Knives"

English Canadians resented the claims and demands of a unique and sovereign Québec and seem convinced of Mackenzie King's sentiment that Québec is a province like any other in Canada. The Québécois, on the other hand, rejected Charlottetown on the basis that the constitutional revisions did not go far enough in ensuring their cultural and ultimately national sovereignty. The "French Fact" again proved an irreconcilable divide in the quest for Canadian nationalism and national unity. The return of the Parti Québécois in 1994 under the leadership of Jacques Parizeau would again bring about the question of whether the "French Fact" could stand alone within its own nation.

In 1995 a second referendum was put to the Québec electorate and asked a single question: "Do you agree that Québec should become sovereign after having made a formal offer to Canada for a new economic and political partnership within the scope of the bill respecting the future of Québec and of the agreement signed on June 12, 1995?"

The referendum was defeated by less than one percent of the vote (50.58% *non* against 49.42% *oui*). The close vote prompted many to dispute the balloting procedures of the PQ and to claim voter intimidation on both sides of the issue. The number of votes in the *oui* camp, however, led many to believe that the sovereignty issue was far from being defeated in the minds of the Québécois. In 1998 the Supreme Court of Canada unanimously resolved that the province did not have the authority to leave Canada although the Court left open the possibility of future constitutional renegotiation. The federal government of Jean Chretien made the issue even more muddied by passing the "Clarity Act (C-20)" that gave the House of Commons authority to edit any proposed sovereignty referendum and to unilaterally determine if an "acceptable majority" had been obtained by the referendum. The definition of "acceptable majority" was left ambiguous. In response the Québec *Assemblée nationale* passed legislation that defined a majority as "50 percent plus one." The legacy of these attempts at legislative clarification remains to be seen. To date, no logistical discussion or planning has taken place in the province to bring about another referendum on Québec sovereignty. Neither has a concerted effort to challenge either the Supreme Court decision, the Clarity Act, or Québec's definition of sovereignty been launched by either federal or provincial parties.

PART THREE

ECONOMIC GLOBALIZATION, LABOR MIGRATION, AND SOCIAL INTEGRATION

INTRODUCTION

Section Three, comprising Chapters Five, Six, and Seven, presents empirical data used to compare the state-level responses to the shifting political economic and demographic conditions emblematic of the so-called "globalization era." Each chapter is focused on a particular aspect of global integration and designed to be cumulative in both scope and presentation.

Chapter Five examines the impact of neoliberal policy convergence, trade liberalization, and foreign investment on Canada and Québec. These criteria are reflective indicators of global market integration and offer a categorical framework to evaluate the integration of both Canada and Québec in the global economic system. More to the point, these indicators allow for a comparison of the effects of so-called globalization on both social entities.

While the chapter is focused primarily on the effects of external market integration, the overall emphasis on strategic state-building remains. In this sense, the comparisons between Canadian federal and Québec provincial experiences are essential. Both with respect to policy (particularly trade liberalization) and the economic impact of global economic integration, the comparison illuminates differences due to expected size differential, but also with respect to the role national identity influences state-building within the context of global market integration.

These differences are tempered with a similar emphasis on strategic efforts to maximize growth opportunities existing as a beneficiary of global capitalism. Both seek economic growth, yet both are faced with a similar need for labor market expansion. Chapter Five establishes that both Canada and Québec are integrated in and benefit from (to varying degrees) global economic integration. The persistent problem of limited population and subsequent (relative) labor shortages are met with commensurate demand as production and growth potential increase. The solution has been the state promotion and management of labor migration. This economic basis for increases in labor migration forms the segue between Chapters Five and Six, the latter being an examination of immigration history and policies in both comparative cases.

Chapter Six does not argue that immigration to either Canada or Québec is the result of globalization. On the contrary, immigration policies have largely defined Canadian growth initiatives since the 17th century. This chapter makes explicit the connection between both economic growth and nation-building initiatives. Besides the obvious connection between economic growth and immigration, there are several other points of particular importance made in this chapter.

First, the state promotion of labor migration carries with it several opportunities and challenges. Through the active promotion of targeted immigration, the state is able to expand its labor force and its overall national population. The expansion of any large group requires managed integration/assimilation initiatives in order to ensure social cohesion – Canada is no exception. With the expansion of Canadian immigration came state efforts to define and redefine a Canadian national identity. Given Canada's aforementioned binational realities, this was no mean task and engendered significant opposition in Québec. The link between immigration policy and national identity, particularly with respect to nation-building efforts, makes the simple equation of economic growth equals labor market expansion through immigration much more complicated. In fact, contention over federal immigration policy often took a backseat of the accompanying nationalist debates that reflected efforts to create a cohesive effort to integrate new arrivals. Much of this debate centered on federal and provincial differences with regards to the definition of a national identity and divergent opinions with respect the necessity of cultural criteria for immigrant selection.

Second, aside from internal debates over national identity and policy criterion, the system of labor migration shifted dramatically. Traditionally, Transatlantic labor migration was typified by European source regions and North American (and to a lesser extent, South Pacific) receiving countries. While time and structural conditions motivated shifts from various European regions to others, labor migration to Canada (as well as other receiving countries) was overwhelmingly European. Following postwar European reconstruction in the 1950's, these traditional sources shifted to a continental migration pattern or were locked in an Eastern Bloc labor market. In need to labor market expansion, North American and European countries began to shift their policies to the Global South. The process is explicated in Chapter Six, however the key point here is that immigration to all receiving countries quickly began to diversify.

The diversification of urban Canada (inclusive of Québec) is commensurate with significant changes in both national immigration policy and systemic global labor supply. It also, however, created challenges for Québec in reconciling its national identity with federal immigration control. As English-speaking Canada emerged as the economic heart of the country, the fear was that immigrants initially settling in Québec would assimilate to this dominant language of business – English in lieu of the national language of Québec – French. As a result, Québec increasingly demanded more and more control over the selection of migrants eventually gaining nearly full autonomy over provincial immigration in 1995. The result has been an explicit link between immigration, as a requisite of long-term economic growth, and both national identity and state-building. Québec was able to redefine its policies to target Francophone migrants from the Global South and enhance its state policy capacities in a key area.

Conforming to the structural realities of the "new immigration" (see Massey 1995) carried additional opportunities for nation and state-building. Chapter Seven builds on both Chapters Five and Six by locating Canadian multicultural and Québec intercultural policies within a specific framework that links state-building with global economic and national cultural motivations. Canadian multicultural policy did not arise out of an increasingly diversifying Canada; rather it was an attempt to redefine Canadian nationalism as unified (obviously, Québec disagreed) and a distinct alternative to American assimilation. Multicultural would soon, however, come to be the overall policy framework that continued to be used in a nationalistic fashion, but more to manage the integration of a rapidly diversifying urban population. The two were not unrelated and multiculturalism soon became the means by which the Canadian state promoted economic growth through immigration as well as a distinct definition of Canadian nationalism.

Québec, understanding the original intent of the multicultural policy as corrosive to Québécois nationalism, soon began to promote its own version of multiculturalism, known as "interculturalism." The primary difference would be understood as a "recognition of difference" in the federal sense, but with the added caveat that this recognition would take place within a defined Francophone linguistic context. As such, Québec's efforts integrate its own diversifying immigrant population was couched in a specific nationalist context. State-building with respect to economic growth and diversifying labor migration is, it would seem, heavily dependent on the ability to link these policies with a national cultural context. These questions are raised in the concluding chapter, but the importance of national cultural definition is here, explicitly linked to state-building processes as both Canada and Québec more fully integrate into the global economic system (and seek to exploit those beneficial advantages).

CHAPTER FIVE

THE GLOBAL MARKET ECONOMY: HISTORY AND IMPACT ON CANADA AND QUÉBEC

How has the global market economic system in the post-World War II era developed and how has it impacted the state-building capacities of Canada and Québec? Similarly, how have shifts in dominant political economic ideologies both complemented this process of global integration and altered the state-building strategies of Canada and Québec? This chapter endeavors to examine these questions in more detail. The chapter itself is divided into three sections.

The first briefly chronicles global market economic history from 1870 to the present. As this project is concerned with explaining globalization's impact on the nation-state, I constrain my definition and view of the global market economy to the period of institutional international global financial and trade control. This perspective begins with the institution of the gold standard in the late 1800s[1], the rise of Keynesian, state-centered, economic dominance, and concludes with the ascendance of the contemporary neoliberal era. The purpose of this section is to illustrate the dynamic nature of global market development and the role of states in both promoting global capitalism and being shaped by these same systemic conditions.

The second and third sections examine the impact of global market integration on Canada and Québec, respectively. I examine the actions and policy responses of the Canadian and Québec governments with respect to issues such as tariff reduction, export expansion, and market integration. The general contention among political economic scholars is that economic globalization, defined as the post-1973 political economic environment, has decreased the political economic autonomy of the individual nation-state (Albrow 1996; Kennedy 1993; Robinson

---

[1] This starting point is not consistent with either world-system or economic globalization approaches, which begin their analyses in the 1500s and 1970s, respectively I use this starting point because this project utilizes social practice, in the form of policy, as a medium of analysis. Thus I am interested in how states and political economic institutions manage and control the global market economy, not necessarily in the analytical nature of the global market economic system in its entirety.

2004; Sklair 1995; Spruyt 2002). The purpose of this chapter is the identification of historical change in the global economic system and the role of the nation-state in this system as well as the deeper examination of *how* these changes have affected Canada and Québec[2].

The Global Market Economic System[3]

The existence of a governed global market economy can arguably be traced back to the institution of the International Gold Standard in the mid to late-1800s[4]. The standard was predicated on two major prerequisites: the fixed, standard value of gold and the hegemonic economic power of a lender of last resort. Due to its position as the dominant capitalist economy, Great Britain assumed the role of lender-of-last-resort with the Bank of England serving as the principal control over interest rates, supply of credit, and issues of trade.

The establishment of a fixed currency valuation system created the stability necessary for international trade and financial exchanges that define an international liberal market economic system. The system worked relatively well in maintaining a stable medium of exchange for financial and trade exchanges due largely to the economic and political hegemony of Great Britain. While the stability of fixed monetary valuation provided the exchange medium necessary for the expansion of international trade, it effectively limited the monetary policy potential of individual states. The value of a national currency and state budgetary capacities was almost entirely contingent on its respective

---

[2] This chapter is concerned with demonstrating global market integration and not in evaluating the benefits or drawbacks from such integrative processes. As such there have been no efforts made by the author to evaluate performance or efficacy of growth such as increasing socio-economic stratification or inequality exacerbation in health care provision, education, or vocational inequalities.

[3] General background information for this section was compiled from various sources including Best (2005), Cerny (1996), Gilpin (2000;1987), O'Brien and Williams (2004), and Woods (2000).

[4] The exact date for the adoption of a global gold standard is difficult to establish as individual nation-states adopted the monetary practice at different times such as Germany (1871), France and Italy (1873), 1879 (Austria), and Russia (1893). Another problematic issue is that practical adoption and political affirmation are often dissociated evidenced by the case of the United States. The U.S. was practically tied to the international gold standard in 1873 with the US Coinage Act that ended the silver dollar standard, however it was not until 1900 that the dollar was officially tied to the American dollar to the international gold standard with the passage of the US Currency Act.

gold stores. This restriction of state-level policy autonomy proved too much for many states, particularly in times of economic recession when states were substantially restricted in their efforts to enact monetary policies to control inflation and stimulate growth. The relative decline of British hegemony in the late-19th and early 20th centuries amplified the instability of the global economic system, particularly affecting confidence that the British administration could administer credit levels and interest rates.

World War I effectively ended the International Gold Standard. The years of 1914 through 1945 were not good ones for a stable global economic system. War, economic depression, and national economic isolationism ensured that a resumption of the global trade system in existence before World War I would not occur. An effort to resume gold convertability was implemented in the early 1920s, but the onset of economic depression motivated the final demise of the "traditional" gold standard in 1931 when both Germany and the United Kingdom eschewed the standard in favor of increased economic/monetary policy flexibility.

The coming end of World War II prompted allied nation-states to consider options for revitalizing global trade. In 1944, delegates from forty-five nation-states met at Bretton Woods, New Hampshire determined to establish a stable international commercial medium to revive the global market economy. The conference was led by the United States and Great Britain, but in reality the United States held the key to reviving the international economic system. By this time the United States controlled fully three-quarters of the world supply of gold and had emerged from the War era as the sole global economic power. A compromise solution[5] to the problem of economic leadership and agreeable management came with the establishment of a "dollar standard." The agreement required the United States to peg the value of the

---

[5] The initial proposal, put forth by John Maynard Keynes, was for the creation of an international non-governmental central bank. The purpose of this bank would be to "monitor trade imbalances and with the power to force deficit countries to adjust their economic policies any time deficits were out of line" (Pool and Stamos 1989, 3). This proposal was soundly rejected by the United States, as it offered no incentive for their economic leadership. This position was a replication of previous British positions in 1870 and again in 1922 when the British, in exchange for the responsibilities of managing and supporting the gold standard and gold-exchange system, respectively, were granted the power of monetary policy power. In short, the British and later American hegemonic economic leadership was not selfless and carried several national economic advantages.

dollar to a $35 per ounce standard, which made the American dollar the official currency of the Bretton Woods global market system.

Another outcome of the Conference was the establishment of two nongovernmental institutions: the International Monetary Fund (IMF) and the World Bank. The former was tasked with the responsibility of monitoring commercial activity within the global market system and be available for short-term, deficit-reduction lending purposes. The latter was established as a fiscal management institution for the rebuilding of Western Europe after World War II. For the first time the global market economic system was supported by international nongovernmental institutions albeit under control of donor states (Best 2005; Endres 2005).

The subsequent era of "embedded liberalism" (Ruggie 1982), lasting roughly from 1944 to the mid-1970s, was predicated on efforts to restart international trade but allow states increased flexibility to adjust national economic conditions and meet specific national socio-economic demands. The result was a concerted effort liberalize international trade (through the institutionalization of the General Agreement on Trade and Tariffs [GATT] in 1948) while at the same time encouraging individual states to regulate and manage national economic conditions including employment promotion, fiscal regulation, and the promotion of consumption through expanded public spending initiatives. This system of "compromise" saw resurgent international trade under the stabilizing mechanism of the US dollar (and IMF oversight) and a massive increase in public sector spending in areas of education, health care, housing, and other social services. Above all, this era was based on the ideological assumption that the state was the primary regulator of national economies and its role as an economic protectionist institution was theoretically and (perhaps more importantly) politically sacrosanct.

This revived global economic system collapsed in the 1970s. Faced with a number of domestic political pressures (demands for protectionism, a trade deficit, and a pending election) and international pressures (a decline in confidence due to the expansion of an inflated dollar and the inability of the US to match its gold-convertibility responsibilities), Richard Nixon ended dollar to gold convertibility in 1971. This action effectively ended the Bretton Woods system by abandoning the primary disciplinary mechanism designed to stabilize the global currency unit (the U.S. Dollar). For much of the 1970s, international trade stagnated and in many areas national economies became increasingly withdrawn. Without the conditioning mechanisms of the Bretton Woods system, many states embraced a reactionary economic nationalism in response to what appeared to be a collapse (again) of systemic global capitalism.

Once again, those promoting a global market economic system were required to find a means to administrate and discipline such a system. For liberal economists and financial interests, the demise of the Bretton Woods system ushered in nearly unprecedented opportunities for global capitalism. One area of particular interest was the demise of fixed exchange and the emergence of floating, market-based rates in 1973. As the FOREX system of floating exchange rates matured, a transnational trade in currency speculation and foreign direct investment emerged that reduced state efficacy in managing economic policy – particularly monetary policy (see Robinson 2004; Sklair 2001). While the "liberation" of financial capital from national regulatory mechanisms created incredible increases in international capital flows, it was soon understood that state monetary policies and national economic conditions were still of utmost importance. Clyde Barrow makes the perceptive observation that:

> It is the political fragmentation of the globalized economy that makes the threat of capital flight and disinvestment operative. The structural power of transnational capital can be effective only in a political world where capital has the ability to move from one state to another in search of competitive advantages. Transnational capital—American or other- wise—would have no long-term interest in constructing a global state or a transnational state, because such an arrangement would jeopardize, or at least mitigate, the political basis of its structural power" (Barrow 2005, 136).

Put simply, a system of states with sustained monetary policy authority facilitates the "shopping" of financial capital from one national location to another, searching for the most amenable conditions for financial capital investment. Even so, if this system of resurgent global financial capitalism was to be sustained by compliant states, guidelines and standards of coordination would have to be developed. A solution was sought by the seven largest industrial economies (G-7[6]) at successive international economic summits in New York (Plaza Agreement of 1985), Tokyo (1986), and Venice (1986). The agreements varied in

---

[6] Canada, France, (West) Germany, Italy, Japan, the United Kingdom, the United States.

content and scope, but one central feature emerged: policy coordination. In short, the G-7 agreed to "coordinate their macroeconomic policies and in effect formulate a macroeconomic policy for the entire world.... Collective leadership of the world economy would be substituted for the decline of American leadership" (Gilpin 1987, 151; see also O'Brien and Williams 2004; Schaeffer 2005; and Slaughter 2005).

The resurgence of national economic foci that occurred following the collapse of the Bretton Woods system began to decline in the mid-1980s. The demise of Keynesian state-centered economic strategies conversely ushered in the beginning of the so-called current era of neoliberalism. In short, the ebb and flow of laissez-faire liberal economic theory, policy, and institutionalization that has occurred since the late 1800s once again flowed toward a liberal market system – at the expense of national economic controls.

The major development centers on the emergence of a supranational organizational structure that reflects the contemporary climate of policy coordination. The Bretton Woods institutions (the IMF and the World Bank) have been reoriented to facilitate the ideological and structural conditions necessary for global market integration in the developing world. In addition, the General Agreement on Trade and Tariffs (GATT), which provided a significant level of trade discipline, was institutionalized in 1995 with the creation of the World Trade Organization (WTO) after the Uruguay Round of the GATT in 1993. The WTO was granted powers of adjudication as well as a central mandate to eliminate national (and other) barriers to liberal trade and financial flows. In a very real sense, the WTO represents the most explicit institutional manifestation of neo-liberal political economic ideology. The fact that developed and developing nations are members of the WTO lends credence to the contention that international non-governmental organizations (and their non-governmental actors) have usurped economic policy-making power from individual states on a global scale. Member states must adhere to the mission and rulings of the WTO, thus the capability of respective states to enact national protections is restricted, albeit by choice.

A significant shift with respect to the contemporary era is purely ideological – the state is no longer understood (in political and economic orthodoxy) as a regulatory and protectionist institution. Instead, the state is regularly vilified as an unwanted and dangerous threat to capital accumulation. This belies the very real necessity of existing states as social stabilizing institutions as well as the only social institution capable of ensuring diverse national economic conditions that Barrow identifies as being central to the mobility of financial capital in the globalization era.

The purpose of this cursory history of the modern global economic system is to show the evolutionary nature of systemic development. No less important is the observation that international nongovernmental institutions and financial capital interests have gained significant power, but a power that is still contingent on the stabilization capacities of state institutions. This is important with respect to Canada and Québec in that their active institutional participation and support is necessary for the global economic system to survive. What we are less clear on, however, is how these conditions impact state-building in an era of supposed "state decline."

Canada[7]

Canada was an autonomous participant in the 1944 Bretton Woods Conference and continued to set its own political and economic agendas independently of British control. Canada's political image as an independent mediator in international disputes as well as its expanding economic sectors led to a series of appointments to high level political economic posts (autonomous membership in the League of Nations (1919) and the International Labour Organization as well as appointment to the United Nations Security Council in 1947). This status contributed to Canada being named as the seventh member of the powerful Group of Seven (G-7) economic powers in 1976[8].

Economic globalization can be roughly defined as the integration of national economies into a global liberal market economic system. Thus, the primary mechanism for the expansion of such a global economic system is the incorporation of liberal market economic structures to govern national economic systems. In other words, integration of national economies into the global economy requires that individual states relinquish a level of economic policy autonomy. As previously stated, a global market economy cannot function without a centralized control structure. In the era of globalization this structure has been

---

[7] General background information for this section was compiled from various sources including Bothwell, Drummond and English (1989; 1987); Chodos, Murphy and Hamovitch (1993); See (2001); and Urmetzer (2003).

[8] The G-7 would become the G-8 in 1997 with the inclusion of Russia.

institutionalized in myriad bi- and multi-lateral trade agreements and in institutions such as the IMF and WTO; however, the primary conditioning mechanism for these institutions is the ideology of neoliberalism. In most cases, national economic integration requires that state economic policy conform to the rules of the liberal market system – with the most obvious consequence being an inability to protect national markets.

Given Canada's position in the G-8 and political status as a core state in the global political economic system, we can safely make two assumptions. First, that the economic policies of Canada will be consistent with those made by other G-8 countries and in accordance with the Bretton Woods system of dollar hegemony and later the position of policy coordination. This consistency is limited to Canada's support for a stable global economic system not stating that global market integration is an egalitarian or consistent process in and of itself. In other words, the ebb and flow of the international global market system should be easily observable in the economic policies of the Canadian government.

Second, as one of the few economic powers in the world, Canada should experience a net gain from its position in the global system. It stands to reason that Canada would promote trade liberalization, state retrenchment, and other requisites of global systemic participation; but we can also assume that since Canada is in an elite position adherence to neoliberalism and support for global systemic dictates is willful. This section will examine the role of international economic policy development, foreign direct investment (financial capital flows), and trade flows in Canada to establish the impact of global systemic integration as well as begin to develop a deeper understanding for the motivation for neoliberal adherence and the conditions created by Canada's position as a beneficiary of economic globalization.

Canada: International Economic Policy

The issue of free trade in Canada has been a long and contentious one. From early liberal reforms that mirrored global economic changes in the 1800s to the entrenchment of national economic protections in the post-war era, Canada has been a reflection of international political economic shifts. The post-war era is most helpful in providing a nation-state level example of global market integration and the problematic acceleration of this integrative process due to demands for national socio-economic protection during periods of transition.

Prior to World War II, the bilateral trade relationship between Canada and the United States was the most active in the world. This relationship continues to grow in the post-war era and remains the largest trade partnership in the world. This relationship was not without contention as evidenced by the 1951 Massey Commission, originally tasked with evaluating the state of Canadian educational, cultural, and arts institutions in the immediate post-war era. The Commission's findings reflected a substantial fear that an "invasion" of American culture through large-scale financing and ownership of Canadian cultural institutions, coupled with the lack of Canadian protections against the free flow of intellectual and cultural capital south, would result in a precipitous decline of Canadian autonomy – particularly with respect to identity. The free flow of American financial capital represented a clear threat, in the minds of the Commission, to the very incubation of a post-war Canadian national identity (Massey and Lévesque 1951). The Massey Commission report offers an important early example of the concern for the effects of trade integration, but other state-initiated research dismissed such fears. The Bladen Report (1961), for example, focused on the inefficiencies inherent in Canadian attempts to build its own automotive industry. Bladen and others promoted a development strategy that emphasized export-oriented production for already established American automotive firms. Put simply, the idea that Canada could protect and nurture its own domestic automotive industry was rejected in favor of transnational production schemes based on a decrease in national economic protectionism and liberalized trade between the United States and Canada (see Anastakis 2005; Wonnacott 1965).

The clearest example of this liberalization initiative was the Canada-United States Automotive Agreement (Auto Pact), signed in 1965. With the post-war explosion of automotive manufacturing the geographic proximity of production centers such as Detroit, Michigan and Windsor, Ontario could not be ignored. Both were significant automotive manufacturing centers, yet trade between the two was restricted by tariff and trade restrictions. In a clear sign that the promotion of trade liberalization trumped fears of nationalist dilution, the Diefenbaker government began to reduce tariff restrictions on select auto parts in 1962. The Pearson government brought the initiative to the international agreement level in 1965.

The Pact eliminated tariffs on most automotive products produced in both Canada and the United States. The Pact had an immediate effect in expanding the market for Canadian automotive products. In 1964, only 7% of Canadian automotive sales went to the world's largest automotive market (the U.S.), but by 1968 fully 60% of Canadian automotive manufactures were exported to the United States. The success of the Auto Pact in expanding Canadian industrial production and American production cost decreases have led many to label the 1965 Auto Pact as the precursor to later bilateral liberal trade agreements (Anastakis 2005; Perry 1982). This agreement was significant, yet focused on a limited economic sector. The idea of opening Canadian markets to American capital was seen as highly lucrative but problematic[9]. Despite the economic success of the Auto Pact, many Canadian remained wary of wholesale economic liberalization.

The legacy of the Massey Commission report and the increasing integration of American and Canadian economic and cultural spheres contributed to a period of nationalist rhetoric and protectionist positions by the Trudeau administration, particularly in the 1970s. It should be noted that this resurgence of economic nationalism was not an isolated case, as the demise of the Bretton Woods system and the economic challenges of the 1970s motivated most advanced capitalist states to withdraw from international trade and emphasize national economic development in relative "isolation."

Efforts to expand the Auto Pact and increase trade liberalization with the U.S. met an unreceptive federal administration[10] occupied with national protectionist demands to resolve several issues such as

---

[9] In 1967, a Task Force on the Structure of Canadian Industry was commissioned. Their findings were published in a then-confidential report chronicling the "double-edged" nature of foreign investment in Canadian industry. Economic analysts clearly saw the advantages of increased foreign capital in promoting economic growth, however they consistently warned that economic autonomy would be the major casualty/cost of such a growth strategy.

[10] This national protectionist tendency should not be construed as an isolated event in Canadian economic history. Many economic historians have commented on the global period of the 1950s through the mid-1970s as a period of national economic retrenchment (Gilpin 1987; O'Brien and Williams 2004; Strange 1985). Therefore, the fact that Canada engaged in a political economic period of protecting its national economic interests should be viewed as neither surprising nor unique with respect to global political economic trends. However, we must consider the national protectionist demands made on the Trudeau administration and the similarities in their occurrence throughout the Western world. The 1960s in particular saw a global explosion of nationalist demands for increased state protection of cultural rights, economic prosperity, and general demands for retributive and social justice.

ethno-cultural unrest (including First Nations and Québécois nation-alism), urban ethnic and racial diversification, and social change rooted in increased urbanization and economic growth. It was not until the election of Brian Mulroney and the Progressive Conservative Party in 1984 that this resistance to liberal market economics faded. The Mulroney Administration's embrace of liberal trade agreements (despite campaigning against such agreements in 1983) effectively ended federal resistance to liberal market integration. The federal Liberal Party (as well as the National Democratic Party) attempted to rally anti-CUFTA support in 1988, but Mulroney was re-elected com-fortably on a platform supporting liberal economic reforms and the expansion of free-trade agreements. The benefits, it was seen, out-weighed national protectionist concerns and in 1994 the Liberal administration of Jean Chrétien finalized the expansion of Canadian free-trade to Mexico with the NAFTA agreements.

Proposals for a North American Trade Agreement were made in the United States as early as 1979. The election of Ronald Reagan in 1980 and his administration's push to liberalize trade created a necessary political pre-condition for such an agreement. It was not until 1985, after the election of the Conservative Mulroney administration, that talks on creating a regional zone of "managed trade" were politi-cally feasible from a Canadian perspective. In 1988, both countries signed the Canada-United States Free Trade Agreement (CUFTA), with agreement implementation occurring on January 1, 1989.

Soon after the CUFTA agreements took effect, Canada was included in ongoing trade talks with United States and Mexico. The negotiations resulted in the North American Free Trade Agreement (NAFTA), which was signed in 1993 with full implementation in 1994. The basic agreement was similar in structure to CUFTA with the main thrust being the elimination of trade tariffs and other national protectionist strategies. This culmination of liberal market political negotiations marked the effective end of political resistance to liberal ideological and structural reforms –the only federal Canadian political party in opposition to liberal market trade policies was the NDP, whose oppo-sition has waned since 1994. In fact, even the NDP has embraced lim-ited "free-trade" in advocating a reduction of inter-provincial trade barriers as well as reorienting NAFTA toward a "fair trade" focus (National Democratic Party 2005). If CUFTA opened the gates to liberal market expansion in North America, NAFTA ensured that those gates would remain open. The past ten years has seen a marked

expansion of liberal political economic agreements. Chile recently lob-
bied for inclusion in the NAFTA agreement and bilateral trade agreements were brokered between Canada and Chile (1995), Costa Rica
(2001), and Israel (1997)[11].

These regional and bilateral agreements, while illustrative of
increased global political economic cooperative efforts, are limited in
scope in comparison with the creation of the World Trade Organization
(WTO) in 1995. The WTO was created as an organizational alternative
to the series of liberal trade agreements known as the General
Agreement on Trade and Tariffs (GATT). Briefly, this organization, of
which over 145 countries are members, establishes rules for trade to
which all participating member states must adhere. This participatory
organization is, in effect, the nongovernmental administrative, adjudicative, and political control mechanism for the global market economic system. Trade disputes and macro-economic policy decisions
are made, in most cases, within the negotiating structure of the WTO.
Canada's active participation in the WTO and its push to increase
bilateral trade negotiations (active negotiations are currently underway with Korea, Singapore, El Salvador, Guatamala, Honduras,
Nicaragua, the European Free Trade Commission, as well as continuing negotiations to establish a Free Trade Area of the Americas
(FTAA)) show that Canada has fully integrated itself into the liberal
market economic system. An examination of (1) trade balances and
(2) foreign investment will provide a clearer picture of what this global
market integration looks like and how is has impacted the Canadian
economy.

Canada: Balance of Trade

A main argument of liberal economic proponents is that export-
orientation must be a primary focus of national economic development (O'Brien and Williams 2004; Woods 2000). In other words, the

---

[11] Agreements such as CUFTA, NAFTA, FTAA (proposed), and numerous bilateral
trade agreements show that the process of global market integration and neoliberal
market reforms are a contentious and fluid process. Adaptation in reaction to national
protectionist demands require constant attention and flexibility. This section, and
indeed this chapter, is designed to present the structure of global market integration,
not to imply that these processes are static.

more integrated a national economy is in the global market economy the higher its exports and, in the best case scenario, the lower its imports. This optimal situation theoretically results in a trade surplus providing capital for additional economic growth. This simplistic theoretical exposition can best be viewed in the construction of the Bretton Woods system and the development of American Dollar hegemony. Only the United States, as the financial keystone of the global market economy, was encouraged to run a trade deficit due to issues of liquidity (Gilpin 1987, 135). All other nation-states were encouraged to work towards a positive balance of payments. This emphasis on positive trade exchanges is a central focus of liberal market economics: barriers to trade are barriers to economic growth.

Canadian integration into the global market system offers interesting insights as to how a core state can profit from favorable global trade. Canada in the immediate post-war period experienced modest economic growth due to increases in industrial production, but ran trade deficits throughout the 1950s. After 1961, Canadian balance of trade experienced only one deficit year in 1975. This consistent surplus should be viewed as a success of liberal market adherence. However, a closer look at specific trends is necessary to determine a commensurate decline in state policy autonomy as a result of economic growth due to global market integration.

One of the major components of the Trudeau administration in the 1970s was its nationalist emphasis both in terms of culture and economic autonomy. This was a difficult road as the United States was (and remains) Canada's largest single trading partner. The stagnant growth of a trade surplus in the 1970s is reflective of increases in domestic spending as well as the stagflation period within the global economy due to high energy costs. Pressure from business and economic interests led to talks on the establishment of a regional managed trade bloc in 1979. Increases in United States deficit spending, as well as reduced energy costs led to a massive increase in Canada's early 1980s trade surplus, with the most massive increase being a jump of $10 billion from 1981 ($7.7) to 1982 ($17.6). The Canadian balance of trade would oscillate from a high of $19.8 billion in 1984 to a low of $7 billion in 1991. Interestingly, the signing of the CUFTA agreement and its implementation in 1989 provided no positive growth in the trade surplus. In fact, the average trade surplus in the four years following the CUFTA agreement was approximately $8 billion. This number was

well below the massive surplus number of the early 1980s, but still a
relatively significant trade surplus.

The implementation of the NAFTA agreement in 1994 seems to
have had a much more dramatic impact on Canadian trade surplus
growth than the bilateral CUFTA agreement. In the first three years of
NAFTA's existence, the Canadian trade surplus grew from $20 billion
(1994) to $42 billion (1996). It must be noted that the creation of the
WTO and its governing structure in 1995 also opened up many markets to Canadian goods. In effect, wholesale Canadian participation in
the global market economy began in the mid-1990s and provided an
incredible profit to the nation-state of Canada. The trade surpluses
reflected in Figure 3 are indicative of Canadian integration into the
global market economy. As Canada has acquiesced to regional and
global trade agreements, its share of global capital from trade transactions has increased.

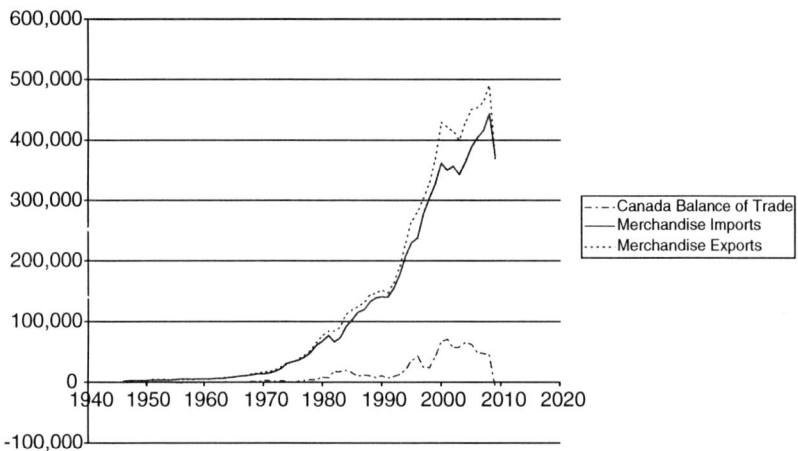

Figure 3. Canadian International Trade, 1946-2009 (In millions)
Source: Wilkinson, B.K. "Section G: The Balance of International Payments, International
Investment Position, and Foreign Trade." 11-516-XIE Historical Statistsics of Canada:
Statistics Canada http://www.statcan.ca/english/freepub/11-516-XIE/sectiong/sectiong
.htm

This rise in production and export-orientation is, however, only part
of the story. Labor demand to fuel this trade surplus has led to
net increases in immigration to Canada since 1990 and will be discussed in the following chapter. The focus of the following section is an

additional measure of global market integration, foreign direct investment, or foreign investment/control of Canadian economic and production entities.

Canada: Foreign Investment

Foreign direct investment is a reliable measure of global market integration due to its reflection of the transnationalization of production (Robinson 2004, 22). As production in core capitalist states increasingly deals in matters of finance, high technology, information, and service provision, the transnationalization of production processes in Canada must be understood as more than simply industrial or manufacturing production. This point is important, as sociological attention to the integrative function of FDI has been focused on the developing world as an impetus for modernization. The contention is that increasing rates of FDI in the developing world is a direct measure of global market integration of these areas (Dicken 2003; Robinson 2004; Scharpf 1999). I do not disagree; however, the power of this measure also illustrates the effect of global market integration on national populations in core states, particularly with respect to national protectionist capacities.

Concerns about the effect of foreign investment and ownership of national economic entities is reflected in documents such as the Massey Commission report (1951) and the Task Force on the Structure of Canadian Industry (1967). These concerns, that Canada was losing the capacity to protect its national economy, persisted despite very low levels of FDI as reflected in Figure 4.

These economic protectionist concerns, however, have not been reflected in the post-Trudeau era (ending in 1984). In fact, one could argue that Trudeau was less of an economic nationalist as his political rhetoric implies, particularly in his second term (1980–1984). Beginning in 1983, FDI inflows into Canada began a relatively rapid (albeit inconsistent) climb through 1999. The acceleration of import and export trade coincided with large-scale increases in both in- and out-flow direct investment. While Canada worked to create conditions amenable to foreign direct investment, it also exploited investment opportunities in a similar fashion. In 2004, Canada actually exported more investment capital than it imported; however, the long-term trends clearly illustrate Canada's status as a destination for transnational capital flows. In keeping with theories of liberal economic growth, the exportation of capital is designed to encourage trade in specific regions. Given the dramatic increases in both merchandise imports and exports, we can easily observe the impact global market integration has on core societies.

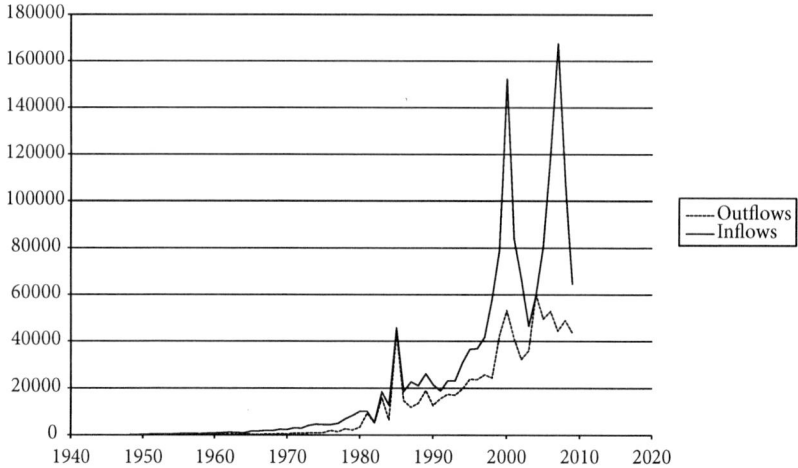

Figure 4. Canada: Foreign Direct Investment (In millions)
Source: CANSIM Table 376-0015, Balance of International Payments, FDI 1946–2004

Of particular importance is the fluctuation in FDI inflows in the past decade. Nearly 90% of inward FDI is from the United States and the European Union (Holden 2008), which ultimately means that any respective recession in either location will have a significant effect on Canadian FDI. This is, of course, exactly what we see in 2001 and 2008 as investment in Canadian economic entities dramatically decreased following each respective Western recession.

The concurrent increase in FDI and export-led trade surplus growth is reflective of Canada's increasing integration into the global market economy. Canada's complete support for WTO regulations and trade authority, its active promotion of the NAFTA agreements, and continuing support for the FTAA portray a willing and active participant in the global market economic system. Canadian liberal trade policies have been consistent with increases in trade surplus growth and FDI inflows. Clearly, Canadian integration into the global market economic system has been beneficial to the general Canadian economy.

A closer look at Québec's integration will offer a comparative example of a state with strong institutions and commensurate spending although with an equally strong desire for full global market integration.

Québec[12]

Understanding the role of globalization in Québec is more problematic, primarily with respect to data collection, but also due to the fact that economic controls in Québec are a relatively new phenomenon. The role of the Quiet Revolution in changing the culture and political power of Francophone Québécois is reflected in the predominant economic concerns of the 1960s and beyond. The push to eliminate the income inequality that existed between Francophone and Anglophone Quebeckers required increased control over the economic mechanics of the provincial economy. This legacy of the Quiet Revolution was massive state-intervention and the nationalization of select provincial industries.

The Canadian federal-provincial economic relationship is unique in that provinces are responsible for funding most of their respective social welfare projects, including health care and education. This means that provinces are also responsible for generating revenues. The federal government, which is also responsible for generating tax income, augments provincial tax incomes with an "equalization payment" intended to ensure a level of provincial financial equality[13]. The case of Québec is unique in that the financial resources that are expended in the province to support Québec nationalism do not exist anywhere else in Canada. The primary example is state support for the monitoring and promotion of French language legislation. Provincial taxation and the highest level of federal equalization payments in

---

[12] General background information for this section was compiled from various sources including Bothwell, Drummond and English (1989; 1987); Chodos, Murphy and Hamovitch (1993); Fitzmaurice (1985); Fry (2000); Pacom (2001); and Urmetzer (2003).

[13] Canada's Equalization Program is run by the Department of Finance and is designed to "address fiscal disparities among provinces" (http://www.fin.gc.ca/fedprov/eqp-eng.asp). Québec is, by far, the greatest beneficiary of these federal payments. In 2010–2011, the province is schedule to receive over $7.6 billion in just "equalization" payments from Ottawa. When added to other "transfer payments" (designed to provide federal financial assistance for social services and health care), Québec will receive over $17 billion from the federal government in the 2010–2011 fiscal year (Source: Finance Canada, http://www.fin.gc.ca/fedprov/mtp-eng .asp#Quebec).

Canada fund these nationalist efforts, including the unique and autonomous educational system of Québec.

Ironically, while conventional scholarship on economic globalization concludes that the state is diminished as it integrates into the market economic system, Québec is actively recruiting foreign direct
investment and external trade relationships based substantially on a
nationalist rationale. In effect, Québec can distance itself from Canada
though its own integration into the global market economy. This perspective is supported by Spruyt:

> ...liberalism reduces the costs of secessionism. In a mercantilist world
> with barriers to the free exchange of goods and services, scale becomes a
> decisive asset. Small states simply lack the domestic markets required for
> the efficient production of goods (hence, small states tend to rely far
> more on trade as a percentage of gross national product than large
> states). But if few barriers exist, size becomes a less important prerequi-
> site. Some scholars have argued that progress on the North American
> Free Trade Agreement (NAFTA) in fact assisted secessionist sentiments
> in Québec (Spruyt 2002, 145).

This perspective is complicated by the combination of liberal and
social democratic ideologies that pervades Québec. The historical provision of social services by the Catholic Church prior to 1960 and by
the Québec state after the Quiet Revolution generates significant
expectations of social and state institutions. The national population in
Québec continues to view social service provision by state institutions
as a primary responsibility of the state. The injection of liberal ideology
after the Quiet Revolution allowed the state to grow in strength, while
at the same time maintaining the social democratic traditions of the
province. This section will examine how increasing participation in
the global market economy has impacted the development of a nation-
state in Québec.

Québec: International Economic Policy

Québec does not have the political authority to enter into international
financial or trade agreements as an autonomous entity. It does, however, have the power to manage and control domestic economic
matters. This situation has resulted in a massive increase in the state-
management of economic matters since 1960. A simple look at state
spending in Québec in the first few years after the Quiet Revolution
reveals this massive expansion of the Québec state. Bradbury notes this

expansion and describes the increase as largely the result of the desire to eliminate the economic inequality/stratification between Anglophone and Francophone populations. One of the many economic indicators he cites is the simple increase in state expenditures during this period. In 1960, provincial expenditures totaled $598 million while only twelve years later total expenditures reached $4.5 billion in 1972 (Bradbury 1982, 46).

The development of a strong nationalist economic orientation has resulted in several significant institutions. Québec effectively nationalized several economic institutional entities during and after the Quiet Revolution. Hydro-Québec and la Caisse de dépôt et placement du Québec are two such examples of state control over national economic interests in Québec.

Hydro-Québec was created in 1963[14] and represented the most successful effort at nationalized energy production and distribution in North America. In fact, initial growth of the state corporation was so rapid that existing production facilities quickly became insufficient to meet demand. Hydro- Québec began to import additional energy supplies in 1969 when it signed an agreement with the Churchill Falls Corporation in Labrador (Newfoundland). Production continued to increase with the development of the James Bay project (see chapter four) and the focus on energy exportation was formalized in 1978 with the creation of Hydro-Québec International (HQI). This focus on exporting (primarily) hydroelectric power culminated with the opening of the Hydro-Québec distribution system to the North American energy market in 1997. This agreement created a new Hydro-Québec division, Hydro- Québec TransÉnergie, and an American subsidiary, HQ Energy Services, to market energy in the United States. The current net income in 2005 was reported at nearly $2.5 billion spread across four divisions (production, distribution, equipment, and exports)[15].

---

[14] An earlier version of nationalized energy production, in the form of Hydro-Québec, was created in 1944. Then-Premier Adelard Godbout partially nationalized Montréal Light, Heat, and Power in an attempt to begin liberal reforms intended to accelerate Québec's modernization process. The election of Maurice Duplessis later in the same year put an end to the nationalization experiment.

[15] Information and data for Hydro-Québec were obtained from financial statements and historical profiles obtained from Hydro-Québec (http://www.hydroquebec .com). Other documents include strategic plans, financial reports, and annual reports available at Hydro-Québec.

La Caisse de dépôt et placement du Québec is a financial management and investment institution that emerged from the same Lesage-reform period of the early 1960s. The institution was originally created in 1965 by an official act of the Québec National Assembly to manage the newly created Québec Pension Plan. Again, the emergence of state supported social service provision in Québec illustrates an emergent state in support of national interests. This is important, particularly with respect to la Caisse, as one of the main goals of the Quiet Revolution was to reduce the Anglophone dominance over financial institutions in Québec. In the words of Claude Castonguay, Special Advisor to Jean Lesage (1960–1966), "it was essential to free the Québec government from its longtime dependence on the powerful alliance of Anglophone brokerage firms" (Castonguay 2002, 2). In this way, the emergence of la Caisse represents the institutional end of the status quo arrangement between elite Anglophone economic and Francophone political and clerical elites. Viewed as a sort of economic reclamation project, the resumption of economic control by Francophones in the province was clearly a primary goal of the Quiet Revolution and Québécois nationalists.

La Caisse was given the responsibility of managing deposits of the Québec Pension Plan, but it was also given a secondary mandate to support Québec economic growth at the same time. The investment responsibilities of la Caisse, combined with the state protect of economic equalization, motivated the organization to oversee the health and development of Francophone business entities. The combination of the cultural and economic goals of the Quiet Revolution are readily apparent in the functioning of la Caisse. The responsibility of managing priovncial pension funds occurs within the context of a healthy provincial economy. All of this economic interaction occurs with the understanding that Québec is first and foremost a Francophone province/nation. Therefore, the mandate of la Caisse also includes responsibilities for overseeing the health and welfare of explicitly Francophone, Québécois economic and business entities (Arbour 1993; Forget 1984; Pelletier 1989).

This implied mandate was dramatically illustrated in 2000 when la Caisse blocked the multimillion-dollar acquisition of the Québec company, Vidéotron, by Ontario-based Roger Communications. The sale of Vidéotron (a Francophone telecommunications company based in Montréal since 1964) to an Anglophone corporation was, in the view of la Caisse, detrimental to the cultural sovereignty of Québec. The sale was effectively disallowed by la Caisse under the authority of their implied mandate to encourage Québec economic growth and protect Québec (specifically Francophone) investments. After a series of settlements and negotiations with Rogers Communications, the sale of Vidéotron to Quebecor, a Francophone communications corporation based in Montréal, was approved by both la Caisse and the Canadian Radio-Television and Telecommunications Commission (CRTC) in 2001.

The inability of the Québec government to develop international economic agreements and arrangements has not stopped the Québec state from participating in the global economy as an autonomous corporate entity. Through the creation of state-controlled economic entities such as Hydro-Québec and la Caisse, Québec is able to directly control its participatory levels in various market economic activities. In fact, the nationalization of Hydro-Québec and the public-private cooperative structure of la Caisse means that Québec participates in the global market economy in a more direct manner than the federal Canadian government (with la Caisse participation limited to oversight as a state control institution). Of course, the level of state control over various economic structures and entities is variable and it remains to be seen whether or not this level of cultural and economic protectionism is compatible with greater global liberal market integration. These changes will be discussed in Chapter Eight, tying Québec attempts to protect national economic sectors with the overall theoretical and methodological project of this dissertation. Our goal now is to simply illustrate the nature of global market integration in Québec.

This is not to say that the Québec state is limited to social-democratic nationalization projects. As previously stated, the federal-provincial relationship is largely defined by provincial social service responsibilities and taxation authority. Québec, with its unique political economic structures and nationalist demands, has a tax structure that reflects these state funding requirements; its provincial personal income tax is one of the highest in Canada[16]. Recently, the Québec National Assembly passed a unique anti-poverty measure, Bill 112,

---

[16] Interestingly, *Investissement Québec*, the state-sponsored promotional institution for foreign investment in Québec, cites the rate of corporate taxation is the lowest in not only Canada, but also North America at 31.02 percent. This illustrates the desire of the Québec state to attract investment and business entities while at the same time maintaining existing levels of state spending on social service provision.

designed to both reduce poverty and eliminate social exclusion. The bill is unique in its dual emphasis and in its drafting by members of both the Québec National Assembly and a collection of community movement activists. The bill will not come into effect until 2006, but its construction and ambitious agenda (chief amongst being the halving of poverty levels by 2015) are reflective of the national economic power of the Québec state.

Clearly, the commitment to social service provision and national protection through economic means remains a significant motivation for the Québec state. This political economic climate seems to show a situation of limited global market integration. However, we must understand that Québec's ability to apparently integrate into the global market economy and maintain national economic protections is highly contingent on the equalization payments it receives from the federal government. Due to this source of additional state income, Québec is able to both facilitate global market integration as well as maintain high levels of national economic protections. Recent events have cast doubt on Québec's ability to maintain this contradictory environment and will be illustrated in Chapter Eight. It must be noted that from this perspective, Québec sovereignty would undoubtedly mean the end of federal equalization payments and therefore the end of additional state income to support such programs. One must question the ability of an independent Québec to profit from global market integration as well as maintain non-liberal national economic protections. Again, these issues will be revisited in the project conclusion.

The power of the Québec state to control its domestic economy and to participate in the global market economy cannot be disputed. In fact, it is the strong state control over a national economy that troubles critics of Québec economic protectionism. New political parties such as the Equality Party have sprung up to directly challenge the sovereignty agenda and social democratic, state-centered national protections. Liberal critiques point to Québec's chronic unemployment and relative rates of poverty as being, per capita, among the worst in Canada. These (and other) problems are exacerbated, according to such critiques, by Québec's refusal to engage in total liberal economic reforms (McMahon 2003).

On the other hand, Québec has recently taken extraordinary efforts to promote foreign investment through active marketing and institutional support from such public-private cooperative groups as Investissement Québec. Québec also is a public supporter of free-trade agreements on both regional and global levels. Jacques Parizeau, then Premier of Québec, argued that Québec had been the strongest Canadian supporter of both NAFTA and WTO participatory negotiations and that Canadian participation in both regional and global trade liberalization was due to Québec's unfailing support (Parizeau 1995).

Québec international economic policy is, undoubtedly, contradictory. Many argue that Québec is missing an opportunity to grow its economy at much higher rates due to its protectionist policies. Québec nationalists argue that without these non-liberal national protections their very culture and social structures would collapse under the onslaught of free-market capital and culture. But what has the effect of globalization been on Québec? Have its national protections inhibited economic growth and discouraged foreign investment? Has Québec been able to encourage investment while still maintaining demanded national protections?

Québec: Balance of Trade

A look at Québec's balance of trade since the early 1980s shows marked similarities and differences with Canada. The first major difference is the fact that Québec seems plagued by trade deficits. The second difference is the fact that when Québec has been able to run trade surpluses, it has not been able to sustain them. The provincial economy, while impressive in comparative context[17], is heavily dependent on importation. These differences are illustrated in Figures 5 and 6, respectively.

The major similarity when comparing Québec and Canada trade balances is the increase in trade surpluses at two points: 1995 and 2000, respectively. The pattern of trade is nearly identical when both are compared in scale (see Figures 3 and 5). The initial 1995 growth in Québec of over $3 million mirrors the surplus growth in Canada at approximately $35 million. Both show a marked decline until 1998 for Québec and 1999 for Canada when rapid growth led to trade surpluses for both Québec ($6.8 million) and Canada ($70.7 million) in 2001.

This similar pattern is reflective of the subordinate economic role of Québec in Canada, but it also shows that, in terms of trade, Québec is similarly embedded in the global economy, as is the whole of Canada.

---

[17] According to the government of Québec, the province would rank 50th in economic importance and 21st within the OECD if Québec were a sovereign state. (http://www.gouv.qc.ca/portail/quebec/pgs/commun/portrait/economie/?lang=en)

It would seem that, from this information, Québec's socio-economic protectionist policies have done little to retard the integration of the province into the global market economic system. In fact, one could easily argue the converse: That both la Caisse and Hydro-Québec are well positioned to take advantage of emergent transnational market opportunities. In the case of the former, investment in commodities, futures, real estate, and other direct investment vehicles have proven both incredibly lucrative (pre-2007) and commonly short-sighted (post-2007) – although la Caisse was hardly alone in its investment myopia. In the case of the latter, Hydro-Québec has successfully exported its product to the United States largely through the efforts of bilateral agreements with individual states (such as New York) and as a beneficiary of NAFTA.

On the other hand, this also suggests that high rates of protectionist legislation (Bill 122, Provincial tax laws) and state control over economic production (Hydro-Québec) and oversight (*la Caisse de dépôt*) organizations have not hampered Québec's economic growth to the extent that some would believe. This, however, is a conclusion that cannot be addressed with simple balance of trade statistics. It should also be noted that the massive trade surplus growth of the Canadian national economy provided a significant buffer during the recession years of the early 2000s.

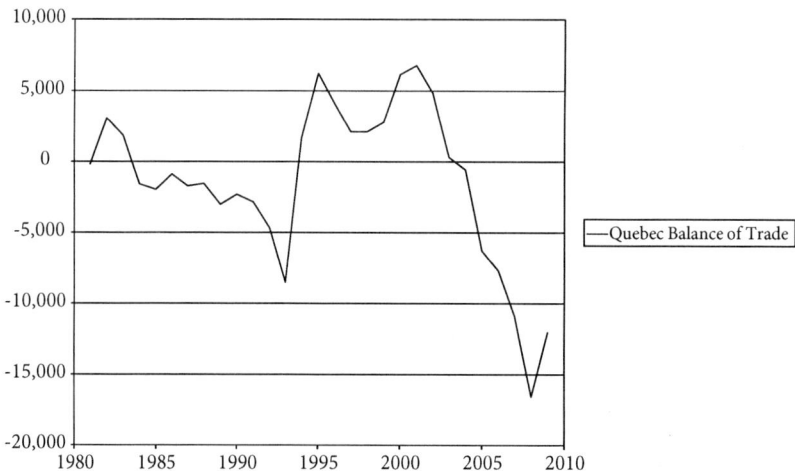

Figure 5. Québec: Balance of Trade (In millions)
Source: Institut de la statistique Québec. "Commerce internationale en ligne." http://diff1 .stat.gouv.qc.ca/hkb/index_fr.html for years 2009–1999. Insitut de la statistique Québec .Commerce exterieur du Québec, 1981–1998.

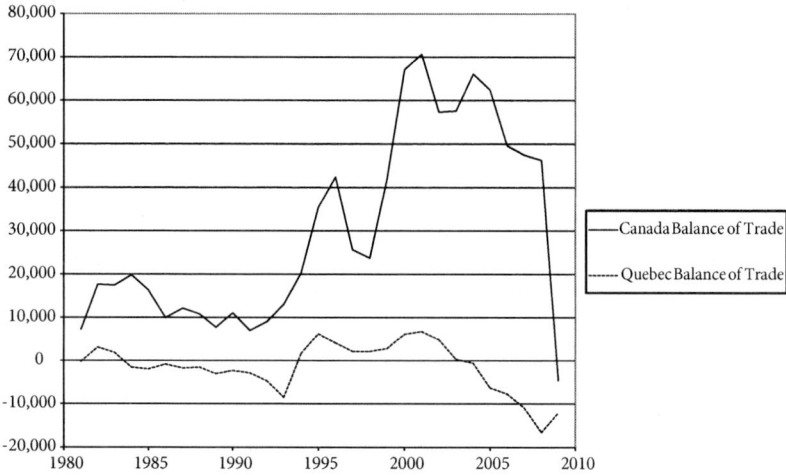

Figure 6. Canada and Québec: Comparative Balance of Trade (In millions)
Sources: Wilkinson, B.K. "Section G: The Balance of International Payments, International Investment Position, and Foreign Trade." 11-516-XIE Historical Statistsics of Canada: Statistics Canada http://www.statcan.ca/english/freepub/11-516-XIE/sectiong/sectiong.htm AND Institut de la statistique Québec. "Commerce internationale en ligne." http://diff1.stat.gouv.qc.ca/hkb/index_fr.html for years 2009–1999. Insitut de la statistique Québec. Commerce exterieur du Québec, 1981–1998.

Canada's long history of trade surpluses ended in 2009 when it posted a CD$4.5 billion deficit (it's first since 1960). The past year was a low-point in a precipitous decline from a 2001 peak (and 2004 recovery) of a more than CD$70 billion positive trade balance. As previously stated, this should come as little surprise given the predominance of Canadian – U.S. trade and the contagious nature of recession in a globalized economy. Québec was similarly affected by recent recessions, falling from a peak surplus of CD$6.7 billion in 2001 to a deficit of CD$16.5 billion in 2008. Interestingly, 2009 saw a decrease in the deficit (to CD$12 billion) as the federal government posted its first trade deficit in nearly fifty years. Increased exports of electricity and aerospace products worked to reduce Québec's trade deficit, but the sustained reduction in sales as a result of the most recent recession illustrates Québec's reliance on global market conditions – and its integration in the global market system, itself.

On the other hand, Québec does not have the economic resources available to the Canadian government. The scope and diversity of

Canadian trade creates a much more uniform pattern of growth (and decline) – implying a stability with respect to trade patterns. Québec, on the other hand, as a simple matter of size is less able to withstand market fluctuations. So while Québec may show a trade deficit reduction in 2009 (as opposed to Canada's continual decline), it will also experience more frequent declines, as evidenced by its trade balance history. Both Canada and Québec have benefited from neoliberal trade policies (NAFTA), but with increased trade comes increased instability. While Canadian trade surpluses have been the norm, annual fluctuations have also accompanied commensurate overall growth in export (and to a lesser extent, import) orientation. Québec's trade balance pattern has been similarly sporadic and reflects the substantial integration of both entities in systemic transnational trade.

Québec: Foreign Investment

Mapping FDI in Québec is problematic. Official investment statistics for Québec have only recently been calculated by the *Institut de la statistique du Québec* and other FDI monitoring institutions such as UNCTAD and OECD do not keep statistics below the nation-state level. Invest in Canada, a department within the federal Department of Foreign Affairs and International Trade, maintained a database (now defunct) of foreign investment in Canada between 2000 and 2006 that was broken down by province. Cobbling together data from these disjointed sources makes a quantitative comparison difficult. There is, however, a practical solution that can at least allow comparative inferences. First, a simple overview of Québec investment recruitment and management will illustrate the problematic nature of foreign investment in Québec. Second, statistics demonstrating recent growth in foreign-owned capital expenditures offers a simplistic but informative view of Québec's financial integration.

Foreign investment is traditionally more problematic politically in Québec than in Canada. Due to Québec's close relationship with the United States with respect to trade, investment flows would logically follow the same pattern. This would, obviously, mean that English would be the dominant language of business and investment in Québec. The (relatively) contemporary nature of the Quiet Revolution and the need to reinvigorate Francophone Québécois business and economic sectors led some to argue against encouraging increases in foreign investment and ownership in Québec economic institutions. This view of economic nationalism, or more pointedly economic decolonization, persisted to the point that actual tangible gains were made in improving Francophone income equality (Vaillancourt 1985)[18].

Once these economic disparities were effectively reduced, the emphasis on economic nationalism has decreased. On the other hand, some saw the emergence of financial capital mobility as an opportunity to give Québec a comparative advantage over the rest of Canada. In 1984, Jacques Parizeau promoted and won passage of Bill 75, which de-regulated Québec's financial infrastructure (see Chanlat and Bédard 1991). The advantage was that formerly restrained investment vehicles were able to diversify and develop a viable, Québécois, financial industry well before similar schemes were launched in Canada. According to Fraser: "Deregulation in Québec gave French-Canadian financial companies the opportunity to consolidate and create huge capital pools in a worldwide financial market which was rapidly concentrating" (Fraser 1987, 97). Yet another in a line of state-building strategies made possible by globalizing trade and financial transnational mobility.

It became increasingly apparent to sovereigntist leaders (primarily in the PQ and Bloc Québécois) that encouraging foreign capital investment in Québec would accomplish two goals: (1) increase Québec's participation and integration into the global economy as an increasingly autonomous entity and (2) show support for liberal economic policies and create a more positive bilateral political economic relationship with the United States as a result. In other words, increasing global market integration and recruiting foreign investment, as a unique and autonomous entity, is viewed in Québec as a strategy to expand Québec's economic base in a more autonomous fashion than simply as a Canadian province. Of course, the extent of arguments promoting FDI as a sovereignty issue varies by political party and ideological affiliation. The interesting point here though is that regardless

---

[18] Albouy (2005) supports this conclusion by measuring change in the log annual earnings gap between Francophones and Anglophones. In 1970, the gap within Québec was -.270 (representing the relative gap between the lower group (Francophones) and the dominant group (Anglophones). In 2000, this gap had been reduced to -.070 (Albouy 2005, 29). Additionally, his research cites annual earnings figures that offer descriptive illustrations of this earnings gap. In 1970, Francophone average annual income was approximately $34,272 while Anglophone annual income averaged $46,857. In 2000, the Francophone average was $43,418 while Anglophone annual earnings averaged $46,656 (Albouy 2005, 30).

of whether Québec political leadership is sovereigntist (PQ) or federalist (PLQ) in orientation, the encouragement of FDI remains constant.

The universality of FDI promotion by the Québec state is apparent in the institutional state support of investment recruitment through organizations such as Investissement Québec[19]. This organization is based on the same public-private cooperative model that structures la Caisse and other partners of the Ministère du Développement économique, de l'Innovation et d l'Exportation[20]. Through such institutional programs, the Québec state is able to encourage and manage foreign investment specifically directed in Québec. These efforts have resulted in positive FDI increases (see Figure 7). A recent evaluation of venture capital investment found that inflows of foreign capital into Québec economic entities were among the highest in North America; in fact, Québec ranks third in North American biotechnology, information

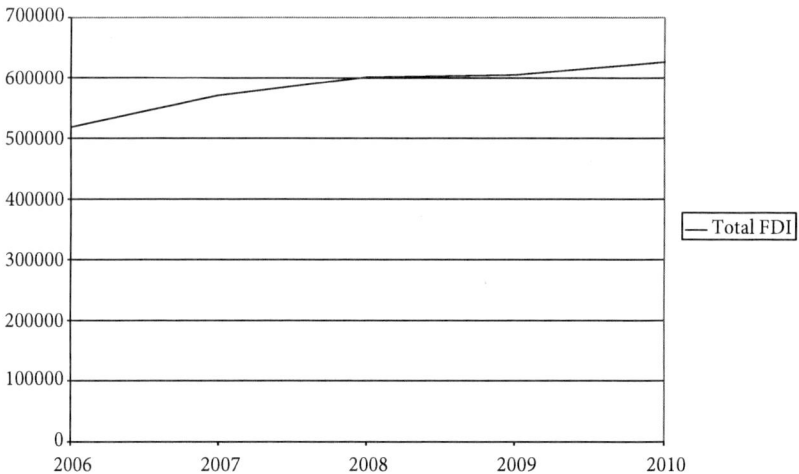

Figure 7. Québec Foreign-Owned Investment: Capital Expenditure, 2006–2010 (In millions)
Source: Investissements – prives et publics: Dépenses en immobilisation selon le pays de contrôle, par secteur du SCIAN1, Québec, 2006-2010 http://www.stat.gouv.qc.ca/ donstat/econm_finnc/conjn_econm/inves/ipp_etr_qc-t3.htm

---

[19] Investissment Québec is a public-private cooperative organization that is organized in a way similar to la Caisse. The Board of Directors is comprised of Québec state ministers and officers as well as private business leaders in the province. The goal of the organization is to promote and facilitate foreign investment in Québec as well as Québec investment abroad.

[20] Ministry of Economic Development, Innovation, and Exportation

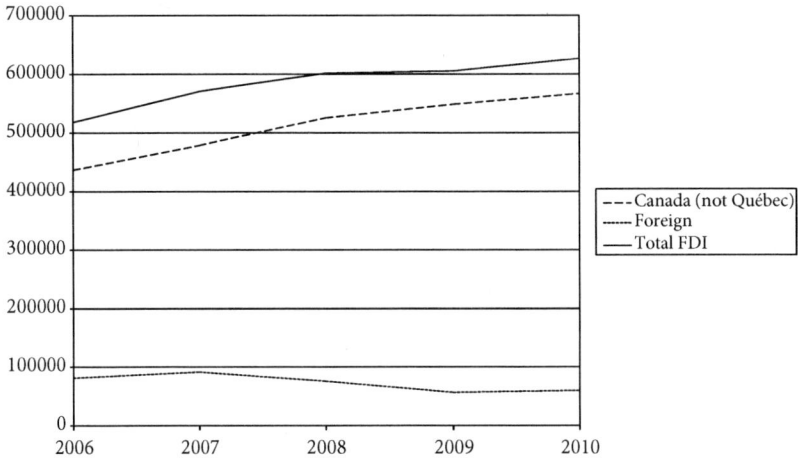

Figure 8. Canadian and Foreign Sources of Foreign Direct Investment
in Québec (In millions)
Source: Investissements – prives et publics: Dépenses en immobilisation selon le pays de contrôle, par secteur du SCIAN1, Québec, 2006-2010 http://www.stat.gouv.qc.ca/ donstat/econm_finnc/conjn_econm/inves/ipp_etr_qc-t3.htm

technology, and venture capital investment behind only California and Massachusetts. The rapid increase in growth, $49 million in 2002 to $51 million in 2003 to $88 million in 2004 (and growing), occurred after implementation of liberal economic reforms by the Charest administration in 2002 (King 2005)[21].

This increase in venture capital is reflected in more material construction and material goods investment in the province. Other than venture capital investment[22], foreign investment in Canada has fallen along with other economic indicators as a result of the most recent recession. This decline in foreign investment has been mitigated by sustained Canadian investment in the province. In fact, as shown in Figure 8, the vast majority of "foreign" investment in Québec is from Canadian sources.

---

[21] "It was just a drop in the bucket in the context of U.S. venture investments - which came to $15.5 billion in the first three quarters of 2004 - but with just under C$500 million in disbursements in all of Canada in the third quarter, the increase in Québec is substantial." (King 2005).

[22] Venture capital investment has all fallen as a result of the most recent economic recession. Efforts to maintain high levels of venture capital investment have been nurtured by Investissement Québec through various capital and seed funds.

The foreign investment and venture capital growth achieved in recent years raises significant attention to the effect of liberal reforms undertaken by the current Charest government. However, the policy legacies of the Parti Québécois and the federal Bloc Québécois have largely mirrored those of their liberal counterparts in both provincial and federal politics. As previously stated, it seems that the political position on sovereignty/federalism is more of a determining difference than is the common desire to integrate Québec into the global economy through both trade and increased foreign investment. While Québec has, for the most part, maintained its tradition of publically funded services and corporations. However, the pressures of neoliberal ideology and the realities of policy convergence as a result of political economic integration have increased privatization initiatives with respect to Hydro- Québec (the PLQ government approved private ownership of wind power production in 2008) and accelerated initiatives to reduce state spending on higher (and secondary) education, child care, and an interesting combination of public and private health care provision following the 2005 Supreme Court ruling striking down Québec's ban on private heath care in competition with Medicare.

While the current PLQ government in Québec is, in fact, attempting to decrease these national economic protections and adhere to neoliberal demands, their efforts are hardly made in isolation. The *Parti Québécois* has moved in a neoliberal direction and the *Action démocratique du Québec* was born as a neoliberal alternative to the (then) social democracy of the PLQ and PQ. This mainstream shift in Québec political economic ideology has motivated the rise of new parties, such as Québec Solidaire, that seeks to combine sovereignty and social democracy in a reminiscence of the inaugural platform of the *Parti Québécois*. The outcome of these limited down-sizing and privatization efforts remains to be seen, however the fact that Québec has utilized policy as a tool to historically promote national economic institutions and protections is significant in defining respective state capacities. More specifically, the ability of Québec to maintain its state-centered approach while at the same time promoting full global market integration is, at the very least, a curious phenomenon.

Comparative Growth

Canadian economic growth in the post-WTO and NAFTA era has been impressive. Trade and budget surpluses, at the federal level, have proven to be some of the largest in the world. In comparison with other G7 countries, Canada was alone in posting a budget surplus in 2004 (CBC 2004). Québec, on the other hand, has struggled to register consistent trade surpluses and has posted consistent budget deficits. This stark position would seem to imply that Canada, exclusive of Québec, was experiencing an economic boom, while the province of Québec remained mired in economic stagnation. A quick look at overall GDP growth illustrates this superficial trend (see Figure 9).

The problem, however, is that measurement at these levels is problematic due to the diversity and levels of economic inequality within Canada. For example, natural resource rich provinces such as Alberta and capital rich provinces such as Ontario tend to show rates of growth that are much higher than poorer provinces such as the Maritime provinces and (relatively) Québec. In addition, regional disparities within provinces are not taken into account. Québec, for instance, has areas of high economic growth (Montréal and Québec) and also areas of large-scale poverty (Gaspé and Côte-Nord). A more accurate measure of comparison would be to examine the rates of annual GDP economic growth in both Canada and Québec. Figure 10 clearly illustrates this trend of similar rates of growth.

This comparison is striking in its ability to show the matching patterns of growth occurring in both Canada and Québec. This pattern

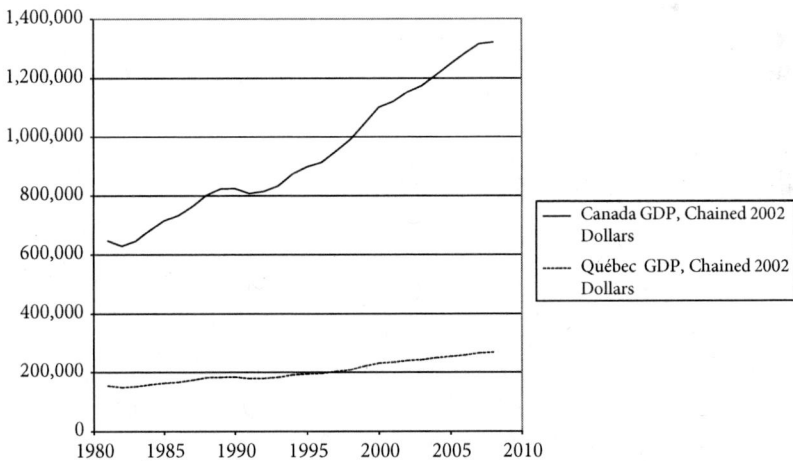

Figure 9. Canada and Québec: Comparative GDP Growth (In millions)
Source: Statistics Canada. Table 384-0013 – Selected economic indicators, provincial economic accounts, annual (dollars unless otherwise noted), CANSIM (database).

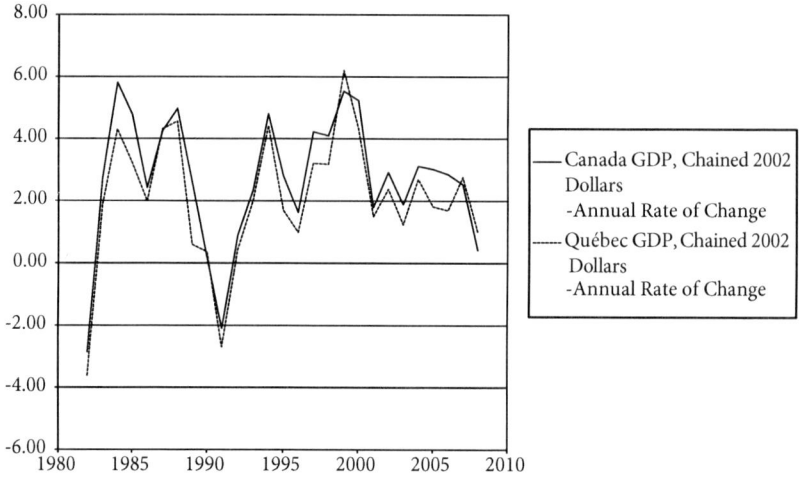

Figure 10. Canada and Québec: Comparative Rates of GDP Growth
Source: Statistics Canada. CANSIM Table 384-0013 – Selected economic indicators, provincial economic accounts, annual

would suggest that while Québec often under-performs in terms of annual GDP growth in comparison with the whole of Canada, its rate of growth is higher at times. We can conclude that aside from rates of absolute GDP growth, the rate of annual growth shows a comparable economic growth trend. The conclusions that can be drawn from this data, with respect to determining global market integration, would imply that Québec has followed a similar path of economic integration (as Canada). We can assume that through comparable rates of annual GDP growth, trade flows, and FDI recruitment efforts that Québec and Canada have achieved at least comparable levels of global economic systemic integration.

Two significant issues emerge from this overall analysis. First, the national population of Québec continues to demand that the state maintain traditional levels of spending. This is in reaction to pressures to decrease state spending by advocates of greater liberal market reforms. Spending cuts and general economic reforms have been received coldly at best in Québec. Béland and Lecours (2006) argue that this phenomenon influenced the difficulty faced by the neoliberal ADQ in mobilizing support in the province. Their contention is that the neoliberal platform of the ADQ was incompatible with prevailing Québécois values, and once d the impact of these neoliberal strategies, support for the ADQ collapsed:

Two things happened to the ADQ as it came under close scrutiny and heavy criticism. First, it backtracked on such things as vouchers and the flat tax, reducing them to 'interesting ideas' and 'long term objectives.' The ADQ also committed to keep Québec's daycare and drug insurance plans intact. Second, its popularity plummeted, which led to disappointing election results (Béland and Lecours 2006, 84).

This strength of national population demands is countered by the universal political will to integrate Québec into the global market economy on an ever-increasing scale. This tension has seen the increasing neoliberalization of Québec, but clearly at a slower rate and in more hybridized fashion. The state is linked explicitly to the nation within the context of Québec – global market opportunities are nearly universally promoted; however, the maintenance of the Québec state is a requisite political responsibility for state actors.

This second issue of liberal market promotion provides an interesting contradictory position – and a potential problem for future Québécois politics. The dual position, advocated by both the PQ and PLQ, has been to promote liberal reforms such as increasing FDI and transnational trade, while also maintaining traditional state-funding for social programs demanded by the national population. This dual position will become increasingly tenuous if political goals for each major provincial party are realized. The desire for PQ leadership to promote sovereignty (elimination of equalization payments) and the PLQ's current desires to dismantle state social service institutions (as will be shown in Chapter Eight) both embrace global market integration as a vehicle for political goals; however, both will result in decreased ability to protect national economic sectors and social service provision. Again, these conclusions will be revised in the final chapter.

Overall, we can conclude that Québec's level of global market integration has been facilitated by its unique position with respect to "foreign aid" in the form of federal equalization payments. This situation allows Québec to promote neoliberal market integration as well as maintain relatively high levels of state social spending. This is a contradictory position that is unique to Québec; however, the existence of this climate raises significant questions about the Québec state and its continuation of such a contradictory and potentially tenuous political economic position (supporting both neoliberal economic reforms and maintaining non-liberal national economic protections). I argue that the relative power of the Québécois national population requires this contradictory state position.

This "inhibited integration" occurs as a result of popular resistance to the effects of such integration. The political elite of Québec has shown a strong willingness to promote greater market integration, but have been unable to adequately reduce the state institutional capacities required for such reforms to fully take hold. Canada, on the other hand, has succeeded in integrating to a fuller extent and the effects of this integration have been reflected in reduced federal spending for health care (Health Canada), education, and other social services once highly prized by the federal government. This conclusion, and the potential dangers of such a political economic position, is revisited in Chapter Eight.

Conclusions

The previous data illustrate two realities with respect to the Canadian and Québec economies. First, they are both unequivocally integrated into global material and financial economic systems. Both have advocated trade liberalization as a means to enhance economic growth and both have attempted (relatively successfully) to attract foreign capital investment. In the case of Canada, trade liberalization was neither popular nor seamless; however, it has become a hegemonic ideological framework for national economic policy due in no small part to Canada's emergent role as a member of the G8 and other multinational trade organizations. Québec, on the other hand, has long supported liberal trade as a means to circumvent the East-West economic orientation promoted by nationalist governments from Macdonald to Trudeau. Québec has certainly been successful in funneling foreign investment to industries it views as nationally strategic (such as Bombardier) and encouraged transnational (i.e., American) sales for crown corporations such as Hydro-Québec. Québec's persistent support for trade liberalization certainly has some roots in economic theory; however, one could easily make the case that nationalist concerns explains Québec support for liberal trade during an era of federal and popular Canadian opposition.

Second, this integration belies severe difference with respect to scale and authority. Canada is, obviously, a much larger economy with far greater resources, labor markets, and capacities than is Québec. The province's limited labor and manufacturing base simply has difficulty meeting provincial market demands while at the same time maintaining a global export orientation – hence Québec's habitual inability to maintain a trade surplus. This has certainly not been the case for Canada as a national whole, for whom liberalized trade has opened significant expansion of transnational markets and production. Surpluses in terms of trade and budgets have become normative, while the opposite is more reflective of the Québec globalization experience.

So what can these conclusions tell us with regards to the impact economic globalization has had on Canada and Québec? With regards to the former, we can clearly see the development of a global capitalist beneficiary, while in the latter, we can see emergent opportunities hidden behind contemporary problems. The problem of persistent trade and budgetary deficits has plagued Québec for decades; however, this is not a problem that has been ignored by successive provincial governments and state institutions. In fact, these conditions have contributed to a fairly distinct reality that defines Québec's contemporary sub-state autonomy.

Québec's distinct brand of economic nationalism (crown corporations and high state spending) has created a unique political economic climate in the province. However, this "Québec Model" is built within a larger Canadian framework and is dependent upon the federal government for a large part of its financial outlays. As stated previously, federal equalization and transfer payments (totaling over $17 billion in the current fiscal year) represent a significant source of revenue for Québec, moreso that any other province (2010–2011 equalization and transfers for Québec represent nearly 30% of all federal equalization and transfer funds). This quasi-Faustian relationship facilitates popular (Québec) state social programs and enhanced the fiscal capacities of the Québec state; however, it is impossible to ignore the condition of dependency that accompanies equalization. In light of this fiscal augmentation and persistent trade deficits – sub-state autonomy in the context of economic globalization takes the form of a negotiated, albeit subordinate, relationship and not one of complete autonomy.

On the positive side, economic growth has occurred in both Canada and Québec, if not in overall volume/scale, certainly at comparable rates. As Canadian history has shown, economic growth necessitates labor market expansion. The contemporary globalization era is no exception. Given Canada's potential for growth and Québec's limitations with regards to production and labor market, the prospect of expanding labor markets. The purpose, of course, is for labor market expansion to fuel increased production (as well as facilitating wage flexibility/depression), which can meet emergent global demand and meet the key criteria of any capitalist enterprise: profit maximization. Demographic conditions in both Canada and Québec require that economic growth be fueled by commensurate increases in labor migration. The following chapter will illustrate this process and the accompanying ethno-cultural diversification or urban Canada and Québec as a result of this economic growth due to increased global market integration.

CHAPTER SIX

ETHNIC DIVERSIFICATION AND LABOR MIGRATION*

The post-World War II period ushered in the dual conditions of expanding economic production in Canada and Québec and an increasingly interactive global political economy. These, of course, were not mutually exclusive conditions as the Keynesian economic growth strategies of the post-war period saw increases in national economic performance along with the institutionalization of global economic mechanisms in the form of the IMF, World Bank, and (less formally) American dollar hegemony. These conditions began to create a more interdependent global political community, dramatically demonstrated by the process of rapid ethnic diversification in Western capitalist nation-states during globalization's early years.

We can understand this development as the causal outcome of several historical and economic forces culminating in the creation of a modern global labor supply system. First, the traditional labor migration from the source countries of Eastern and Southern Europe was limited in the post-War era. New sources of labor migration were required and subsequently filled by migration from the Global South.

Secondly, the political economic shifts that resulted from economic reorganization following World War II, and again after the collapse of the Bretton Woods system and the energy crisis of the early and late 1970s, created conditions conducive to the liberalization of immigration policies in many advanced capitalist nation-states. These conditions included significant motivation for source countries to participate in the global labor supply system due to the same global economic pressures that were functioning in the developing world.

Finally, the transnationalization of production and the expansion of centers of capital in non-Western areas created a new class of educated and skilled labor migrants. These migrants would be increasingly in demand for two reasons: (1) their skills in information technology, which were increasingly in demand as Western states moved toward

---

* Portions of this chapter appear in Cory Blad and Philippe Couton. 2009. "The Rise of an Intercultural Nation: Immigration, Diversity and Nationhood in Quebec." *Journal of Ethnic and Migration Studies* 35(4): 645–667.

information-based economies and (2) their immediate resources, as often these are monied migrants who possess the skills and resources to immediately contribute to the expanded economic growth of the receiving country.

This chapter chronicles the experience of both Canada and Québec in promoting and managing labor migration in accordance with the demands and constraints of the global market economic system. The diversification of national populations in Canada and Québec has been a result of increasing integration into the global economic system. The contemporary ethno-cultural diversification of Canada and Québec must be understood as a consequence of globalization; an economic growth requisite that must be managed in order to maintain national-state stability that is essential for global economic systemic maintenance. The state response to these national demographic changes takes the form of multicultural and intercultural policies and will be examined in the following chapter. This chapter provides an important link demonstrating that multicultural policies are, in fact, outcomes of globalization processes. More to the point, I argue that these cultural pluralist policies offer significant clues as to the strategies state-building options available in the globalization era.

Understanding Labor Migration

Labor migration and immigration have been popular topics in the post-World War II era. The ubiquitous nature of immigration is reflected in the many disciplinary theories of its origins, functions, mechanics, and outcomes. Predictably, disciplinary theories are concerned with respective dominant questions. For instance, economic theories of migration are concerned with explaining the economic motivations and conditions that promote or discourage migration. Sociological theories of migration are more concerned with social integration and incorporation into receiving societies. A focus on networks of labor and ethnic affinity/identity complement perspective examining migration as motivated by the transnationalization of production (Cordero-Guzmán et al. 2001; Light and Bhachu 1993; Portes 1998; Sassen 1991). Political theories of migration are largely focused on issues of governmental control and management of immigration (Brettell and Hollifield 2000; Brochmann and Hammar 1999; Foner and Rumbaut 2000).

The discipline-specific nature of migration studies is made even more problematic by two trends in the literature. The first is a general attempt to develop theories of migration with respect to out-migration, immigration management, migrant integration, migration flows, and many other specific aspects of the migratory process. The second trend is typified by case studies intended to show the unique and historically dependent nature of migrations. Russell King comments on this diversity of questions, issues, and approaches in the study of migration:

> A sampling of even a small portion of migration's vast literature reveals a tension between attempts to create models and theories on the one hand, and the numerous empirical case-studies which tend to emphasize unique circumstances on the other. The case-studies are nearly always interesting but have limited theoretical validity or general application; the theories either state the obvious or involve unrealistic assumptions... it is perhaps precisely because it is so difficult to make generalizations about migration that it is such an important and fascinating subject to study (King 1996, 7)!

The effort to integrate these divergent approaches is a difficult one. For instance, an identified sociological bias is to focus on the receiving country, particularly on assimilationist or identity-centered questions of social integration (Brettell and Hollifield 2000; see also Gordon 1964; Kramer 2003). While some have pointed to the inherent interdisciplinary nature of sociology as providing a natural position of authority in migration studies (Waters 1999) others have moved beyond disciplinary limitations to embrace a methodological common ground of systems theory.

Systemic perspectives of international migration are superior to the traditional "push-pull" models of migration due to their ability to incorporate structural variables in addition to traditional agent-centered choice models. Briefly, traditional models explain migration as a dynamic process involving "push" conditions (high population density, generally poor social, political, economic conditions, or extreme cases such as famine or war) in source countries and "pull" conditions in receiving countries (notably demand for labor, high economic growth, and favorable living standards, social condition, and political stability). While these explanations are often accurate, the methodology is limiting due to its emphasis on migration as a rational decision-making process on the part of the individual migrant. This approach is only able to tell part of the story of migration, specifically "the supply of foreign workers is only a necessary condition for the phenomenon of international labor migration. The decisive condition is the demand for foreign labor in the immigration country" (Straubhaar 1986, 853).

In other words, immigrant choice is an important but limited portion of the labor migration process.

Systemic studies of migration develop divergent conclusions on the motivations and functions of international labor migration from those of traditional rational-choice "push-pull" models. Straubhaar (1986; 1988) makes the case that labor demand in receiving countries is the determining factor in motivating migratory flows. The ebb and flow of labor demand can be measured through immigration controls enacted by respective receiving countries. The resulting conclusions of this perspective are that individual migrants have relatively little power as larger networks of regional and international migration are dictated by receiver demand and established cultural connections (such as lingering political colonial relationships or linguistic affinity). These networks are contingent on conditions of cultural affinity (generally linguistic and ethnic) that encourage the immigration of specific group to specific locales. The mechanical operation of migration networks facilitates the creation of ethno-cultural communities in receiving states.

Harris further critiques traditional migration theory by pointing out its obvious limitations with respect to the actuality of available choices:

> International migration, with all its problems, is only for the better-off workers – those who have escaped the unremitting misery of labour experienced by the millions of workers left at home (Harris 1995, 84).

These conclusions are significant advancements over rational-choice perspectives of traditional migration theory and allow research to investigate the emergence and development of labor migration as a premeditated system (Hollifield 2000; Potts 1990; Salt 1989).

The Global Labor Supply System

Integrative attempts at understanding systemic international migration is best demonstrated in Sassen's *The Mobility of Labor and Capital* (1988).[1] One of the more important aspects of this study is the ability

---

[1] While Sassen's work contributed to the initial development of the concept other authors have contributed significantly to an understanding of the global labor supply system including Abowd and Freeman (1991); Nash and Fernández-Kelly (1983); Portes (1978); Potts (1990); and Straubhaar (1986; 1988).

to examine expansion of international capital in conjunction with an expansion of the international labor market. Her analysis builds on the observations of Portes (1978) and others that international labor migration as a non-coercive process corresponding with the "consolidation phase of the world capitalist economy (Sassen 1988, 31).

The expansion of economic globalization has resulted in a dramatic increase in foreign direct investment for both developed and developing countries, which Sassen links directly to increases in out-migration from source countries. Increases in FDI facilitate economic reorientation to encourage industrial production and increases in export-oriented production. This industrial shift from traditional economic activities also results in internal migration and accelerated urbanization. The process of FDI investment in developing countries contributes to conditions that typify contemporary international labor migration:

> (a) the incorporation of new segments of the population into wage labor and the associated disruption of traditional work structures both of which create a supply of migrant workers; (b) the feminization of the new industrial workforce and its impact on the work opportunities of men, both in the new industrial zones ad in the traditional work structures; and (c) the consolidation of objective and ideological links with the highly industrialized countries where most foreign capital originates, links that involve both a generalized westernization effect and more specific work situations wherein workers find themselves producing goods for people and firms in the highly industrialized countries (Sassen 1988, 120).

The connections between the acceleration of economic globalization and the changing of economic structures in the developing world are clear. The link to migration is, largely, due to the creation of a labor supply through modernization/industrialization funded, in part, by FDI. The removal of a viable market for traditional agriculture or rural economic pursuits encourages urban migration resulting in the proletarianization of national populations in the developing world.

With a ready labor supply, developed countries are able to establish networks of labor migration that can be adjusted in accordance with demand. The evolution of this labor supply system is an outcome of economic adjustment strategies (or modernization processes) that are a consequence of global market integration that defines economic globalization. The question of why this market emerged after World War II is essential to understanding how Western receiving countries are ethnically diversified through the process of labor migration.

Source Region Shifts

In accordance with Portes' (1978) contention that voluntary labor migration patterns begin with the consolidation of capitalism, we can view the development of Western labor migration networks as an outcome of the emergent liberal market economy of the late-1800s. Early Twentieth Century migration patterns were generally consistent with cultural affinity in that colonial relationships, linguistic familiarity, and political management ensured established networks of labor supply. In the case of Canadian labor migration the common denominator was a European lineage. That is, Europe was the source region for labor migration to Canada and Québec until the mid-Twentieth Century. These patterns are easily observed and follow a general historical pattern of Western European migration shifting to Southern and Eastern European sources in the expansionist period of the mid to late 1800s (Bailyn 1986; Games 1999; Hansen 1940). European (read: Caucasian) migration typified immigration to the West. This pattern of European out-migration would come to a halt as a result of World War II and the re-emergence of a global economic system.

The reconstruction and recovery of European industrial production and accompanying economic growth by the 1950s effectively reduced European labor migration to Canada and Québec. At that point labor demand within Europe was sufficient to motivate continental migration patterns between European nation-states and stem the flow of out-migration. In addition, the political stalemate of the Cold War ensured that migration from Eastern European countries tied to the Soviet Bloc would be restricted, if not eliminated. If labor demand was to continue in both expanding North American and European markets, new supplies of labor migration were required. The result was a global shift from the traditional source countries of Eastern and Southern Europe to the developing countries of the Global South.

This shift to the Global South for labor supply needs brought a rapid and dramatic demographic change to many advanced capitalist nation-states. While ethnic diversity has been a hallmark of (voluntary) labor migrations, much of this diversity was Caucasian, Judeo-Christian, and European in general cultural orientation. Shifting global labor supply sources to the Global South resulted in a more true diversity of culture, traditions, values, and race/ethnicity.

This shift is reflected in Sassen's description of the mechanics of the global labor supply system. Economic relationships and capital flows

influence emigration. Briefly, capital investment facilitates modernization and industrialization of developing countries. The moderniza-
tion/industrialization of the developing world is further fueled by the
resultant proletarianization of national populations. This predictable
pattern follows the same history of European industrialization as identified by Marx (1964) and Thompson (1968) – the mechanical capitalist process of creating a centralized (urban) supply of manual labor out
of disparate, rural, and agrarian populations. Thus, for Sassen and
others, individual receiving countries are able to influence migration
by increasing FDI flows into individual source countries or regions.
In addition, Sassen alludes to the existence of certain perceptual "pull
factors" that influence the destination of labor migrants. For example,
the image of the United States as a "land of opportunity" works in conjunction with massive foreign investment in several source countries to
motivate and support this modern global labor supply system (Sassen
1988, 20).

Migratory flows to countries experiencing economic growth, and
thus labor demand, demonstrate a network logic (Light and Bhachu
1993; Portes 1998; Salt 1989). In the case of Canada and Québec, these
networks follow traditional lines of cultural affinity, and will be demonstrated in later sections of this chapter. It is the role of the state in the
creation and maintenance of these networks that is of primary importance in understanding the role of the nation-state within the global
economy.

General Canadian Immigration Prior to 1945[2]

As mentioned in Chapter Three, early Canadian migration was colonial
in nature and predicated on mercantile relationships with respective
mother countries. The first half of the 1800s saw small numbers of
emigrants from Western Europe, mainly from the United Kingdom
(most notably Scotland and Ireland). British colonial authorities
actively promoted a pro-British immigration policy that encouraged
loyalist migration, particularly following the War of 1812. The pre-
Confederation years were, however, ones of relatively low migration to
Canada.

---

[2] Background information for this section was derived from several sources including Cameron (2004); Citizenship and Immigration Canada (2000); Halli and Driedger
(1999); Hawkins (1972); and See (2001).

The political autonomy afforded the Canadian government following Confederation in 1867 allowed greater flexibility in matters of immigration, specifically with respect to source county selection. It also provided Canada with a powerful ability to promote autonomous economic expansion through increased industrial and agricultural production. Immigration and economic development/growth are inexorably connected in Canada. Economically, Canada is an under-populated country requiring inflows of migrants to supplement a limited domestic population.

This focus on migration as essential to the manpower needs of the Canadian economy is well documented (Danysk 1995; Green 1994; Green and Green 2004; Hawkins 1972; McInnis 1994). The chronic Canadian economic problem is that vast natural resources and the economic potential that represents meets a low national population. This need for external labor to fuel economic growth has led to Canada being an excellent case to illustrate the "tap-on/tap-off" pattern of immigration policies that is able to manage labor migration (Ongley and Pearson 1995: 767; Straubhaar 1986). This pattern is quite simple. In times of economic recovery or growth, immigration policy is altered to allow greater numbers of immigrants to enter the country. Conversely, in times of economic recession or depression, the "tap" of immigration policy is turned off to reduce migration inflows (Cameron 2004; Green and Green 2004; 1999; Hawkins 1972). The reality of labor demand in times of economic expansion is pronounced in Canadian history. The fact that economic expansion can be documented through immigration policy is significant and adds empirical credence to the methodology of this project; namely, that state action and motivations can be discerned through embedded policy analysis.

The traditional focus on loyalist emigration from the UK was replaced with a more expansive focus on labor market expansion in the latter half of the century. Westward expansion and the desire to increase Canada's agricultural production dominated Canadian immigration policy during the late 1800s to the early 1900s. The Dominion Lands Act of 1872 allowed free land grants to those willing to settle the interior of Canada. The Sifton policies during the turn of the century effectively reversed years of targeted UK immigration to Canada. American and later Eastern European sources were targeted. A less typical case was that of Chinese migration in response to the construction of a Trans-Canadian railroad (1881–1885). These migrants had a different experience as several anti-Chinese legislative actions created conditions of official discrimination not felt by Caucasian ethnic communities.

World War I effectively ended the large flows of UK and Eastern European migration to Canada. Intermittent attempts were made by both Canadian and United Kingdom authorities to restart immigration flows. The Empire Settlement Act of 1922 was the British governments answer to lagging immigration throughout the British Commonwealth by providing financial and logistical assistance to UK citizens wishing to migrate. The Depression years of the 1930s saw a near complete shutdown of Canadian immigration. High unemployment and limited growth opportunities represented the most extreme historical example of the "tap-off" tendency in Canadian immigration policy.

The end of World War II ushered in an era of dramatic growth in industrial production and economic growth in Canada. This growth was made possible by large numbers of European (Western, Eastern, and Southern) immigrants in the immediate post-war period as Canada encouraged massive migration to fuel this economic expansion. As previously stated however, European reconstruction in the mid-1950s would restrict this source of labor for Canada and Québec. Demographic change and immigration policy designed to facilitate labor migration necessary for economic growth are the two foci of the remaining sections on Canada and Québec, respectively.

Canada: Immigration Policies[3]

The Canadian legacy of discriminatory immigration policies began to dissolve shortly after the end of World War II. In 1947, the Chinese Immigration Act was repealed, eliminating such racial measures such as the provincial "head tax" and outright limits on Chinese immigration. The Department of Citizenship and Immigration was created in 1950, yet preferences based on race continued to be enforced. Small changes occurred in the early 1950s when agreements with Ceylon, India, and Pakistan allowed limited numbers of immigrants necessary to sustain Canada's post-War economic boom. This limited "de-racialization" would not be sustained as recession in the late 1950s created high

---

[3] Background information for this section was derived from several sources including Cameron (2004); Citizenship and Immigration Canada (2000); Halli and Driedger (1999); Hawkins (1972); and See (2001).

unemployment and reduced immigration levels until 1962. It was not until the 1960s that wholesale change began to emerge in Canada's immigration policies.

By 1960, Canada was confronted with the reality that their traditional sources of labor migration were evaporating. Western investment in European reconstruction proved successful and by the mid-1950s the European economy began to require its own sources of labor. What was formerly a trans-Atlantic migration system began to shift to an intra-continental system (Potts 1990; Straubhaar 1988). Canada, along with the rest of the Western World, was faced with the need to develop and encourage new sources of labor migration. As previously shown, that solution was found in the developing states of the Global South.

In 1962, Canada began the process of facilitating migration from the largely non-Caucasian regions of South Asia, Africa, South America, and the Caribbean. Immigration regulations were significantly liberalized with the elimination of race as a selection criterion, although other criteria such as education and "desirable" skills were granted higher selective authority. Canadians of European-descent also retained greater ability to sponsor immigrants from primarily European sources. This system also began to break down in 1966 when the Assisted Passage Loan Scheme (APLS)[4], formerly limited to European immigrants, was extended to Caribbean migrants. Finally, in 1967 the Canadian immigration system was fully de-racialized with the implementation of selection criteria based on a systems of points with no preference to region or racial category. In 1970, the APLS was extended to all potential Canadian immigrants with an established interest rate of six percent.

These reforms led to massive increases in immigration, particularly from source regions of the Global South. The facilitatation of immigration was extended beyond traditional labor categories with the development of Canadian refugee protection programs. Canada's support of the 1969 Africa Refugee Convention created a distinct category of refugee migrants with distinct selection criteria. These selection criteria were essential in allowing humanitarian migration from

---

[4] The Assisted Passage Loan Scheme was effectively a way for the federal government to subsidize immigration and encourage targeted economic growth. Loans were provided, interest-free, to desirable migrants with the understanding that the loan would be repaid within a two-year span and that the migrant would work for at least one year in a selected employment category. The expansion of this system in 1966 prompted the Canadian government to begin charging interest on these loans in 1967.

Czechoslovakia (1968), Tibet (1970), and Uganda (1972), to name a few. Domestic support for the liberalization of Canadian immigration was also expanded. Federal funding of immigration was expanded in 1974 with the Immigrant Settlement and Adaptation Program, which provided funding for new Canadian immigrant initial settlement.

The importance of labor migration to the health of the Canadian economy is indisputable, however larger national concerns would come to define issues of labor migration. Nationalist concerns over the increasingly diverse nature of immigrant populations and the potential for destabilizing existing legitimating structures became increasingly vocal. Nowhere in Canada was this more immediate than in Québec. The main point of contention from Québec was that the federal government did not understand the unique and distinct nature of Québec society and therefore could not make commensurate selection decisions. Many Québécois pointed to the potential for destabilizing French language and Québécois culture due to an immigrant base determined to use English as their primary language of Canadian integration. The lack of selective control was a significant point of contention between the federal and provincial governments. In 1978, the Cullen-Couture Agreement gave Québec the power to select its own immigrants, albeit an autonomy with ultimate oversight by the federal government.

A new Immigration Act in 1978 continued large-scale organizational reforms by establishing four migrant categories: independent, family, assisted-relative, and humanitarian. The Act also eliminated migratory prohibitions for homosexuals, certain criminal convictions, and those with particular health problems such as epilepsy.

The Foreign Domestic Workers Program was implemented in 1982 as a way to provide a pool of temporary service workers to areas of demand in Canada. These temporary visa holders could apply for permanent resident status after two full years in Canada. Liberal immigration reforms experienced a political backlash in 1987 with debates over Bill C-55 and C-84. The former would create a separate Immigration and Refugee Board to evaluate credibility claims of those requesting refugee status. The latter was a legislative attempt, sponsored by the Mulroney administration, to discourage additional refugee claimants from arriving in Canada. Proponents viewed both measures as necessary to prevent potential migrants from taking advantage of Canadian refugee status designations. Québécois critics saw this as an opportunity for the federal government to increase its control over the immigration process and determination of migrant "desirability" (Hardy and

Phillips 1998). Both bills were implemented, in less contentious forms, in 1989.

In 1986, the business class designation of desirable immigrants was expanded to include an investor category. In effect, immigration was approved based on the migrant's ability to invest in Canadian business or economic sectors. As Green and Green state:

> While business classes have never become more than a small part of the inflow, this represents a philosophical shift toward an idea that immigration could be used as a source of capital and as a means of establishing trade links (Green and Green 1999, 434; see also Head and Ries 1998).

The minor demographic, but significant economic role of these business-class migrants offers an excellent insight into the economic nature of Canadian immigration. An example of this process was the desire to attract wealthy Hong Kong emigrants following the Chinese resumption of political authority in 1997 (Abu-Laban and Gabriel 2002; Green and Green 2004; Harrison 1996). Fears of economic repression led many monied residents of Hong Kong to consider leaving for more economically friendly environments. The facilitation of this movement through the business and investor categories led many of these migrants to choose Canada over other destinations.

The early 1990s was a period of economic recession, but despite this traditional discouraging condition, the federal government announced its Five-Year Plan (1990) to increase immigration. This was the first time the federal government engaged in long-term immigration planning and only the second time that immigration was promoted during a time of economic recession (the first being in 1962). The Québec-Canada Accord was also signed in 1991. The Accord gave full authority over immigration selection and settlement to Québec.

Refugee immigration was again restricted in 1992 and 1993, although in 1993 Canada became the first state to issue gender-based guidelines designed to identify gender persecution. The mid-1990s was a period of active reduction in immigration levels as well as a resumption of the Right of Landing Fee in which $975 was charged to all immigrants seeking permanent residency.

Problems of refugee detention, definition, and settlement largely defined Canadian immigration at the turn of the century. Canadian labor migration continues to be dominated by sources of the Global South with issues of integration and settlement being significant contemporary issues. In 2002, the Immigration and Refugee Protection

Act was passed to reorganize and codify immigration changes and refugee claimant status.

These policy shifts, including various mechanisms to manage immigration flows by the federal government, provide a brief overview of the changes in Canadian immigration after World War II. The reduction of European migration, development of Global South labor sources, and development of refugee and business class designations all denote managed contributions to the contemporary ethnic diversity existing in urban Canada. The following section examines, in detail, the changes that have resulted from these immigration policy changes.

Canada: Immigration Trends[5]

The history of European immigration to Canada can be traced back to the beginnings of the country. The post-World War II era presented Canada with a rapidly changing world in which European labor migration was no longer viable in isolation. As Figure 11 shows, several trends can be identified since the mid-1960s when Canadian immigration began to become a more open and inclusive process.

The two most obvious trends are the dramatic decrease in European immigration from 1966 through 1985 and the equally striking increase in immigration from Asia. The decrease in European immigration is the result of continuing European economic recovery and growth that inhibited further labor emigration from the continent. Interestingly, European immigration rises in 1990 due in part to Soviet social and political economic reforms (*Perestroika* and *Glasnost*) in the mid-1980s and later by the pending dissolution of the Soviet Union. These changes greatly increased out-migration opportunities for many Eastern Europeans.

The massive increase in Asian migration is reflective of Canadian (along with most other core countries) liberalization/ deracialization of immigration policies and its embrace of the Global South as a new source of labor migration. China and India are consistently at the top of Canadian immigration source countries both in

---

[5] Statistical information used in this chapter (including sections on Canada and Québec immigration trends) was obtained from Citizenship and Immigration Canada statistical collections, archival collections, and databases.

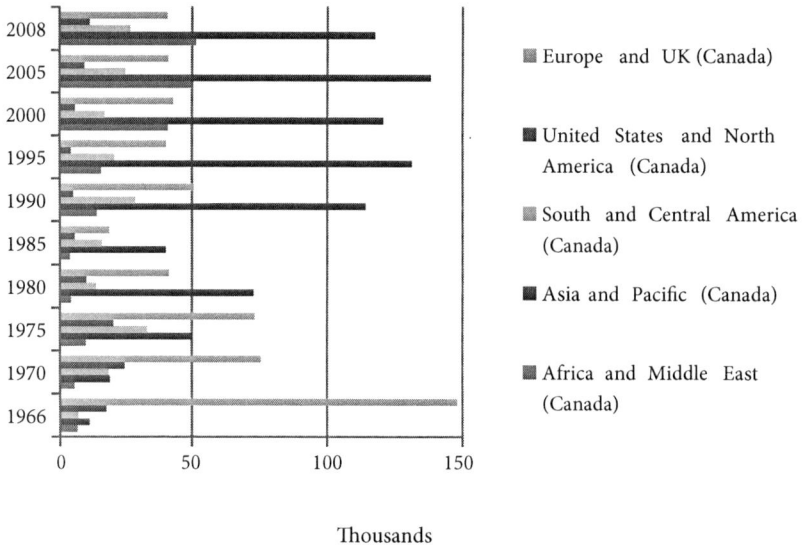

Figure 11. Total Canadian immigration, selected years, 1966–2008
Source: Citizenship and Immigration Canada. Facts and Figures: Immigration Overview 1998 (http://www.cic.gc.ca/english/pdf/research-stats/facts2008.pdf) and Citizenship and Immigration Statistics Archives, 1966–1996 (http://epe.lac-bac.gc .ca/100/202/301/immigration_statistics-ef/index.html)

Table 2. Canada immigration by top five source countries, 1996–2003

Source country	1996	1997	1998	1999	2000	2001	2002	2003
China	17,533	18,526	19,785	29,119	36,723	40,328	33,237	36,116
India	21,286	19,614	15,372	17,430	26,103	27,869	28,822	24,560
Pakistan	7,760	11,239	8,090	9,297	14,196	15,345	14,156	12,330
Philippines	13,158	10,872	8,185	9,171	10,091	12,921	11,003	11,978
South Korea	3,157	4,001	4,917	7,216	7,635	9,604	7,324	7,086

Source: Citizenship and Immigration Canada. Facts and Figures 2008. Immigration Overview: Permanent and Temporary Residents. http://www.cic.gc.ca/english/ resources/statistics/facts2008/permanent/10.asp

terms of independent and business-class migration, with Pakistan, the Philippines, and South Korea ranked as the most recent top five source countries (see Table 2).

Table 3. Canada immigration by top five source counties, 2003–2008

Source country	2003	2004	2005	2006	2007	2008
China, People's Republic of	36,252	36,429	42,292	33,079	27,013	29,336
India	24,594	25,573	33,146	30,754	26,052	24,549
Philippines	11,988	13,303	17,525	17,718	19,066	23,724
United States	6,013	7,507	9,263	10,943	10,449	11,216
United Kingdom	5,199	6,062	5,864	6,542	8,129	9,243

Source: Citizenship and Immigration Canada. Facts and Figures 2008. Immigration Overview: Permanent and Temporary Residents. http://www.cic.gc.ca/english/resources/statistics/facts2008/permanent/10.asp

Interestingly, a more recent look at sources of Canadian immigration show a resurgence of migrants from the United Kingdom and the United States (see Table 3). While the causes for these respective increases are largely speculative, the impact of the recent economic recession in both the United States and the United Kingdom is the most likely factor. According to Citizenship and Immigration Canada, "the economic downturn in the United States as a top possibility, followed by social and political considerations" (CIC 2007). What should be noted, however, it that the top three countries not only remain unchanged, but the combined totals of Chinese, Indian, and Filipino migration easily outpaces that of any other group. In fact, despite the interesting increases in UK and American immigration (particularly in light of popularized emigration "promises" following the 2004 re-election of George W. Bush), the doubling of Filipino migration only solidifies the dominance of Asian (and Pacific) source regions in Canadian immigration.

Episodic increases in source countries reflect both geopolitical conditions (particularly displacement resulting from regional conflict) and Canadian refugee policies. For example, the former Yugoslavia and Bosnia-Herzegovina appear as top source countries due to recent warfare and civil unrest in the region. Similar increases in African emigration are also reflective of these policies, particularly following the 1969 Africa Refugee Convention.

Deteriorating political economic conditions in many African regions have made this humanitarian immigration designation an important component to Canadian immigration as well as foreign policy. This is not to imply that all or even the majority of African migration is refugee based. In fact, African migration provides an interesting point of difference when Canadian and Québec immigration is compared.

Québec: Immigration Policies[6]

In 1966, the Union Nationale provincial government created the Ministère de l'immigration (MIQ) under the Ministère des Affaires culturelles.[7] Not only was Québec expanding the structure and power of its state apparatus, it was also creating a political foundation from which to differentiate Québec from the rest of Canada. Federal control over immigration was viewed as insufficient for Québec's needs. More to the point, by allowing federal control over immigration into Québec to continue, the province was actively handing Anglophone Canada the tools to effectively dilute the Francophone influence in Québec, and eventually Canada.

In 1968, the province struck an agreement with the federal government to place Québec officials in several overseas immigration offices to better monitor the selection of potential immigrants to Québec. This agreement led to the 1975 *Entente Bienvenue-Andras*[8] in which Québec immigration officials were granted the authority to interview and recommend the selection of specific immigrants to federal immigration officers.

The 1976 Immigration Act presented an additional opportunity for the federal government to delegate a portion of immigration power and responsibilities to provincial governments. Section 108 of the Act allows federal-provincial interaction with respect to provincial immigration and settlement patterns. This allowance has led to several

---

[6] Background information for this section was derived from several sources including Rossard (1967); Cameron (2004); Citizenship and Immigration Canada (2000); Doran and Babby (1995); Halli and Driedger (1999); and Pâquet (1997).

[7] Ministry of Immigration under the Ministry of Cultural Affairs.

[8] The *Entente Bienvenue-Andras* was the result of continuing dissatisfaction on the part of the Québec government in matters of immigration control. The Entente was the result of ongoing negotiations between Canadian and Québec government immigration officials designed to grant increased immigration authority to Québec.

federal-provincial agreements on immigration, with the 1978 Cullen-Couture Agreement representing the most significant agreement to result from this policy provision. This agreement allowed greater autonomy in the selection of immigrants destined for Québec. The Cullen-Couture Agreement represented a significant step toward autonomous Québec immigration policy, but the goal of fully Québec control over immigration processes would not come until 1991.

The Agreement was a victory for the PQ (elected in 1976) as it explicitly recognized that Québec immigration must contribute to Québec's cultural and social health. This statement of federal recognition was accompanied by practical reforms allowing Québec immigration officials more authority in selecting immigrants bound for Québec. In addition, the Agreement granted Québec greater authority in establishing financial, skill, and other selection criteria. The Cullen-Couture Agreement was a significant step in Québec's development as a state: it had begun the process of gaining official autonomy in its demographic development.

Québec's authority in matters of immigration was expanded in 1991 with the signing of the Canada-Québec Accord. This agreement grants sole authority for immigrant selection to Québec as well as sole responsibility to provide equivalent settlement and integration programs. Québec is the only Canadian province to retain authority over selection criteria, although there are several other federal-provincial agreements that grant provincial advisory authority to recommend policy and selection changes. Québec is also the only Canadian province to have independent immigration offices for the sole purpose of promoting immigration to the province. Québec operates such offices in Argentina, Austria, Belgium, France, Hong Kong, Mexico, and Syria that serve as regional administrative and recruitment centers.

The most recent federal Immigration and Refugee Protection Act (2002) does not alter the Canada-Québec Accord in any way. The federal government retains authority over total immigration inflows and establishing overall admissibility criteria (largely health requirements), but selection, administration, and settlement remains the exclusive responsibility of Québec. This situation is one of the strongest indicators of Québec's status as an autonomous state entity. The increasing authority of Québec over immigration policies and practices is reflected in the analysis of immigration to the province since the mid-1960s.

Québec: Immigration Trends

Immigration flows into Québec reflect the same shift in source region during the 1960s and 1970s. High European immigration typified the Québec immigration environment as it did in the larger Canadian case. In fact, until 1980, European immigration constituted an even greater proportion of total Québec immigration than in the larger Canadian total. When the immigration source countries for Québec and Canada are compared the proportions are strikingly similar, that is until 1995 (see Figures 11 and 12). After the Canada-Québec Accord in 1991, Québec gained full control over the selection and recruitment process. This is dramatically reflected in the source country shift that occurs in Québec immigration starting in 1995. As total immigration from Asia rises for Canada, the total Asian immigration flow into Québec actually decreases (from 21,567 in 1990 to 9,329 in 2000). Instead of the trend of increased Asian migration, Québec shows increases in African (from 4,732 in 1990 to 9,680 in 2000) and South and Central American (including the Caribbean) (from 4,314 in 1990 to 7,830 in 2000) migration.

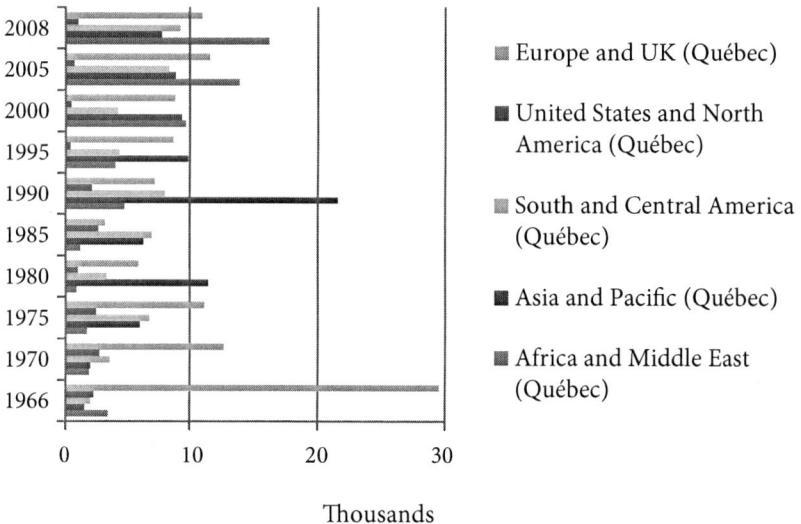

Thousands

Figure 12. Québec immigration, selected years, 1966–2008
Source: Citizenship and Immigration Canada. Facts and Figures: Immigration Overview 1998 (http://www.cic.gc.ca/english/pdf/research-stats/facts2008.pdf) and Citizenship and Immigration Statistics Archives, 1966 – 1996 (http://epe.lac-bac.gc.ca/100/202/301/immigration_statistics-ef/index.html)

This difference in immigration source regions is made more explicit when Canadian immigration is controlled to exclude Québec (Figure 13). This comparison shows a similar pattern of source region shift from Europe to the Global South in both Canada and Québec, thus confirming the initial contention that a shift in global labor supply due to increasing economic globalization has effectively diversified the demographic composition of core states, in this case Canada and Québec respectively.

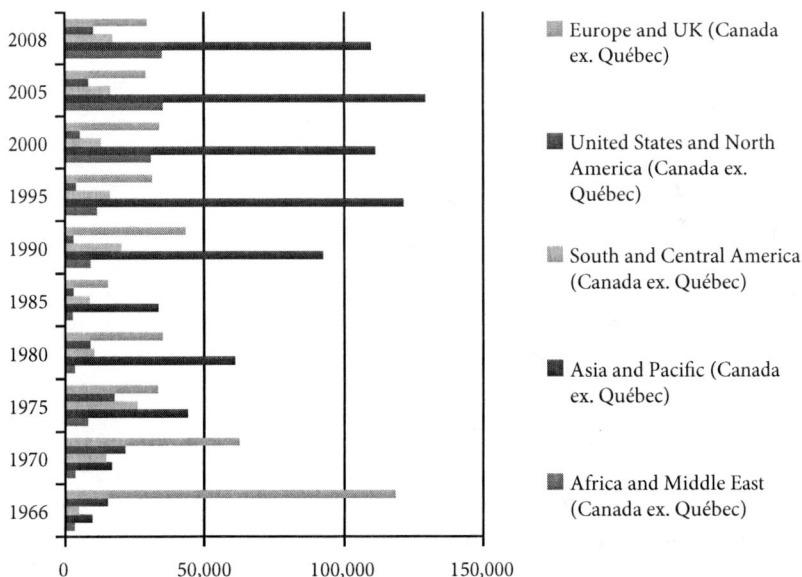

Figure 13. Canadian immigration (excluding Québec), selected years, 1966–2008
Source: Citizenship and Immigration Canada. Facts and Figures: Immigration Overview 1998(http://www.cic.gc.ca/english/pdf/research-stats/facts2008.pdf) and Citizenship and Immigration Statistics Archives, 1966 – 1996 (http://epe.lac-bac.gc.ca/100/202/301/ immigration_statistics-ef/index.html)

The power of states to control regional migration patterns is an additional observation that can be made from the comparison of Canadian and Québec immigration. Canadian immigration reforms in the 1960s contributed to the rapid growth in migration from the Global South, predominantly from Asian source countries. This pattern was replicated in Québec until the early 1990s when Québec immigration controls could be fully enforced by the Québec state.

The result is a concerted effort to recruit and promote migration from regions (also of the Global South) with Francophone cultural and linguistic affinity. This has led to increased recruitment and migration from former French colonies in North and Western Africa and the Caribbean. It is also interesting to note that European immigration to Québec has also increased in recent years, although African migration constitutes the dominant source region for Québec immigration (14,082 in 2004, representing 32% of total Québec immigration).

From this cursory comparison of Canadian and Québec immigration we can conclude that both have, in fact, conformed to the dominant systemic shift in the global labor supply system and encouraged increased migration from regions of the Global South (as shown in Figures 11 and 12, respectively).

Québec, in line with its nationalist project and state development since the Quiet Revolution, has worked within this systemic change to recruit and encourage migration from specific regions of the Global South. The result in both cases, however, has been a rapid and consistent increase in the ethno-cultural diversity of new arrivals in Canada and Québec. This dissertation argues that ethno-cultural diversification in Canada and Québec is the result of increased global market integration and shifts in global labor supply. Economic growth opportunities afforded by increased global market integration *in core states* is made possible through increased labor migration.

This is particularly true in Canada and Québec where regressive population growth presents long-term economic problems with respect to labor market maintenance[9]. Diversity in Canadian and Québec immigration is the result of shifts in source regions in the global labor supply system. Therefore, ethno-cultural diversification is the result of labor market demand motivated by economic growth that is, in turn, motivated by increasing global market integration.

This rapid ethnic/racial diversification (only in the past 40 years) has created a situation of social change and a series of national demands to which the state must respond. These social changes have been dually motivated by integration into the global market economy and

---

[9] In order to maintain current population levels, exclusive of immigration, in Canada and Québec the native fertility rate must be 2.06. Current birth rates in Canada are 1.5 and in Québec, 1.46. Neither rates are sufficient to sustain current population levels nor meet increased labor demands resulting from continued economic growth (Statistics Canada 2003; Dai et al. 1996).

changes in the global labor supply system, thus globalization-motivated change has pressured the individual state to react in turn. Major questions that must be answered are how the impact of these changes has affected state policy-making processes? If global market integration inhibits state economic policy, what avenues for national protection remain?

Conclusions

The explicit connection between economic growth and labor market expansion is particularly lucid in the contexts of Canada and Québec. Both seek labor market augmentation through the promotion of immigration, the majority of which is recruited from the Global South. As beneficiaries of the emergent global market system, both entities can arguably promote economic growth, standards of living, and job creation as attractive conditions for potential migrants. Both also actively recruit and take advantage of adverse conditions in the Global South and actively promote migration to Canada and Québec as a socio-economic alternative.

While these conditional recruitment efforts illustrate the causal motivation for migration promotion, the relevance here is the assumption of autonomous policy control over provincial migration that Québec assumed in 1995. While early Canadian migration in the late-1800s was certainly driven by a nationalist framework (officially, in the context of the Conservative "National Policy"), the development of the Canada-Québec Accord was in direct response to provincial concerns about the future of a francophone Québec. These concerns were exacerbated as Canadian migration began to diversify from European sources and Ontario's emergence as the center of Canadian economic growth (and job creation). The former is a universal condition that Québec has clearly embraced through its active recruitment of migrants from *la francophonie*[10], while the latter poses a significant challenge to immigrant retention for Québec. The concern, of course, was that economic growth in Ontario (and eventually Alberta and British Columbia) would attract migrants not only from abroad but also within Canada. If Québec was unable to compete economically with

---

[10] The French-speaking world; in this context, the reference in to former French colonial countries.

Ontario (and other provinces), it would have to find other means to recruit and retain valuable additions to its citizenry.

The proposed solution was increased control over the selection of potential migrants, which focused extensively on the French-speaking developing world. In this way the Québec state could at least attempt to attract culturally-amenable migrants who would, hopefully, chose to remain in a Francophone province as opposed to moving to Anglophone Canada. The result has been a dramatic distinction in Québec immigration that reflects the province's success in targeting and attracting francophone migrants. While this is certainly not a reflection of complete sovereignty and a significant reflection of the decentralization of federal authority that has accompanied Canadian neoliberalization in the past two decades, it is important to recognize the efficacy of national culture in the construction of sub-state autonomy.

Although the first, Québec is not the only province with a federal agreement granting autonomy over immigration policy. It is, however, the only province to radically alter the regional composition of its incoming migrant population. As previously illustrated, the top source region for Canadian migration is Asia. In 2008, nearly half (47.8%[11]) of all permanent migrants were from Asia. These 2008 percentages are relatively identical in Ontario (50.4%) and Alberta (50.7%) and higher in British Columbia (68.5%) for several historical and geographic reasons. Asian migration to Québec, on the other hand, was only 17.1% for the same year.

Comparatively in 2008, 35.8% of all permanent migrants to Québec were from Africa, while Ontario (20.7%), Alberta (17.3), and British Columbia (8.5%) all had far fewer African migrants. The percentage of African migrants in all of Canada represented 20.8% of total permanent immigrants – clearly, Québec is anomalous with respect to migration demography. While this divergence is easily explained, it is important to not that Quebec, as a sub-state beneficiary of global capitalism (and migrant-receiving society) clearly understands immigration to be *both* an economic and nation-building process. More to the point, Québec's emphasis on francophone migrants is clearly linked to its overall goals of maintaining the cultural distinctions that characterize a national population.

---

[11] Author's calculations. Source: Citizenship and Immigration Canada. 2009. *Facts and Figures*, http://www.cic.gc.ca/english/pdf/research-stats/facts2009.pdf.

It would be foolish to claim that Canadian immigration policies were not "nationalist" in some form; however, the decentralization of policy control and the lack of a unifying cultural tendency that might link respective migrants severely minimizes the argument that a distinct Canadian nationalism underlies federal immigration policies. Québec, obviously, can augment its labor force and *national* population through both centralized policy control and a singular, albeit not exclusive, cultural (i.e., linguistic) definition of desirable immigrant characteristics. In this sense, globalization in both economic and population terms facilitates sub-state autonomy through cultural means.

Despite the nationalist tendencies inherent in Canadian and Québec immigration efforts, both must reconcile immigration promotion with the reality that their efforts are rooted in a global labor supply system. Ironically, state and sub-state efforts to promote national economic growth are intertwined with its geographic proximity to the United States, which simultaneously creates advantages and challenges to both entities. On the one hand, this proximity has engendered the largest binational trade relationship in the world (see Chapter Five) and allowed Québec to regularly promote a reoriented North-South trade axis in support of trade liberalization initiatives. Canada, as a whole, has largely benefitted from both proximity and policy, as trade liberalization basically opened the largest consumer market in the world to Canadian products – as well as facilitating the importation of American and Mexican products to fuel Canadian consumption.

On the other hand, Canada and Québec are sensitive to the fact that sustained (or expanded) economic growth is heavily dependent on respective labor markets, which in turn are dependent on migration. In this sense, both national entities are at a distinct disadvantage due to their proximity to the largest economy in the world with a global reputation for job creation. Put simply, many migrants, particularly skilled or monied migrants, have choices with respect to their potential destinations. Why might a potential migrant choose Canada over the United States, especially when perceptions of economic growth potential and employment opportunities favor the southern destination?

Both federal and provincial state institutions recognize two important needs. First, migration into Canada and Québec must be sustained if future economic growth is feasible in the long-term. Second, both Canada and Québec must somehow differentiate themselves from the United States (and in the case of Québec, the rest of Canada) if they are to successfully attract and retain these valuable additions to its labor force. The following chapter examines one of these strategies, policies designed to facilitate the social integration of new arrivals to both Canada and Québec, as a means to both maintain social cohesion in the face of rapid cultural diversification and state efforts to differentiate Canada from the United States.

CHAPTER SEVEN

MULTICULTURALISM, INTERCULTURALISM, AND THE CHANGING DEFINITION OF NATIONAL CULTURE*

The confluence of international political economic and domestic demographic change poses a challenge to both Canada and Québec. On the one hand, demand for labor continues to exceed domestic Canadian supplies with the expansion of source migration to the Global South providing an immediate remedy. On the other hand, the rapid urban diversification that accompanied this solution carried significant problems for both Canadian and Québec nationalist projects. The development of multicultural policies in Canada, and later intercultural policies in Québec, offer an explicit example of the Polanyian "double movement" in which the state must actively work to maintain balance between the demands of a neoliberal market economic system and a national population demanding protections from these systemic forces. This chapter chronicles the emergence and evolution of both Canadian multicultural policy and Québec intercultural policy in the context of this "double movement," albeit with a focus on culture that is much more explicit than in Polanyi's original thesis. Table 4 provides a brief chronology of Canadian multicultural policies and institutional development in support of the following section.

Canada: Multicultural Policy[1]

Canada's unique multicultural policy (the first of its kind among capitalist democracies) was the result of the 1963 Royal Commission on Bilingualism and Biculturalism (B&B Commission), which was in turn the result of the equally unique dual colonial legacy of French and

---

* Portions of this chapter appear in Cory Blad and Philippe Couton. 2009. "The Rise of an Intercultural Nation: Immigration, Diversity and Nationhood in Quebec." *Journal of Ethnic and Migration Studies* 35(4): 645–667.

[1] Background information used to compile this section was derived from sources including Abu-Laban and Gabriel (2002); Hawkins (1988); Jansen (2005); and archival sources from Heritage Canada, the Ministry of Multiculturalism, and the Ministry of State.

English "founding peoples" (Jansen 2005). The dramatic and immediate changes that occurred in Québec as a result of the PLQ-led
Quiet Revolution[2] motivated the federal government to "explore new
approaches toward greater Canadian unity" (Canada 1973). Canada's
long history of promoting a specifically Eurocentric[3] nationalism
through immigration regulations and nationalist cultural policies was
increasingly challenged by its entry into global economic and labor
systems after World War II. Marc Lehman points to the post-war
changes as being the end of Canada's traditional national definitions:

> For the most part, central authorities dismissed the value of cultural
> heterogeneity, considering racial and ethnic differences as inimical
> to national interests and detrimental to our character and integrity. Only
> the massive influx of post-Second World War immigrants from Europe
> prompted central authorities to rethink the role and status of "other
> ethnics" within the evolving dynamic of Canadian society (Lehman
> 1999, 3).

This post-war reality was, on the whole, not a significant challenge to
the Canadian national "vision" due to the fact that these were largely
Caucasian migrations from various regions in Europe. It was not until
the 1960s that shifts in labor supply to the Global South resulted in a
more racially and ethno-cultural diverse immigrant population.

Lehman's focus is on what would be termed the "Third Force" of
Canadian political demography: those who did not claim aboriginal,
English, or French ancestry yet did claim Canadian citizenship. The
formation of the B&B Commission in response to the acceleration of
tension between English and French Canada and its framing as a bicultural conflict in a bicultural nation-state irked the many "Third Force"
citizens of Canada. The most visible and vocal of these groups self-
identified as Ukrainian and many traced their "Canadian-ness" back to

---

[2] As a final statement of clarification, the Quiet Revolution is the historical culmination of long-standing Québécois nationalism, not a singular and isolated event
denoting the beginning of any Francophone nationalist project. The political economic reforms undertaken by Jean Lesage and the PLQ begin the process of building
an autonomous Québec *state*. The existence and cohesion of the Québec nation is not
in question.
[3] This Eurocentric nationalism was specifically Western European and it could be
argued, British. Ethnic diversity was not viewed as a positive social trait. In fact,
Canadian leaders such as King and Diefenbaker consistently lionized the British
nature of Canadian political, legal, social, and cultural national structures. The shift in
immigration by Sifton at the turn to the 20th century brought thousands of Eastern
Europeans to Canada. The active recruitment of Ukrainian groups for agricultural settlement in Manitoba and Saskatchewan would return in the 1960s as larger number of
Southern and Eastern Europeans immigrated to Canada following the war.

the opening of the Canadian West in the late-1800s. Their stake in the Canadian nation, it was argued, constituted more than a subservient role in the greater national society (Bibby 1990; Kelner and Kallen 1974; Smith 1981). Their vocal opposition resulted in the production of an additional section to the B&B Commission's report, Book IV, "The Cultural Contribution of other Ethnic Groups" (Canada 1970).

The role of Ukrainian advocacy groups in the "Third Force" response to the B&B Commission has been well documented and the existence of a well-organized Canadian population of non-aboriginal, English, or French ancestry was essential to the success of the movement. I would argue that Lehman's point that the influx of European post-war immigration be taken more seriously as a motivating force in generating Book IV of the B&B Commission Report. Commonly, studies of the B&B Report view existing Eastern and Southern European groups as primary motivators for the inclusion of Book IV (Armour 1981; Bell 1992; Brooks 2002; UCC 1968). This fact is not in dispute. I would add that the changes in Canadian immigration policy and shifts in global labor supply also contributed to the Commission's decision to add Book IV to its official report. Passaris comments on the inexorable connection between immigration and economic growth:

> Economic considerations have always been a paramount influence over the scope and substance of Canada's immigration program. Indeed, it is those economic considerations that have determined the gradual change in the multicultural composition of immigrations to Canada in the post World War II period and are likely to define the more substantive ethno-cultural diversity and racial pluralism of immigrants admitted to Canada in the future (Passaris 1986, 17).

In fact, by the time Book IV was published, Canadian immigration had been completely de-racialized and the cumulative effect of these policy changes resulted in gradual increases in Asian and South and Central American immigration as early as 1970 (see Chapter Six). The combination of a more diverse European immigrant population and the expansion of immigration policies to include migrants from the Global South resulted in a rapid increase in Canadian diversity. The fact that Canada's national demographic composition was rapidly changing as a result of its core political economic position in the post-World War II world could not be ignored.

The confluence of issues organized around ethnic recognition movements presented a significant problem for the Canadian government. Not only was Québécois nationalism a significant threat to Canadian stability and cohesion, but Third Force and First Nations groups were

Table 4. Chronology of Canadian multicultural policies and institutions

---

1963 – Royal Commission on Bilingualism and Biculturalism commences

1971 – Policy Statement by Prime Minister P.E. Trudeau, "Multiculturalism within a Bilingual Framework

1972 – Creation of the Multicultural Directorate under the Department of the Secretary of State

1973 – Creation of the Ministry of Multiculturalism

1982 – Canadian Charter of Rights and Freedoms officially recognizes the multicultural character of Canadian society (Section 27)

1984 – Special Parliamentary Committee on Visible Minorities produces the Equality

Now! report emphasizing the need to enforce non-discrimination legislation

1985 – House of Commons Standing Committee on Multiculturalism is created

1987 – Standing Committee on Multiculturalism publishes a report advocating for the creation of a Department of Multiculturalism and a stronger policy of multiculturalism designed to address discrimination.

1988 – Multiculturalism Act provides singular legislative support for defining Canadian society as multicultural and reinforces anti-discriminatory language of the Charter of Rights and Freedoms.

1991 – Department of Multiculturalism and Citizenship is created with a mandate to improve race relations and cross-cultural understanding as well as support minority community development and cultural preservation.

1993 – Department of Multiculturalism and Citizenship is divided. Multicultural programs would be subsumed within the Department of Canadian Heritage and Citizenship programs would be subsumed within Citizenship and Immigration Canada.

1994 – Liberal administration of Jean Chretien eliminates federal settlements payments for federal actions deemed illegal and grievous by various groups (including formerly interred Japanese-Canadian and several Native Canadian groups). This action reversed years of settlement payments by Liberal and Conservative administrations to aggrieved groups.

Table 4. (*Cont.*)

1996 – Canadian Race Relations Foundation is created by the federal government with an initial endowment of $24 million. The CRRF assumed race relations research and monitoring responsibilities formerly of the Department of Multiculturalism.

1997 – Comprehensive review of Canadian multiculturalism revised the federal goals of multiculturalism to include: identity (recognition of ethno-cultural diversity within a Canadian national context), civic participation (promoting democratic participation among immigrant and minority community groups), and social justice (with respect to equality and non-discrimination).

2002 – Declaration of June 27 as "Canadian Multiculturalism Day"

2005 – Federal initiative to combat racism with the declaration of $56 million in funding to implement recommendations in *A Canada for All: Action Plan Against Racism.*

Source: Author's Compilation.

also demanding recognition. Federal attempts to examine and recognize the bilingual and bicultural nature of Canadian society seemed to be expanding into a multicultural context in which all Canadian ethno-cultural groups were contending for recognition. The development of Canadian multicultural policy, however, embraced these contending demands in the creation of a national cultural framework intended to promote a singular Canadian nationalism.

The Institutionalization of Multiculturalism

The diversification of the Canadian population was underway by the early 1970s; however, it is important to note that the initial implementation of the Multicultural Policy in 1971 had little to do with diversifying immigration trends. This policy was, in effect, a statement of Canadian nationalism that was intended to address lingering issues and complaints of ethnic minorities with respect to their *cultural* identification and survival. In other words, the 1971 Multicultural Policy was a direct result of the three forces (aboriginal, Québécois, and the diverse "other" category, largely comprised of Eastern European groups) and their potential to disrupt the national stability of Canada[4]. More importantly, the Trudeau administration's focus on national economic development required a consistent and stable definition of Canadian nationalism to harness the productive capacity and potential of the Canadian labor force, including non-Anglo Canadians.

In 1971, Prime Minister Pierre Trudeau announced a new federal government framework designed to foster a unique and inclusive form of Canadian nationalism: multiculturalism within a bilingual framework. The policy had four central components: (1) to allow minority cultures the opportunity to retain traditions and self-identification, (2) an equal opportunity mechanism to facilitate the removal of economic stratification based on race and ethnicity, (3) to increase intergroup communication for the purpose of education and fostering understanding, and (4) to facilitate the acquisition of either English or French language skills by immigrants (Trudeau 1971).

In order to support these policy initiatives, the Multicultural Directorate was created under authority of the Department of the Secretary State in 1972. One year later the Directorate was expanded into an autonomous Ministry of Multiculturalism with the added responsibilities of monitoring governmental compliance with non-discrimination measures prompted by the Multicultural Policy. Almost immediately, the institutional responsibilities of the Ministry of Multiculturalism began to shift. While the initial policy statement focused on recognition and the protection of relative cultural autonomy within the context of a bilingual Canadian nation-state, the primary mission of the Ministry became the facilitation of equal economic opportunity and economic integration of newly arrived immigrants. These responsibilities were hampered by the lack of legislative authority to enforce the edicts of non-discrimination.

---

[4] Polanyi refers to these destabilizing effects in economic terms; specifically, his "tension of classes" phrase refers to social strain and instability produced in times of high unemployment, high prices, and other conditions producing socio-economic hardships. The same argument is made in Piven and Cloward's (1993) conceptualization of the rise and fall of welfare regulatory efforts on the part of the advanced capitalist state. In this case, the effects of global market integration are increasingly articulated through a cultural medium namely, ethno-cultural diversification. As the state increases its capacity to manage and control national cultural definitions and symbols, maintaining a stable national cultural environment becomes necessary for ensuring control over these universal (and monolithic) definitions of national culture. Strong ethno-nationalist sentiment (outside of the "official" national culture) is destabilizing because it withdraws legitimacy for a universal, state supported nationalist definition.

The need for non-discrimination legislation grew exponentially in the decade of the 1970s. Although shifts in immigration source regions did not provide a primary motivation for the initial 1971 Multicultural Policy, these shifts would come to define both Canadian diversity as well as drive multicultural policy shift in response to this rapid demographic transition. Lehman makes a particularly direct connection between the rise in ethno-cultural diversity and changes in multicultural policies:

> The architects of the 1971 policy had perceived barriers to social adaptation and economic success largely in linguistic or cultural terms. The marked increase in the flow of visible minority immigrants whose main concerns were employment, housing, education and fighting discrimination required a shift in policy thinking. Equality through the removal of racially discriminatory barriers became the main focus of multicultural programs and race relations policies and programs were put in place to discover, isolate and combat racial discrimination at personal and institutional levels (Lehman 1999, 5).

The need to match ethno-cultural protections with economic development would come to define Canadian multicultural policy. Until 1982, however, the Multicultural Policy was simply a federal initiative with no legal authority. The larger goal was to encourage the national population to accept the reality of Canadian multiculturalism, while at the same time promoting a unified Canadian nationalism. In 1977, the Minister of State for Multiculturalism, Norman Cafik, commented on the motivation for official multiculturalism:

> We don't have a second class culture or a first class culture in Canada. We have a multicultural society not because we created it that way as a government, but because that's the way it is (Cafik 1977).

Cafik's statement is typical of policy defenses in that his arguments present a state seeking to support the nation during a period of dramatic social change. That is, the state is simply reacting to socio-economic changes outside of its control and therefore must respond in a reactionary fashion to protect its national population. His implication that the state did not create a multicultural society is flawed as evidenced by the previous chapter. This implies that the "reactionary" nature of multicultural policy is not accurate.

Multicultural policy supports the diversification of Canada and therefore maintains a proactive function. By presenting multicultural policy as reactionary, the Canadian state is able to publicly absolve itself of complicity in facilitating socio-economic conditions requiring political attention. In other words, the Canadian state presents itself as protecting Canadian national populations from social changes motivated by external forces and processes. The fact that the multicultural policy also facilitates ethno-cultural changes promoted by global market integration is overlooked in the public presentation of Cafik's policy statement.

Cafik was correct in his assessment of the historical nature of Canadian multicultural society. At no time in Canada's post-colonization era was there a single ethno-cultural entity that existed without challenge. Cafik was incorrect in his general statement about the lack of culpability on the part of the Canadian state. As chapters five and six have shown, the Canadian federal state actively promotes ethno-cultural diversification in support of economic growth. From the recruitment of Ukrainian and other Eastern Europeans in the Western Expansion era to the current shift of the global labor supply system to the Global South, the federal government has relied on immigration to fuel economic growth. The labor required to produce economic growth is increasingly of an ethnic and culturally diverse nature. Therefore, the Canadian federal government had a strong role in the ethno-cultural diversification of Canada due to its willingness to integrate into the global market economic system. The collapse of any semblance of national economic protections in the late 1970s (after the first Trudeau administration) required that expanded economic growth be accompanied by continued immigration and accelerated ethno-cultural diversification. The task of the federal government, unencumbered by economic protections, would be how to manage this rapid diversification while ensuring a stable economic (production) environment.

The 1982 Charter of Rights and Freedoms, as part of the Constitution Act, gave legal support and authority to the Ministry of Multiculturalism with respect to the enforcement of non-discrimination. For the first time, Canada was legally able to prosecute discriminatory actions in hiring, housing, and public interaction. The Charter defined Canadian society as being one of equal opportunity, particularly with respect to the demographic composition of the country. Section 27 of the Charter specifically codifies the multicultural character of the Canadian nation, while Section 15 specifically provides legal discriminatory protection for all individuals "in particular...based on race, national or ethnic origin, colour, religious, sex, age, or mental or physical disability" (Canada 1982).

The Charter provided important legal authority for anti-discrimination goals of the revised multicultural policy[5]. As the face of Canadian immigration continued to grow increasingly diverse, the federal government began to realize that the official recognition of cultural diversity and legal protection from discrimination required additional augmentation. In 1984, the Special Parliamentary Committee on Visible Minorities was commissioned and one year later the House of Commons created a Standing Committee on Multiculturalism. On the recommendation of these two Committees, Canadian multiculturalism was officially codified by the 1988 Multiculturalism Act.

The Multiculturalism Act did not institute any new changes to Canadian multicultural policy. What it did was provide specific legislation officially defining Canada as a multicultural society, protecting individuals from discrimination, continuing the process of cultural diversity education and understanding, and facilitating cultural preservation for ethno-cultural minorities. The specificity of the Multiculturalism Act meant that the sporadic mention of multicultural and diversity protection in the Charter of Rights and Freedoms was superseded. The Act also created the Department of Multiculturalism and Citizenship that eventually commenced full operations in 1991. The responsibilities of the Department were three-fold. The primary mission was monitoring race relations (for example, receiving and evaluating discrimination complaints) followed by cultural preservation (largely through grant support for cultural education programs and celebratory functions) and then community support (facilitating integration activities and sponsoring events designed to encourage inter-group dialog). This emphasis on race relations is an important shift that was prompted by the rapid diversification of urban Canada and reflective of the changing nature of national demands in the face of these local changes wrought by global market integration.

> Where early multicultural policies concentrated on cultural preservation and intercultural sharing through promotion of ethnic presses and festivals, the rejuvenated multiculturalism program emphasized cross-cultural understanding and the attainment of social and economic

---

[5] Enforcement of anti-discrimination legislation was limited within the Ministry of Multiculturalism. The Ministry was able to monitor compliance and cite offenders, but had no adjudicative authority. Ultimately, the institution of official multiculturalism was enforced by the court system through adherence to both the Charter of Human Rights and Freedoms and the Multiculturalism Act.

integration through removal of discriminating barriers, institutional change and affirmative action to equalize opportunity (Lehman 1999, 7).

The Decline of Institutional Multiculturalism

The institutional position of multiculturalism led many neoliberal critics to question the effectiveness of state spending on multicultural programs. The nearly universal neoliberal calls to decrease state spending on social service provision heavily affected the state decision to downsize the mission and institution of official multiculturalism. As the Canadian state became more and more integrated into the global market system, the more intense and persistent the calls to reduce and/or privatize the state's role in social services.

As a result, the institutional emphasis on official multiculturalism was revised yet again in 1993 as the Department of Multiculturalism and Citizenship was downsized to become a subdivision within the Canadian Heritage Department. The administration of federal multicultural policies was removed as a primary emphasis and placed on par with official language programs, among many other programs of national interest (media, national park administration, and support for the arts).

Canadian multicultural policy was revised again in 1996 as a result of increased criticism from many neoliberal and national interests. The renewed emphases returned to the original 1971 policy statement in that Canadian multiculturalism would increasingly emphasize the recognition of cultural identity while de-emphasizing the authoritative role of multiculturalism in managing issues of discrimination and diversity. The new policy focused on the development of community-centered initiatives to promote inter-cultural understanding and cooperation. The multicultural program within the Canadian Heritage Department was largely divorced from larger race relation issues with the establishment of the public-private Canadian Race Relations Foundation (CRRF) in 1997[6]. Initially funded by a federal grant, the CRRF is now a completely self-financed organization that is responsible for

---

[6] The Canadian Race Relations Foundation was established by an act of Parliament in 1996 and initially funded by a $24 million grant. The Foundation is run on a corporate model with a Board of Directors with day-to-day operations administered by an executive officer. A descriptive statement on the CRRF website (www.crr.ca) offers a more complete view of the public-private model of operation:

generating research and awareness of racial/ethnic relations and problems in Canada. The CRRF has no legal enforcement authority and the federal government has largely returned to the general non-discrimination statements inherent in the Charter of Rights and Freedoms.

This de-institutionalization of multiculturalism in Canada was the result of neo-liberal attacks on perceived excesses in both state spending and state involvement in market economic processes (Frow 1999; Joppke 2004). In fact, Mitchell goes even further in declaring multiculturalism and neoliberal ideology incompatible (Mitchell 2004). I argue that the conflict between (neo) liberal ideology and multiculturalism is, in fact, indicative of the "double movement" process of neoliberal market encroachment and national protectionist demands. The incompatibility of liberalism and multiculturalism (as articulated by Taylor, Kymlicka, Joppke, Mitchell, and others) is the manifestation of neoliberal (global political economic) pressures generating a non-liberal (national protectionist) reaction.

The issue of multicultural (and later intercultural) policy is that it is designed to mediate these impulses (liberal and non-liberal) – thus we can view the mechanics of the "double movement" through such policies. In other words, the effects of global market integration encourage social destabilization at which time national populations demand protections from these destabilizing effects. The state must negotiate these dual pressures through policies intended to meet both demands (global market integrative and national protectionist). This dynamic will be revisited in the final section of this chapter as well as in the following chapter.

Returning to the example of Canadian multicultural policy, the return to the liberal foundations of the Charter is a significant development. In view of neoliberal critics, the institutionalism of federal multiculturalism could be easily replaced with a simple judicial adherence to the liberal equality espoused in the Charter. The pressures of adherence to the neoliberal ideology of limited state spending and control have been identified as a ubiquitous condition of global market integration (Baiman et al. 2000; Boyer and Drache 1996; Harris and

---

CRRF is a Crown corporation with a national mandate operating at arms length from the federal government from which we receive no funding. Our primary operating funds are derived from the investment income on the one-time endowment fund.

Seid 2000). The case of multiculturalism's decline as an institutional entity in Canada seems particularly telling of this process.

This decentralization of multicultural responsibilities beginning in 1993 is a direct result of these neoliberal pressures to reduce social spending. Increasing criticism of multicultural programs in general centered on program costs (Breitkreuz 1997), the inability to enforce non-discrimination legislation (Jansen 2005), the incompatibility of multicultural ideology and Canadian social welfare distribution (Barbaro 1995) and the ideological danger to a cohesive Canadian nation-state (Barry 2001; Bissoondath 1994). The declining role of multicultural policy in Canada is reflected in consistent decreases in federal funding and the privatization of one of the once central responsibilities of the Department of Multiculturalism. Of course, one of the central tenants of neoliberal economic governance is decreased state spending for social services that hinder economic growth.

The decline of institutional multiculturalism in the 1990s represented a success for neoliberal critics; however the program continues to play a significant role in support of Canadian immigration goals. In fact, Canadian business entities now support the ideal of multiculturalism as being a facilitator of skilled and monied labor migration (Abu-Laban 2003; Abu-Laban and Gabriel 2002). The current challenge is no longer from neoliberal global market proponents, but from national popular groups claiming that multiculturalism as a state policy has failed to adequately provide a common socio-cultural medium. Critics argue that national cohesion and stability (see footnote 4 in this chapter) are threatened by a policy that, in fact, creates divisions and separation as opposed to provided its promised unity under a common nationalist environment (Bibby 1990; Bissoondath 1994; Gwyn 1995).

Before I enter into a discussion of increasing national popular dissatisfaction with multicultural policies, it is necessary to compare the emergence and decline of multiculturalism with that of *interculturalism* in Québec. This comparison will illuminate one of the central nationalist pressures facing the federal multicultural policy and provide a more fluid transition into the final concluding section of this chapter.

Québec: Intercultural Policy

Official Canadian multiculturalism, particularly the 1971 policy framework and the 1988 Multiculturalism Act, is a significant achievement. Both the policy framework and the legislation of official multiculturalism were the first of their kind in the world. The promotion of official multiculturalism on the part of the federal government was initially intended to define the parameters of the Canadian nation and promote a specific articulation of Canadian nationalism as inclusive and culturally egalitarian. Specifically, the federal government understood the changing nature of the Canadian population as an inevitable outcome of larger socio-economic forces.

> Canada should set its immigration levels on the basis of long-term objectives, rather than on that of short-term considerations...Given the uncertainties involved in deciding both on an appropriate population size and on its fellow age composition, Canada should follow that course which...is, a less restrictive policy than that currently in place...In recommending this approach to immigration policy, this Commission is fully aware of the cultural, linguistic, economic and racial implications (Canada 1985, 668).

The threat of globalization, it would seem, played an important role in the initial conceptualization of Canadian multiculturalism – as did Québec nationalism. In fact, the original motivation for official multicultural policies as a protection against the dangers of cultural homogenization:

> ...Central to the Government's philosophy is the belief that cultural diversity throughout the world is swiftly being eroded by the impact of industrial technology, mass communications and urbanization. Much attention has been given to the denaturing and depersonalization of man by mass society, mass-produced culture and entertainment and the ever-increasing development of large impersonal institutions.

> One of man's basic needs is a sense of belonging and a good deal of contemporary social unrest, at all age levels, exists because this need has not been met. Ethnic groups are not the only way in which the need for belonging can be met, but they can be an important one in the development of Canadian society...Ethnic loyalties need not, and usually do not detract from wider loyalties of community and country. Canadian identity will not be undermined by multiculturalism. Indeed, the Government sincerely believes that cultural pluralism is the very essence of Canadian identity (Canada 1973, 1–2).

Trudeau's 1971 policy framework included two non-stated but implied nationalistic goals. The first was to differentiate Canada from the United States with respect to its national culture and independent nature. The second was to address the threat of Québécois sovereignty by clearly defining Canada as a diverse nation within a singular nationalist framework.

The first aspect of differentiation from the United States is more overt. Kelner and Kallen (1974) point to numerous statements made by Trudeau concerning the nation-building nature of the 1971 Multi-cultural Policy. Of significance is the desire of the Trudeau administration to distinguish Canadians from Americans through ideological uniqueness, which could be represented by social policies reflecting the recognition of a *recognized* cultural pluralism in contrast with the "melting pot" model of assimilation to the south (Bibby 1990; Breton 1986). More to the extreme, scholars have pointed to past animosity toward Americans due to perceived "economic and cultural imperialism" (Richmond 1978, 120) as a broader cultural motivation for incorporating such a diametrically different policy on diversity and culture.

The second implied goal of the 1971 multicultural framework was to reduce the legitimacy claims of the Québec sovereignty movement.

> He [Trudeau] repudiated dualism; the concept of two nations or of a binational Canada; and even biculturalism, as advocated by the B&B Commission…He was implicitly asking his fellow Quebecers to trade their identity as a people against the promise of bilingualism… He [Trudeau] advanced the concept of multiculturalism…thus reducing the global culture of French-speaking Québec to one ethnic component of the Canadian mosaic. They (Québécois) would have accepted multiculturalism if it had not confused their own global culture with the ethnic cultures of immigrants (Balthazar 1995, 47).

This was understood implicitly by the Québec government and national population, but largely denied by federal government officials (Gendron and Sarra-Bournet 1998; Maclure 2003; Vachon and Langlais 1983).

Public opinion in Québec about federal multicultural policy ranges from skeptical to suspicious to openly hostile (Charbonneau and Maheu 1973; McRoberts 1997). The announcement of the federal policy in 1971 by a Trudeau administration already critical of Québécois nationalism motivated a string of protective measures in Québec. Table 5 provides a brief chronology of Québec language legislation and intercultural policy development in support of the following two sections.

Québec Language Legislation

In 1974, Bill 22 (*Loi sur le langue officielle*[7]) was passed by the Québec National Assembly. The primary purpose of the law was to grant

---

[7] Official Language Law.

French official language status. The law also created an administrative body, Régie de la langue française[8], to oversee enforcement of language legislation and other requirements such as making French the official language of provincial administration, legal contracts, provincial advertisement, and encourage French as the primary language of business. The law contained protections for English-speakers, including the ability to "opt-out" of French-only requirements at the behest of *both* parties. The law was widely criticized by the Anglophone minority for its promotion of French as an official provincial language while the federal policy required both French and English as official languages. Many Francophones were disappointed in the law due to its compromises in allowing Anglophones to opt-out of the dominant culture and language.

The election of the PQ in 1976 provided additional opportunity to increase the dominance of French throughout Québec. Bill 101 (*Charte de la langue française*[9]) was passed in 1977 and eliminated any question of the linguistic or cultural nature of Québec. The measure required that all public administrative, legal/judicial, educational, and business entities use French as its operational language. All public advertisements were required to be posted in French only. The most far-reaching aspect of Bill 101 was its focus on the public education system. The only students allowed to attend English-language institutions were those already in attendance, siblings, or the children of existing Québec citizens who were both Anglophone. This meant that all new immigrants and those with mixed-cultural parentage were required to receive a Francophone education. The educational requirements of Bill 101 are arguably the most far-reaching cultural protectionist legislation enacted by the Québec National Assembly.

In 1982, the federal government and all provinces, except Québec, signed the Constitution Act and the Charter of Rights and Freedoms. The Charter explicitly recognized the multicultural character of Canadian society and gave the Supreme Court legal authority to declare many portions of Bill 101 unconstitutional, which it did in 1982[10].

---

[8] Office of the French Language.

[9] Charter of the French Language.

[10] This is an excellent example of the ambiguity surrounding federal-provincial relations in Canada. Québec has, to this date, not signed either the 1982 Constitution Act or the Charter of Rights and Freedoms. This was of little consequence as the Supreme Court ruled on the legality of Bill 101 as if Québec was an operational member of the Canadian Federation. In fact, Québec operates as an inclusive Canadian

Table 5. Chronology of the Québec intercultural policy framework

Language Legislation

1969 – *Loi pour promouvoir la langue française au Québec* (Bill 63) (Law for the Promotion of the French Language) is passed by the Québec National Assembly giving parents the right to have their children educated in the French language.

1974 – *Loi sue le langue officielle* (Bill 22). The "Official Language Law" establishes French as the single official language of Québec

1974 – Establishment of the *Régie de la langue français* (Office of the French Language)

1977 – Bill 101, *Charte de la langue français* (Charter of the French Language), is passed requiring French as the legal, political, and public language of Québec. In addition, the children of new arrivals (immigrants) to Québec were required to be educated in French-language educational institutions.

1982 – Supreme Court of Canada rules that Loi 101 is discriminatory under the multiculturalism and equality sections of the Canadian Charter of Rights and Freedoms.

1984 – Bill 142 is passed ensuring that basic social services, including health care, are available in English.

1991 – Bill 120 is passed, reaffirming the right of English-language social service provision in the province.

1992 – Bill 20 is passed, again re-affirming the bilingual nature of social service provision but also reaffirming the dominance of the French language in Québec.

1993 – Bill 86 allowed English language advertisement and business service provision, granted that French be given a position of priority.

Intercultural Policies

1975 – *Charte des droits et libertés de la personne* (Charter of Human Rights and Freedoms) is passed in response to the increasingly diverse nature of Québec immigration and designed to encourage an equal socio-economic environment.

province from receiving equalization payments to participating in national political, military, and cultural institutions. It would seem that the inclusion of Québec as a member of the Canadian Federation is a given despite the provincial refusal to officially recognize its subordinated place in Canada.

Table 5. (*Cont.*)

1978 - *La politique du développment culturel au Québec* (Quebec Cultural Development Policy) is published to promote the "convergence" of diverse cultures around a central Quebecois national identity. The policy was designed to articulate a pluralist integration policy, but one distinct from federal multiculturalism.

1981 – *Autant de façons d'etre Québécois* (Many Ways to be Québécois) is published stating that Québec is legally an egalitarian society and officially recognizes the right to diverse ethno-cultural communities and traditional adherence. This policy statement also stresses the idea of "convergence" that requires the public language and culture of the province be explicitly French and Québécois, respectively. In other words, traditional (non-Québécois) culture is recognized and encouraged; however, this recognition does not extend to public affirmation of these languages and culture in a public context, particularly government and education.

1990 – *Au Québec pour bâtir ensemble: énoncé de politique en matière d'immigration et de l'intégration* (We are Building Québec Together: Policy Announcement on Matters of Immigration and Integration) is published affirming three main defining features of Québec society: democracy (particularly the requirement that all citizens participate in shared governance), cultural pluralism (or the recognition of ethno-cultural diversity), and French as a common language.

2005 – Creation of the *Ministère de l'Immigration et Communautés culturelles* (Ministry of Immigration and Cultural Communities) to both manage Québec immigration as well as the integration of diverse cultural communities into Francophone Québec society.

Source: Author's Compilation.

Several legislative reforms were implemented in later years in response to the legal rulings deeming Bill 101 unconstitutional. Bill 142, passed in 1986, provides additional linguistic rights to Anglophones by making health and general social service provision available in English. In fact, today most governmental institutions in Québec offer at least reception services in both English and French, although French is practically and legally the official language of the province. Further legislation, Bill 120 (1991) and Bill 20 (1992), further solidified the right of Anglophone service provisions, but clearly articulated the granting of English-language rights as a process governed by the Francophone government and national population of Québec.

Bill 86 was passed in 1993 and reduced the emphasis on reducing English as a public language. English advertising and service provision was allowed with the provision that French be given a priority position. This is largely accomplished through order and size. French phrases are listed first (or above) English phrases and are generally in a larger font size than the English phrases. English language education was made available to the children of Anglophones, provided that the parents or child previously received English-language education *in Canada*.

Québec enacted protectionist policies that would ensure the dominance of a singular linguistic and cultural medium in the province. The promotion of a singular cultural medium becomes increasingly problematic given the labor migration requirements of global market integration. Increasing ethno-cultural diversification of Québec immigration makes the autocratic promotion of a singular cultural nationalism practically impossible. Thus, the protection of the French language and a distinctive Québécois culture must occur in accordance with the recognition of cultural pluralism and the multicultural realities of increased global market integration.

The provincial response to the Supreme Court ruling and the demands of global market integration is telling. Québec refused to rescind protectionist language legislation, but instead created a largely intercultural policy framework that would define Québec as distinct within a larger Canadian legislative context. The intercultural distinction is an important one and shows the unique manner in which Québec has developed a state strategy to facilitate global market integration yet maintain a stable national populace.

Québec Interculturalism

While federal Canadian multiculturalism maintains equal protection and recognition for all cultural, ethnic, and racial groups it does so within a bilingual framework. In short, the federal government makes a clear distinction between language and culture by maintaining a multicultural outlook that is designed to facilitate inter-ethnic relations and immigrant accommodation but requiring economic and political functions to operation within either an English or French linguistic context. This has led some to question the reality of Canadian multiculturalism as simply providing a "choice of two dominant cultures to assimilate to" (Kymlicka 1995, 14).

The initial multicultural policy framework comments specifically on the multicultural yet bilingual social nature of Canada, although this is viewed through the perspective of a singular national population and nationalist ethos:

> We may have two official languages in this country, but we do not have two official cultures (Canada 1973).

The province of Québec responded to this and many other claims of ethno-cultural pluralism by the federal government by questioning both the distinction between language and culture as well as the logic of multiculturalism, itself.

> In Canada the "national" government recognizes linguistic rights to the Francophones. But these are linguistic rights only and not cultural rights (Québec 1984, 3)

> The various ethno-cultural communities do not really inter-communicate. This results in stratification whereby some groups are at the top of the ladder and others at the bottom. The Canadian policy on multiculturalism which seems to appeal to many New-Quebecers can only accentuate this isolation, as well as the mistrust and conflict that result there from (Québec 1984, 6).

The difficulty in implementing federal multiculturalism in Québec centers explicitly on the federal position that Québec, while distinct linguistically, is not culturally distinct from any other ethno-cultural group in Canada. This implied critique of Québécois nationalism was not only deemed unacceptable by the Québec nation and state, it contributed to the solidification of French as the official language of the province. That is, federal multiculturalism and the reduction of Québécois culture to "equal status" among Canadian ethno-cultural groups contributed to the election of the sovereigntist Parti Québécois in 1976 and allowed French language legislation to be passed in the latter half of the decade (Fitzmaurice 1984; See 2001; Vineberg 1987). Recently, the threat of federal multiculturalism has been articulated within the context of cultural survival and labor migration:

> Indeed, the bilingualism policy allows them to integrate into the English-speaking community anywhere in Canada, and this includes Québec, while the multicultural policy conceals the existence of a welcoming community in which French is a common language. Their primary loyalty is to the country that welcomed them, Canada, a country which incidentally still makes its new immigrants swear allegiance to the Queen when they

become citizens. Some of them mistakenly fear that the same problems that led them to leave their native countries will recur in their new country, and for this reason mistrust Québec nationalism (IPSQ 1999).

The active promotion of Canadian mulitculturalism by the federal government, linked with the financial resources expended by the federal government in failing to defeat the PQ in 1976, was viewed in Québec as another attempt to dominate and reduce Québécois culture. The socio-economics of increased labor migration and its connection to ethno-cultural survival make this position both salient and immediate, as show by the previous IPSQ quote.

The issue that soon faced the Québec state was, however, not an attack on its national sovereignty by the federal government. Rather the larger challenge was the increasing ethno-cultural diversity in Québec as a result of global market integration. As shown in the previous chapter, the ethnic and cultural face of Québec grew increasingly diverse as a result of the larger global shift in labor source regions. The autonomy for immigration selection and acculturation granted by the Canada-Québec Accord provided Québec with a unique opportunity to produce a nationalist social policy of its own. Québec's focus on interculturalism is distinct from the Canadian model in its explicit endorsement of French as the dominant language while recognizing and protecting cultural pluralism.

Québec's intercultural framework is more of a collection of legislation and policies that simultaneously strengthens the dominant position of the French language while facilitating the accommodation and integration of immigrants commonly referred to as "neo-Québécois." As is often the case, the impetus for this policy position is derived from the ideological nationalism and structural state apparatus developed during the Quiet Revolution. The recent history of the Quiet Revolution and the growth of the Québec state contributed in part to Québec's strong involvement in the process of global market integration. In fact, it could be argued that the Québec state responded to demographic and cultural changes in a timelier manner than their Canadian federal counterparts.

From the 1960s on, Québec pressed the federal government for more control over immigration to Québec, and in 1975 the National Assembly officially responded to the challenges posed by this integrative process (ethno-cultural diversification) with the Québec *Charte des droits et libertés de la personne*[11]. This policy document officially

---

[11] Charter of Human Rights and Freedoms.

protects the rights of all citizens of Québec and protects individuals from discrimination based on race, ethnicity, gender, age, and pregnancy (Québec 1975). This document was modeled on the United Nations' Universal Declaration of Human Rights (1948) and predates the federal Canadian Charter of Rights and Freedoms by seven years.

In 1981 the Québec state again addressed the diversification of Québec immigration and demography with the *Autant de façons d'être Québécois* (Québec 1981)[12]. This document provided an overview of provincial cultural integration without reverting to the assimilationist patterns of past Canadian efforts at national construction. The policy position stresses "convergence[13]" of culture and community in the desire to create a strong, stable, yet ethno-culturally diverse Québec national population (Québec 1981).

The provincial government adopted an official policy of interculturalism with the publication of *Au Québec pour bâtir ensemble: énoncé de politique en matière d'immigration et de l'intégration* (Québec 1990)[14]. This document established a clear guiding framework for defining the nation of Québec. Three main points create this general nationalist definition: the democratic nature of Québec, a pluralist society that is protected by law, and finally that French be the "langue commune" (common language) of the province. Gagnon and Iacovino clearly describe the purpose of this document and general intercultural framework.

> This view contends that the incorporation of immigrants or minority cultures into the larger political community is a reciprocal endeavor-a "moral contract" between the host society and the particular cultural collectivity with the aim of establishing a forum for the empowerment of all citizens... (Gagnon and Iacovino 2004, 326–327).

Québec interculturalism recognizes the contemporary fact of cultural pluralism through its very political existence. The Québec state must politically facilitate the integration of an increasingly diverse labor migrant population if it (Québec) is to continue to benefit from the

---

[12] "Many Ways to be Québécois." Author's Translation.
[13] Cultural "convergence" in this context refers to the process of cultural integration. Specifically, "convergence" occurs in Québec as diverse ethnicities and cultures maintain traditional cultural norms and practices however do so within the integrative context of a common language (French).
[14] "We are Building Québec Together: Policy Announcement on Matters of Immigration and Integration." Author's Translation.

economic growth opportunities assisted by global market integration. National protectionist demands, however, require that the Québec state also enact high levels of cultural protections to ensure a common national socio-cultural medium.

Intercultural policy clearly promotes the liberal ideal of social equality and the multicultural ideals of diversity recognition, although the institutional framework supporting these ideals is focused primarily on the Francophone social medium in which these ideals reside.

The institutions supporting the intercultural framework are the *Secrétariat à la Politique linguistique* under the *Ministère de la Culture et des Communications*[15] and *les Relations civiques et Interculturelles* under the *Ministère de l'Immigration et des Communautés culturelles*[16]. It is important to note that the current institutional framework supporting intercultural policies in Québec remain strongly supported by the state. Contrary to Canadian multiculturalism, whose institutional support has been greatly reduced, Québec continues to fund and support both support of French language legislation oversight and intercultural programs designed to facilitate immigrant "convergence."

At first glance, it would appear that this understanding of interculturalism reflects the goals and mechanisms of Canadian multiculturalism, although privileging French as the language of common and official interaction. The most glaring difference between Canadian multiculturalism and Québec interculturalism is the belief (in Québec) that language is inexorably connected to culture.

> But the logical consequence would be that a language is the expression of a way of life. Therefore if French is the common language in Québec this implies that French culture although not "abolishing" other cultures, would become the "focus of convergence" for the various communities (Québec 1984, 4).

Clearly, Québec society, while embracing pluralism, is an enclave of Francophone language and culture under the protection of the state.

This difference represents a clear ideological division between the two social policies, but also mirrors each respective history. That is, both are experiencing a demographic shift that is effectively diversifying the ethno-cultural nature of Canadian and Québec societies. This fact

---

[15] Language Policy Secretariat under the Ministry of Culture and Communications.
[16] Civic and Intercultural Relations under the Ministry of Immigration and Cultural Communities.

is the common denominator between both state entities; however the divergence of independent histories works to create independent policy solutions. For Canadian nationalists, the greatest threat to national cohesion is Québec sovereignty (Carens 1995; Doran 2001; McRoberts 1988; Richler 1992). Therefore, any policy designed to address the increasing ethno-cultural diversity of the nation can also be designed to reduce the threat of Québécois nationalism.

For Québec nationalists, the greatest threat to an autonomous Québec is the threat of cultural homogenization or colonization on the part of a dominant English Canada. Therefore, any policy designed to address the increasing ethno-cultural diversity of Québec can also be designed to strengthen French linguistic and cultural dominance and authority. Both policies were driven by global market integration, however the development of both policies are, by necessity, defined by distinct national histories and different nationalist goals.

The interesting aspect of Québec's intercultural framework is its relative stability in comparison with Canadian multiculturalism, with respect to institutional support and to policy revision. While federal multiculturalism has undergone significant growth, reduction, reorientation, and redefinition, Québec's broad intercultural framework has remained constant. The only significant alteration to the policy position has been a reduction in the universal dominance of French as a public language. This change (see Bills 142, 120, and 20 in the previous section) has been limited to social service provision and the production of relevant government documents in both French and English. Thus, the dominance of French as the common language of Québec has not been seriously threatened.

Conclusions

A focus on the commonalities and differences between multicultural and intercultural policy frameworks is important. The similar political economic patterns of increased integration into the global market economic system in addition to full integration into the global labor supply system illustrate a common goal and therefore similar social consequences of increasing integration. The differences, described in the previous two sections, are numerous; however there is a trend of policy convergence that seems to be occurring. This process of policy alteration and evolution can provide a more telling picture of how states respond to the challenges of the neoliberal global economic system and, perhaps the power of that system.

Policy Decline and the Role of National Populations

The decline of multicultural policy in Canada has been debated by those who view this policy position as being successful in its political positions (Kymlicka, Jansen) and those who view this policy as being an anti-liberal political position that hinders social integration and exacerbates stratification (Barry, Bissoondath). Christian Joppke addresses this "debate" by showing a distinct pattern of multicultural policy "retreat in the liberal state" (Joppke 2004).

Joppke points to three indications of the decline or "retreat" of multicultural policies: (1) a lack of public support for multicultural policies (but not necessarily programs), (2) the practical failure of multicultural policies to reduce ethnic conflict or socio-economic stratification based on factors of ethno-cultural diversity, and (3) "a new assertiveness of the liberal state in imposing the liberal minimum on its dissenters" (Joppke 2004, 244). A cursory assessment of these three factors would point to a direct connection between the first two. Policy failure and popular support often coincide. The third aspect of liberal retrenchment raises a more pertinent question with respect to the relationship of these policies to the double movement of neoliberal economic demands and national protection.

The initial motivation for federal multicultural policy was clearly nationalist in its intent. That is, it provided a political definition of Canadian nationalism as diverse, multicultural, and egalitarian. This definition worked to elevate "Third Force" ethno-cultural groups to positions of equal social standing while simultaneously de-emphasizing the claims of ethno-cultural uniqueness and claims of sovereignty by Québécois nationalists. The initial goals of multicultural policies as tools for building minority community support structures and ideological national cohesion was altered by demographic changes resulting from increased ethno-cultural diversification. Multicultural policy shifted to address growing conflicts and tensions that accompanied rapid ethno-cultural diversification, primarily with respect to non-discrimination initiatives. The recent de-centralization and privatization of multiculturalism marks yet another policy shift. As Joppke points out, the contemporary policy shift (to de-centralized and privatized organization) is indicative of a global reduction, or "retreat," from multicultural policies. I would argue that this "retreat" on the part of the state is reflective of double movement tension resulting from continued struggle between global neoliberal market pressures and national protections. A brief revisitation of Québec interculturalism supports this claim.

The unique historical and demographic nature of Québec motivated the development of an alternative policy to Canadian multiculturalism. The common experience of ethno-cultural diversification as a result of migration shifts and national population demands for domestic stability required some form of policy on the part of the Québec state to maintain national stability. As previously mentioned, Québec's intercultural policy framework (comprised of language and cultural legislation) has undergone limited changes in comparison with its federal counterpart. The changes that have occurred are reductions in the promotion of French as a singular language in Québec, but not to the nature, scope, or definition of what it is to be a Québécois (or neo-Québécois) or how daily communication and co-habitation should function in the province. Why has Québec's intercultural policy framework remained relatively unaltered? I believe that the answer is exposed with closer attention to the dynamics of the double movement.

Global market integration is a desirable goal for both Canada and Québec, as evidenced by their policy initiatives and support for neoliberal economic policy reforms. Both Canada and Québec are active participants in the global labor supply system and have experienced rapid ethno-cultural diversification as a result of the systemic shift from European to Global South sources for labor migration. Multicultural and intercultural policies are largely responsible for promoting a comfortable atmosphere and stable environment for these new arrivals and ensuring that the destabilizing potential of rapid ethno-cultural diversification does not affect economic growth or productive capacity. In this light, multi/intercultural policies are an outcome of national market integration into the global market system. Several scholars have commented on the economic benefits of multi/intercultural policies, particularly with respect to attracting business-class migrants whose capital, skills, and education are highly valued by competing core states (Abu-Laban 2003; Abu-Laban and Gabriel 2002; Li 2003).

Conversely, the reality of ethno-cultural diversification is uneven and often conflictual. "Native" groups are often hostile to new residents whose language, religion, traditions, values, and even appearance may differ from conventional national norms. Added tension often arises in times of economic recession or depression when ethno-cultural minorities are often targeted as "causes" or "contributors" to general conditions of hardship. In addition to these ethno-cultural tensions national populations continue to construct and negotiate national identities within the context of the neoliberal nation-state[17]. The issue of liberalism is an important one, as the basic tenant of liberal political ideology is egalitarianism. The promotion of equality, however, is problematic. There are few regions where a particular group (often based on ethnicity or culture) has not maintained some form of dominance or hierarchical authority. The "equalization" process inherent in multicultural policies inevitably causes a backlash by those fearful of losing their positions of prominence. The result is commonly an attack on these multicultural policies as privileging a specific group or groups over traditionally dominant groups. This is the case in Canada where attacks on multicultural policies are increasingly articulated in nationalist language and context. The lack of a common cultural medium in Canada and the promotion of a common nationalist discourse/identity by the state has resulted in increased dissatisfaction by national popular groups (Barry 2001; Bibby 1995; 1990; Bissoondath 1994; Frow 1999).

The demand of true economic neoliberals for limited, if not non-existent, state intervention is an added problem for multicultural policies. State spending on social services, particularly those that make demands on business entities and economic institutions, is an anathema to neoliberal market ideology...the same market ideology that currently maintains a dominant position in this era of globalization. As such, multicultural programs that seek to attain social and economic equality outside of the market system are, in effect, non-liberal. Thus, the national protections (of "native" populations and immigrant populations) of multicultural policies run counter to the demands and requirements of pure neoliberal market ideology.

Interculturalism appeared to have weathered the neoliberal storm (due in no small part to the unique nature of Québécois skepticism concerning state retrenchment) until 2006 when resurgent debate over "reasonable accommodation" began with a series of events that were heavily covered by Québec media outlets. In March 2006, the Canadian

[17] This is, of course, a limited view of national identify construction. This project is limited to the discussion of the effects of global market integration on a specific type of nation-state: Western, advanced capitalist, and republican/democratic. This project makes no theoretical claims outside of this limited empirical scope.

Supreme Court ruled that allowing Sikh individuals to wear ceremonial daggers in schools was consistent with a "reasonable accommodation" of religious rights under the Canadian Charter of Rights and Freedoms. Later the same year a series of publicized conflicts were brought into the public sphere such as the accommodation of Muslim prayer space, the installation of frosted windows at a Montreal YMCA to address Hasidic Jewish concerns, and the institution of women-only prenatal classes at a Montreal CLSC (*Centre local des services communautaires*) clinic to meet requests by various religious communities.

The latter CLSC issue was deemed "not reasonable" by the head of the neoliberal *Action démocratique du Québec*, Mario Dumont in November 2006 and signified the beginning of the ADQ's political defense of monolithic Québec national culture. This opportunity was augmented in January 2007 when the town of Hérouxville issued a "Publication of Standards" that was geared towards potential immigrants and designed "to inform the new arrivals to our territory, how we live to help them make a clear decision to integrate into our area" (Municipalité Hérouxville 2007). These standards included declarations on the rights of women, children, education, and other normative cultural issues including oft-cited references to prohibitions of slavery, burning women, and the prevalence of co-ed leisure activities. The publication of these standards set off a vociferous debate both provincially and internationally about the role of cultural pluralism and "reasonable accommodation."

The resultant *Commission de consultation sur les pratiques d'accommodement reliées aux différences culturelles* (CCPARDC), or more commonly the Taylor-Bouchard Commission, was an effort by the sitting Liberal government to address this debate. The final report of the commission could be easily read as a standing defense of both cultural pluralism and Québec's intercultural approach. The rise of the "reasonable accommodation" debate and the government's response will be further addressed in the following chapter, but it is important to note here that both Canadian and Québec efforts to reconcile liberal economic trends and cultural diversification have both proven difficult to sustain.

It would seem that the "retreat" of multicultural policies means that neoliberal market ideology has become supreme in the context of the double movement. If we attribute some level of legitimate power to national populations, however, the dominance of neoliberal market ideology seems less obvious. National popular support for federal

multicultural policies has waned. Criticism of state multicultural policies reflect previously mentioned failures in policy efficacy; however, a
notable observation is that attacks on multicultural policy are increasingly focused on the need to protect Canadian national culture. The
demands have largely centered on populist critiques of national dete-
rioration or the potential divisive outcomes of diversity recognition.
That is, national demands for a common cultural medium have grown
as both ethno-cultural diversity and multicultural policies have
expanded. While the decline of neoliberal criticism of multicultural
policies has contributed to the idea that multicultural ideology is "good
for business" (Abu-Laban 2003), national support for these programs
has deteriorated:

> Back in 1985, 56% of Canadians supported the mosaic and only 28% the
> melting pot. But in 1995, 44% supported the mosaic and 40% the melting
> pot – almost equal (Bibby 1995, 54).

The ambiguous definition of Canadian nationalism is increasingly
attacked as a failure of multicultural policy. These criticisms are heavily
muted in Québec due to the emphasis of a common cultural medium.

Interculturalism, on the other hand, is heavily criticized by neoliberal proponents on the grounds that the level of institutional support
for these programs is unnecessary and, in fact, a deterrent to increased
economic growth (Boyer 2001; McMahon 2003; Migué 1998; Paquet
1999). On the other hand, intercultural policy in Québec meets the
demands of its national population to maintain the traditional social
dominance of French language and culture. When compared with federal multicultural policy the ability of Québec intercultural policy to
maintain its core structure, responsibilities, and overall framework
allows us to conclude that it is better able to function in the context of
the double movement[18], largely due to the strength of national demands
for Québécois cultural protection. Both policies are attempts by the
state to address global market integration and labor demand; however
the emphasis on recognizing difference and the promotion of state
programs to institutionalize those differences has been received coldly

---

[18] Federal multiculturalism, as a political institution, grew throughout the 1970s
and early 1980s to ministerial status (Ministry of Multiculturalism), but was disman-
tled in the late 1980s and early 1990s and subsumed under the Department of Canadian
Heritage. Québec interculturalism is still institutionally strong and supported by the
Ministère de l'Immigration and Communautés culturelles and the *Ministère de la Culture
et Communications*.

by both national populations and neoliberal market proponents. Interculturalism, while providing a level of state involvement that is not desirable for most neoliberal ideologues, facilitates global market integration and meets the protectionist demands of its national population through cultural means.

The ability of a state-centered policy to negotiate the conflicts of the double movement is clearly necessary for policy survival. The final chapter will expand on this conclusion and integrate it into a larger examination of the initial theoretical propositions of this project. We have examined the background and conditional motivations for multicultural and intercultural policies, but we must now come full-circle in the attempt to understand what these policies can tell us about the contemporary nation-state.

CHAPTER EIGHT

THE EMERGING ROLE OF CULTURE IN NEOLIBERAL STATE-BUILDING

Despite common exhortations to the contrary, state-building and global political economic integration are not mutually exclusive projects. Globalization, as a broad moniker for the integration of individual nation-states into a larger systemic articulation of global capitalism, is built on a consistent capitalist logic privileging profit maximization and facilitating growth in both production and consumption. State institutions have long been complicit with this overall logic and worked to create amenable conditions to satisfy capitalist demands. In this sense, the extended history of the nation-state is one of maximizing profit and growth opportunities for capitalist enterprises (see Poulantzas 1978; Miliband 1969; Jessop 1990, Barrow 1993). This persistent relationship between political institutions and economic systems is at the heart of state building efforts: Any form of strategic state-building must be understood in the context of promoting conditions amenable to capital accumulation. Canada and Québec's efforts are no exception. Regardless of the importance of nationalism or the intractable complexity of a binational history, both state-building enterprises have been preoccupied with enhancing the economic viability of their respective nations.

Despite this economic foundation, viewing states through a mono-causal lens as such is both limiting and highly problematic. In other words, understanding the role of the state as *only* building and maintaining positive conditions for capital accumulation minimizes or ignores the role of national populations in legitimating the authority necessary for states to enact growth-oriented legislation. The legitimating role played by national populations is an essential, yet indirect, element of the capital accumulation process. In fact, many critiques of Marxian state theories have focused on exactly this relative economic determinism as an inherent weakness in explaining the modern state. Many have argued that states must be receptive to a wide range of constituencies – while corporate entities may be dominant they do not hold an exclusive monopoly over state action (see Block 1988; Evans 1995; Seabrooke 2002).

There are two points here that are particularly relevant to the current essay. The first is the aforementioned capitalist basis for both Canadian and Québec state-building endeavors. Regardless of attention to nationalism, culture mobilization, and historical conflicts, both states are primarily tasked with creating conditions amenable to capital accumulation. The form of adherence certainly differs, although this does not diminish the fact that Canada and Québec are, first and foremost, capitalist states.

The second is the equally important role of national legitimation of state institutional authority. Without legitimation, the stability and acquiescence necessary to create amenable production and market conditions in any national context are significantly threatened. This latter point requires a reoriented understanding of the state as not simply a capitalist institution, but rather a mediating institution that attempts to meet both national popular and capital accumulation demands. The relationship between these two points largely informs this study: In relatively conforming to dictates of the former, differences in the latter illustrate a significant need to shift the means of maintaining state authority. Specifically, as capitalism "goes global" so too do Canadian and Québec economic growth strategies. The caveat is that contemporary global capitalism calls for a decrease in state regulatory capacities, which are, as previously stated, at the core of many national economic protectionist demands.

The key point here is that in the economic realm, these countervailing demands on the state are not always congruous. Policies designed to facilitate capital accumulation may result in adverse conditions for those who are not end-beneficiaries of profits. For instance, state legislation removing wage regulations would be welcomed by business interests as enhancing wage flexibility and therefore profits; however, for the wage laborer, such a policy would be extremely unpopular due to the likelihood of wage decreases. Steven Lukes, summarizing the work of Adam Przeworski (1985), makes this point succinctly: "So the 'consent' of the wage-earners to the capitalist organization of society consists of a continuing, constantly renewed class compromise where 'neither the aggregate of interests of individual capitals nor the interests of organized wage-earners can be violated beyond specific limits." (Lukes 2005, 8).

This "class compromise" reflects a mediating role for the state as illustrated in Chapter Two; however, the context of this mediation is of particular importance. If we assume this compromise to be an exclusively class centered relationship, then we can understand state legitimacy to be explicitly tied to the satisfaction of *economic* demands. The state must somehow create conditions to facilitate capital accumulation and growth while at the same time meeting the socio-economic demands of the laboring national population that may require the regulation of certain capitalist functions (labor, financial and material markets etc...) or provide some form of assistance to mitigate the adversities of a deregulated capitalism (job loss or underemployment, housing and sustenance costs, etc...). If we take a more holistic view of the state's strategic management of capital-friendly social conditions, we can easily see that this mediating role is fraught with constant adaptation and negotiation.

The key problem with this perspective though is the explicit determinism inherent in such an approach. What happens, for instance, if the pendulum swings too far in one direction or another? If capital interests gain disproportionate influence and not only promote deregulation but also limit the state's ability to meet national *economic* protectionist demands – what should we expect to see? Well, according to the aforementioned perspective, we can expect a severe decline in state legitimacy and accompanying instability as the state's ability to manage and mitigate social order declines. Contemporary neoliberalism demands decreased state regulatory capacities as well as decreased public spending. One could easily make the case that the integration of neoliberalism is swinging the pendulum too far in the direction of capital interests and leaving laboring populations without a means to satisfy their economic demands. Shouldn't we expect to see large-scale class resistance to this trend? If the state grants more and more autonomy to capital interests and ignores the economic demands of subordinate classes we should expect that a decline in legitimacy will be accompanied by a commensurate decline in state institutional capacities.

The purpose of Part III (Chapters Five, Six, and Seven) is to offer a focused empirical illustration of how global economic integration facilitates social change and motivates twin demands for the state to (1) facilitate further integration and (2) mitigate the social conditions resulting from such adherence to capitalist demands. The implication of these demands is that the state is both a requisite socio-economic institution and one of sustained authority. This is somewhat perplexing in light of vociferous neoliberal calls for the retrenchment of state capacities and authority. This neoliberal hegemony creates particular challenges for state institutions, particularly in the realm of maintaining national popular legitimacy. The following sections move beyond these developmental comparisons to examine several important questions: Has integration into a global neoliberal systemic context inhibited the regulatory/protectionist capacities of Canada and Québec? Can global economic integration occur with a resistance of neoliberalization? If so, can the integration of a national cultural definition really enhance legitimacy and therefore state policy capacities? What might the implications be for state-building in an increasingly neoliberal era?

Globalization on the Ground: Economic Opportunities,
Diversifying Nations and Cultural Legitimation

Both Canada and Québec are beneficiaries of global capitalism. As illustrated in Chapter Five, both state policy and private market development have been explicitly linked to emergent global market opportunities (with respect to both material trade and finance). More to the point, both Canada and Québec actively pursue trade liberalization as well as increasing foreign direct investment opportunities (both inward and outward) – both of which are reflective of state involvement in expanding economic growth opportunities on a larger, global, stage. These growth opportunities have substantially benefitted Canadian GDP, overall trade and foreign investment. In comparison, Québec's degree of beneficence is certainly more varied and less obvious, although it has consistently promoted expanded international trade and facilitated foreign investment as vehicles for national economic growth. This historical support is also built on the belief that economic liberalization would increased economic autonomy by diversifying Québec economic activities outside of the Canadian national economic sphere. While these points are all evident in the chapter, the purpose is to highlight the extent and form of Canadian and Québécois global economic integration. The underlying assumption driving economic policy convergence in both states is that expanded market, production, and investment opportunities will facilitate national economic growth. This simplistic but dominant theoretical assumption places both Canada and Québec in ideological accordance with systemic and national capitalist demands and carries with it certain ramifications for respective national societies.

While the exploitation of growth opportunities inherent in a globalizing capitalism certainly drives policy, the problem of meeting increased market opportunities with increased production requires a sustained labor supply. More so, the opening of local markets to global producers has emphasized price competition as a key strategy to gain market share. Increased competition for shares of emerging markets encourages producers to focus on maintaining wage flexibility through an expanded labor market in skilled and unskilled sectors (see Eliofotou 2008; Duca and van Hoose 2001). These factors have contributed to the sustained emphasis on immigration policy as a key long-term economic development strategy.

Chapter Six chronicles the historical motivations linking labor market expansion in Canada to the contemporary demographic shifts that have increasingly diversified labor immigration into the country. The economic motivations for sustained immigration are obvious; however, the purpose of the chapter was to highlight the socially transformative nature of this so-called "new migration." As Canada and Québec continue to seek additions to their respective populations, these efforts are centered on recruitment from the developing regions of the Global South. This is, as stated in Chapter Six, the result of structural changes in global labor migration that link to European reconstruction following World War II, the Cold War, and political economic development initiatives accompanying the nascence of what we now call globalization (particularly direct investment in the Global South).

There are two primary links between global political economic integration and global labor migration. The first is that beneficiary states, such as Canada and Québec, are afforded emerging market opportunities that motivate increased production at ever decreasing costs in order to maximize competitive advantages. This creates significant demand for a healthy labor market – and a corporate preference for lower cost labor either through wage decreases/reduction in respective labor or through increased labor market flexibility.

The second key point is that globalization has motivated significant changes in the Global South that contribute to the creation of a surplus population that facilitates this global labor supply system. The decline in access to domestic agricultural markets accompanied by land reforms designed to facilitate foreign investment has regularly pushed rural populations into urban areas. This "proletarianization" of a region formerly dominated by disparate rural populations engenders an urban labor force for production efforts in the developing world, although it also creates a substantial supply (to speak of human beings in a brutally crass way) of surplus labor. Put simply, the shift from European to

Global South labor migration sources mirrors emergent political economic interests and investment in the developing world.

These global structural conditions ultimately mean that net beneficiaries of global capitalist integration tie future growth to an expanded and lower-cost labor force – a demand met through sustained (and state facilitated) labor immigration. It also means that in-migration societies such as Canada and Québec now attract the majority of their labor migration from non-traditional source regions in the Global South. As such, global economic integration is explicitly linked to an increasing cultural diversity (primarily in urban areas). This diversification carries with it increased integrative challenges that must be mitigated through state institutions if the social (and labor market) stability required for sustained capital accumulation is to be achieved.

One of the strategic policies employed by both Canada and Québec to promote cultural integration are the multicultural and intercultural approaches described in Chapter Seven. While both policies emerged in the 1970s from a distinctly nationalist context, both have since been employed as integrative policies designed to articulate a national cultural definition into which new arrivals can integrate. This integrationist end is theoretically based on the premise that cultural pluralism is a more stable approach toward integrating new arrivals than alternative assimilationist approaches – the latter, of course, typifying integration policies in the United States. By embracing a multicultural model, Canada was essentially pointing to a key distinction from the United States: If you choose to immigrate to Canada, we will respect your cultural traditions, and essentially, your differences from dominant cultural norms established after centuries of European, Judeo-Christian immigration to Canada and Québec. This non-discriminatory theoretical approach was codified as official national social policy, but also served as a tangible reason for potential labor migrants to choose Canada (or Québec) over the United States.

The cultural pluralism underlying these integration policies belies the fact that the policies emerged as a means to promote respective nationalist projects. Even today, the celebration of diversity inherent in the "Canadian Mosaic" commonly overshadows that fact that these policies still articulate a common socio-cultural medium into which immigrants must integrate[1]. That is, while Canadian multiculturalism is an

---

[1] Will Kymlicka (1995, 14) summarizes this argument: "This shared commitment to Anglo-conformity is obscured by the popular but misleading contrast between the

integrative social policy it is intended to facilitate such integration in a specifically defined cultural direction. The federal articulation of cultural pluralism is somewhat nebulous – which should come as little surprise given the impossibility of a singular Canadian national identity.

This nationalist milieu is more explicit in Québec's intercultural policies, which are based on the same pluralist foundation. Social integration is promoted through an official recognition of cultural diversity; however, that recognition exists within a defined Francophone and liberal social environment. A new arrival is welcome to maintain their cultural traditions including language and religion; however, there is to be an explicit understanding that public life in Québec, including legal, political, and discursive interaction, will occur in the French language and in a liberal political economic context (including adherence to French civil law that has been in place since 1774).

Obviously, the rapid diversification promoted by Canadian and Québec immigration policies will elicit a national reaction – either through socio-cultural strains/conflict or through conflict emanating from increased labor market competition. On the one hand, these policy approaches to integration can be viewed as concerted efforts to maintain social stability during a period of significant socio-cultural change. On the other hand, neither multi- nor interculturalism can be understood without attention to the norms associated with each respective national definition. The primary difference between the two is, of course, the explicit singularity of Québec's definition: Canada must define itself in a fundamentally plural way (binational foundations, official bilingualism, and official multiculturalism), but Québec is not bound by these "constraints." Québec is structurally encouraged to promote some form of social integrationist policy in order to mitigate potential conflict resulting from diversification – in this instance, based on a pluralist approach to social integration. However, Québec is not obligated to extend this pluralism beyond its integrationist policies. On the contrary, Québec's colonial legacy and official recognition as a "distinct society" within the Canadian federation creates an opportunity for the Québec state to link its legitimacy directly with a singular national cultural definition.

American 'melting-pot' and the Canadian 'ethnic mosaic.' While 'ethnic mosaic' carries the connotation of respect for the integrity of immigrant cultures, in practice it simply meant that immigrants to Canada had a choice of two dominant cultures to assimilate to."

On it's own, the explicit singularity of Québec's national cultural definition is not particularly novel. The importance of this singularity is in the central role this definition plays in state level policies – particularly the link between national definitional identity and policies developed by the (sub) state as a means to facilitate economic growth. This connection is even more apparent when the gradual autonomy of Québec immigration policy is understood as a culturally defined response to the promotion of economic growth opportunities through labor market expansion. For both Canada and Québec, economic growth is linked to global market integration, although for Québec, it seems that conforming to this idea has augmented sub-state political and institutional autonomy. Put another way, Québec has long relied on national cultural definitions to legitimate its respective state institutions and agendas; however, efforts to exploit emergent global market opportunities coupled with shifting social demographics have seemingly amplified this connection and enabled Québec to integrate into the global economic system while at the same time maintaining a relatively high level of state institutional spending and enhancing its political capacities as an autonomous sub-state.

Neoliberalism and Challenges to State-Building

The next logical question is, of course, what about this process of globalization enables national culture to play an increasingly important role in legitimating state authority? More to the point, can the legitimating power of nationalism enhance the autonomy of sub-state entities? The answer lies at least partially in the neoliberal ideological structures of contemporary global capitalism.

Trade liberalization and increased investment opportunities work to create market opportunities and facilitate expanded production. In this way, capitalist enterprises regularly support trade liberalization and limits on state authority to regulate emergent economic opportunities. The latter is consistent with overall capitalist logic in that the external management and/or regulation of emergent opportunities would be understood as an inhibiting condition and therefore not amenable to capital accumulation. The state, being the institutional facilitator of capital accumulation, must meet these demands to a relatively satisfactory degree. Put simply, a state that does not promote economic growth is a state that will soon be lacking in sufficient legitimacy.

In this sense, economic policy is not limited to the fiscal. As previously stated, when global market opportunities expand and become more competitive, producers seek reductions in overhead expenses in the hopes of maintaining price competitiveness without sacrificing profits. In this sense, the demands placed on state institutions to facilitate capital accumulation include sustained (if not expanded) support for labor market flexibility – in the case of Canada and Québec, this is inexorably linked to immigration policies.

On the other hand, the neoliberal ideology underscoring calls for increased capital mobility and freedom also includes demands for the reduction of not only state regulatory capacities but also public spending. This is significant as the ideology explicitly ties economic growth to reductions in state regulatory capacities, which ultimately means that global economic integration occurs in a larger context of varied state regulatory retrenchment. As *many* scholars have shown (see Brenner 2002; Harvey 2007; Peck et al. 2010, in addition to similar studies cited in Chapters One and Two), adherence to neoliberal demands for state retrenchment is quite multifarious between states. For example, beneficiaries such as the United States and Canada continue to maintain domestic subsidies in certain sectors (see Hertel and Keeney 2006), while non-beneficiaries in the developing world are commonly limited (or structurally prohibited) in their ability to support or protect domestic producers and markets (Portes 1997; Robinson 1996; Shefner et al. 2006; see also Soderberg 2004). While neoliberalism may be ubiquitous it can vary significantly in degree and effect.

These differences also exist between beneficiary countries as well as, in the case of Canada and Québec, between state and sub-state entities. Both Canada and Québec are willfully integrated into the global political economic system and both have been confronted with neoliberal demands to reduce state regulatory capacities through institutional retrenchment (primarily through reduced revenues and spending). Integrating neoliberal demands into state-level reform has produced significantly different results in both Canada and Québec. The federal state has gradually integrated a level of neoliberalism as it seeks to reduce economic regulation and state spending in accordance with neoliberal dictates. The partial privatization of Multiculturalism Canada through the development of the Canadian Race Relations Foundation (see Chapter Seven) is a particularly salient example.

In contrast, the integration of neoliberalism in Québec has been much more halting. The Québec state has been able to maintain a significant level of institutional control (particularly in the areas of energy and pensions) and sustained public spending (particularly in social service provision) for two primary reasons. The first is that sustained federal equalization and transfer payments provide an essential funding source that enables the Québec state to maintain spending levels that would be otherwise difficult (if not impossible) without alternative revenue sources.

The second is that any reduction in state social spending would be quite unpopular in the province. From $7-a-day childcare to heavily subsidized higher education, many social services are unique to Québec due in large part to their explicit connection to the protection of the province's distinct national identity. In this sense, the maintenance of public services is the maintenance of the mechanisms of national culture and identity. To advocate a reduction in or alteration of these programs and institutional management would be problematic from a political economic perspective (increasing costs rarely result in sustained political popularity), but also would threaten the marriage of the Québec state and national culture that emerged in its contemporary form following the Quiet Revolution. Béland and Lecours (2008; 2006) and Nicola McEwan (2006; 2005) draw similar conclusions in their examinations of the link between so-called "welfare state" maintenance and national identity.

Interestingly, it is this reliance on nationalist foundations that enables the Québec state to maintain programs and relationships that look, at least superficially, more Keynesian than neoliberal in form. While this "Québec Model" may not be sustainable over the long term, the basis for this resistance to wholesale neoliberalization is explicitly tied to national cultural definition. The divergence between Québec and Canada with respect to neoliberalization is surely not exclusive to nationalist causal explanations; however, a cursory look at the divergent experiences of both states illustrates the challenges facing state-building strategies and how a closer link between institutional policies and national cultural definitions can enhance state and sub-state building in an era of neoliberal dominance.

State Political Capacity and Responsibilities

Neoliberal demands to limit public financing are commonly tied to reductions in several key areas: health care, education, and pensions.

In that these are regularly the most expensive and most popular areas of public spending, they provide a useful context for "comparative neo-liberalization." Health Canada[2], for example, has experienced declining federal funding despite the lack of universal private health care alternatives. Generally, neoliberal ideology and integration requirements discourage state spending for social service provision. This is particularly true with respect to privatization that encourages market integration of all aspects of social services, including health care, education, and pension management. Specifically, the decline in health care funding in Canada is linked to encroaching market pressures for privatization (Johnson 2002). The NAFTA agreement weakens the state's ability to protect its public health care system as certain sections or categories of health care provision in Canada are subject to foreign investment and must conform to adjudicative trade rules established in the agreement. This means that the increasing privatization of Canadian health care is a direct result of global market integration.

> By introducing foreign investment into areas of health care service delivery that were previously delivered on a not-for-profit basis by the public sector, private clinics and hospitals open the door to trade challenges and foreign investor claims. These incursions may in turn have profound impacts on the entire health care system (Canadian Health Coalition 2002).

Québec, on the other hand, has a similar tradition of state social service provision that has generally succeeded in avoiding neoliberal "reforms." Recent events have challenged this resistive capacity and raise serious questions about whether Québec can continue to maintain current levels of state spending, contrary to neoliberal demands.

Organized under the *Régie de l'Assurance Maladie*, health care delivery in Québec follows the larger Canadian model (as well as a significant portion of its financing) with a few exceptions. As is the case across Canada, each province is able to administer its own health care systems – as long as they are in accordance with the Canada Health Act. Québec has a public prescription benefit (which is not common provincially) and until 2006, a ban on private medical insurance in the province. Health care in Québec has been, much like other social services in the province, the exclusive domain of the Québec state.

---

[2] Health Canada is the federal institution tasked with overseeing and managing national, public health care delivery. (see also, Health Canada, *Mission, Values, Activities* http://www.hc-sc.gc.ca/ahc-asc/activit/about-apropos/index-eng.php)

The Canadian Supreme Court, in the case of Chaoulli v. Québec in June 2005, ruled that Québec's ban on private insurance for private health care services was unconstitutional. This ruling gave the PLQ government the ability to draft legislation requiring the privatization of portions of Québec's formerly public health care system. Representatives of Québec's five law schools criticized this legislation as "going far beyond what the Supreme Court ordered" (Brun *et al.* 2005). In fact, the representatives argue that the judgment merely required that citizens be able to purchase insurance for private care, not to privatize portions of the public system as the Charest (PLQ) government is doing (Brun *et al.* 2005).

The case of declining public health care provision and the rise of privatization in Canada is consistent with the effects of global market integration. I would argue that the intentional nature of this integrative process can be seen in the actions of both the Canadian and Québec governments. In the case of Canada, ample budget surpluses are available to augment funding short falls for Health Canada. Fuller (1998) argues that these consistent decreases in federal health care funding, despite ample financial resources, is the result of intentional efforts on the part of the state to weaken public health care services. The purpose of intentionally under-funding Health Canada is to contend that public health care is untenable and thus must allow for private health care provision (i.e., global market integration).

Efforts by the Charest administration in Québec are similar in their intent. The Québec state is actively opening the door to health care privatization in accordance with neoliberal/market demands by relying on judicial opinion that does not demand the privatization of the provincial health care system. In both cases, state efforts to decrease state spending and control over social service provision are an intentional act. The crisis of health care provision in Canada and Québec is consistent with conclusions made in this essay that increased global market integration decreases the state's capacity to enact national protectionist legislation (namely, social service provision) that is contrary to neoliberal market demands.

If the state economic protectionist capacity is, in fact, reduced as a result of the demands and requirements of the global economic system, what then is the purpose of the contemporary nation-state? The role of the contemporary state is to ensure local stability required to maintain a functional global economic system. This is consistent with Polanyi's descriptions of the "peace interest" promoted by international financial institutions for international liberal market growth.

> Trade was now dependent upon an international monetary system that could not function in a general war. It demanded peace, and the Great Powers were striving to maintain it. But the balance-of-power system, as we have seen, could not by itself ensure peace. This was done by international finance, the very existence of which embodied the principle of the new dependence of trade upon peace (Polanyi 2001, 16).

The issue of stability is a central requisite of any global economic system. Without such a cooperative medium trade and financial exchanges could not function as freely as they currently do. This case demonstrates that in the pursuit of "double movement" satisfaction, the state has moved into the realm of national cultural policy. The role of the state in ensuring social stability has shifted from economic to cultural protection; however, the dynamics that govern the interaction between nation, state, and global economic system remain constant. The complexities of the state in addressing economic issues with cultural policies require greater attention. That is, although state capacity to meet national protectionist demands through cultural means has increased, the protectionist demand is still motivated by economic changes and demands of the global economic system.

The existing system of nation-states provides for local political institutions of power that are able to legitimately control national populations and provide local stability that facilitates global trade, financial capital flows, transnational production, and consumptive patterns. The mechanics of the "double movement" ensure that this facilitation of liberal market forces will result in a national protectionist outcry. This demand for national protection was met in the post-war era with Keynesian state-centered strategies leading to the development of the Western welfare state. Esping-Andersen supports this contention through his understanding that "the welfare state was therefore also a political project of nation-building: the affirmation of liberal democracy against the twin perils of fascism and bolshevism" (Esping-Andersen 1996, 2). The welfare state, in accordance with the mechanics of the "double movement," was the state response to national discontent and the threat of anti-systemic alternatives (namely, fascism and bolshevism). The "double movement" is a conservative mechanism in which the goal is systemic maintenance and stability.

These conditions no longer exist and state capacity to respond to national protectionist demands through economic means has decreased. Esping-Andersen comments on this shift as well:

> The advanced Western nations' welfare states were built to cater to an economy dominated by industrial mass production. In the era of the

"Keynesian consensus" there was no perceived trade-off between social security and economic growth, between equality and efficiency. This consensus has disappeared because the underlying assumptions no longer obtain (Esping-Andersen 1996, 3).

The core shift from industrial production to service provision is pervasive. The decline of welfare state protectionism in Canada and Québec can be easily mapped through liberal trade agreements signed in the 1980s and 1990s that were once shunned as detrimental to national economic growth (Clarkson and McCall 1990).

The decline of economic protectionist capacities in Canada and Québec came at a time of increasing ethno-cultural diversity (again, motivated by global market integration). This demographic transition offers the state an opportunity to shift its focus from national economic protection to national cultural protection. The institutionalization of multicultural policy throughout the 1980s occurred as hostility to free-trade agreements decreased (notably beginning CUFTA negotiations in 1984). As opposition to neoliberal trade agreements continued to wane in the 1990s (NAFTA and WTO leadership support was promoted by the Liberal Party, who formerly opposed free-trade policies – at least as a political issue) so too did the institutional power of multiculturalism in Canada. However, the continued diversification of urban Canada and the increasing inability of the state to protect national populations through economic means also promoted an increase in criticism of multiculturalism from a popular and nationalist perspective. In other words, multiculturalism as a national cultural ideal is increasingly attacked as being unable to promote a singular nationalist Canadian medium. These attacks are nearly universal in their use of culture as a discursive tool of criticism. The original idea of multiculturalism as the "recognition of difference" is proving to be an untenable position as Canadian popular demands for protection and stability take on an increasingly nationalist tone, generally demanding a common cultural medium.

Québec's response to global market integration is equally focused on culture, but its approach has proven more stable in its ability to meet the protectionist demands of its national population. I argue that this stability is the result of greater national legitimating support for state protectionist policies such as interculturalism. That is, Québec is able to meet the national protectionist demands of its national population in a more effective manner than does the Canadian state. While global market pressures are equally demanding of both Canadian and

Québec state entities, Québec's ability to resist such pressures is due to higher levels of legitimacy in its use of national culture in protectionist strategies.

Urban Québec is experiencing the same rate of diversification as the whole of urban Canada; however the intercultural context to which Québec immigrants must integrate creates the common cultural medium in demand throughout the rest of Canada. Clearly, intercultural policies are designed to protect Francophone Québécois culture and the fact that its policy framework is not generally challenged by Francophone Québécois is telling.

Interestingly, the strength of the national population in Québec has allowed its social service provision role to be maintained in contrast to the demands of neoliberal proponents. The main points of attack against Québec intercultural policy have been from neoliberal critics who view the program as providing excessive state support for national protectionist measures. Again, this is consistent with the mechanics of the "double movement" in which liberal market pressures will increase in response to increased national protectionist pressures. Recent neoliberal economic reforms undertaken by the Charest administration have been deeply unpopular and have resulted in increased national protectionist demands.

An example of this occurred in the spring 2005 when the Québec government announced its plan to decrease state spending by converting provincial student bursary grants into loans. This caused a vociferous reaction among public university students throughout Québec, but the reaction was most vocal among CÉGEP[3] students in Québec urban areas[4]. The loan conversion plan resulted in a student strike (numbering 170,000 students) at ten Montréal area CÉGEP campuses. The strike lasted from February to May and forced the capitulation of the Charest government who ultimately withdrew the proposal and reinstituted the bursary funds. While the fact that student action forced

---

[3] CÉGEP, or Collège d'enseignement général et professionel, are the relative equivalent of junior colleges or vocational colleges in the United States. The strengths and responsibilities of each CÉGEP campus are unique and ranges from general education to fine arts to mechanical vocations to information technology. In many cases, post-high school students are required to attend CÉGEP colleges before enrolling in a provincial university. In other cases, a CÉGEP vocation or technical education is the goal.

[4] Information concerning the CÉGEP strike was compiled from several sources including University Affairs, "Charest Government Weakened by Québec Student Strike." (Peggy Curran, May 2005); several reports from daily news sources including the Gazette, Le Devoir, and the CBC from September 2004 through June 2005.

the government to rescind its neoliberal reform measure is significant, the rejection of a government compromise is even more applicable to the conclusions of this essay.

On March 16, the Minister of Education, Jacques Fournier, offered to replace the $103 million in converted grant funds with $95.5 million. Student leadership rejected this offer due to the fact that the $95.5 million would come from federal government educational funding. In the words of one student leader, "The present offer, in our view, is unacceptable because the extra money comes essentially from the federal government" (Lampert 2005).

The rejection of a compromise effort deemed insufficient in its adherence to national protectionist demands illustrates the importance of culture within the context of the "double movement." In other words, the economic compromise solution was rejected on cultural grounds. This action coincides with the overall conclusion of this essay; namely that culture has become increasingly important as a tool for meeting the demands of the national population for social protection. The question that arises at this point is: does the reliance on culture by the state in meeting challenges of an economic nature prove effective? Developing conclusions of the capacities of the contemporary *nation* will help answer this question.

Neoliberalism and the Problem of National Legitimation

The comparative cases presented here illustrate the importance of culture in maintaining state protectionist capacities. This appears to be the case in *both* state and sub-state scenarios. The Québec state has long relied on a legitimation strategy of linking state-formation with a singular national cultural definition. This strategy has proven effective in promoting both political autonomy and giving rise to the sovereignty movement; however, the demographic diversification accompanying contemporary Québec immigration creates difficulties in employing this monolithic nationalistic strategy. While Québec's version of cultural pluralism clearly integrates this legacy of "monologic" (Beauchemin 2004) national definition within a civic, intercultural nationalism, recent events have illustrated the efficacy of monolithic forms as political legitimation strategies. (Sub)state-building in Québec may be facilitated by its abiding cultural roots; however, the combination of neoliberalism and cultural diversification (both artifacts of global political economic integration) has made the state's defense of a pluralist, intercultural nationalism problematic. The "reasonable accommodation" debate, briefly illustrated below, offers an excellent opportunity to observe these tensions.

Conversely, Canadian efforts to articulate a singular national identity have been much more problematic – not in the least due to the bicultural legacy codified in the Québec Act. Despite state efforts to engender a singular, *Canadian*, identity state-building strategies along first bicultural then pluralist lines, the question over what is exactly "Canadian" has led to myriad conclusions with many simply settling for the explanation that Canadian national identity is simply defined as being "not American" (*cf.* Brown1954).

Obviously, this reactionary nationalism is problematic, particularly due to the fact that increased cross-boarder political, economic, and cultural exchanges made the dubious line between Canadian and American culture much more permeable. Regardless or reactionary or dichotomous definitions of "Canadian-ness," significant attempts to address the "national question" were undertaken in the 1970s – and significantly led by the federal state. The integration of neoliberalism in the mid-1980s has promoted an ideological (and practical) reduction of state socio-economic capacities which raises the question as to how the federal state engages in the process of state legitimation with the substantial hindrance of neoliberal reforms and the lack of a singular nationalist legacy? Its institutional protectionist capacity willfully reduced and (in the case of Canadian multiculturalism) privatized, the state must clearly find alternative legitimation strategies. But how does a state with a history of pluralism articulate a common national cultural definition? One emergent strategy has been distinctly contemporary, particularly with respect to its foundation in marketing strategies: Branding.

As illustrated in Chapter Seven, neoliberalism has had a more corrosive institutional effect on Canadian multiculturalism than Québec interculturalism, but are these limited examples reflective of larger pressures on state-building in the neoliberal era? The following sections illustrate some of the contemporary outcomes of both global socio-economic integration and neoliberalization in both Québec and Canada. While Québec may be well positioned to utilize its monolithic legacy as a means of resisting the state reductionism and maintaining a statist approach to state-building, neoliberalism has clearly emerged as an increasingly dominant ideology in the province.

The neoliberalization of Québec has had an impact on the efficacy of intercultural pluralism as a political approach to cultural diversification, as the "reasonable accommodation" debate illustrates. This implies that neoliberalism makes a civic, pluralist approach to socio-cultural diversification difficult, at best. Conversely, Canadian efforts to develop and promote the "brand of Canada" is exactly the counterpoint necessary for evaluating the aforementioned claim. If Canada can successfully promote a singular, yet civic/pluralist, national cultural definition, then the claim that neoliberalism reduces the efficacy of such pluralist approaches much less tenable.

Reasonable Accommodation in Québec

"Reasonable accommodation" is a term that emerged out of Canada's official embrace of cultural pluralism, or multiculturalism. While the question of respect for cultural practices and traditions has an extended history in both Canada and Québec, the specific "debate" concerning cultural pluralism in Québec began in 2006 with a series of events that were heavily reported by provincial media outlets. In March 2006, the Canadian Supreme Court ruled that allowing Sikh individuals to wear ceremonial daggers (kirpan) in schools was consistent with a "reasonable accommodation" of religious rights under the Canadian Charter of Rights and Freedoms. The case was prompted by a 2001 incident in which a Sikh youth was prohibited from wearing a kirpan in his Montréal school.

Later the same year a series of highly-publicized conflicts were brought to public attention such as the provision of Muslim prayer space in public buildings, the installation of frosted windows at a Montréal YMCA to address Hasidic Jewish complaints (the frosted windows were removed in 2007), and the institution of women-only prenatal classes at a Montréal CLSC (*Centre local des services communautaires*) clinic to meet requests by various religious communities. Other popularized examples included Muslim women being banned from participating in sporting events while wearing the *hijab* and a 2007 Elections Canada dictate that women wearing veils would not have to show their faces to be able to vote – a federal dictate that ran contrary to established Québec electoral protocols.

The dramatization of these events in the Québec media and perceived encroachment of federal electoral authority on provincial affairs made this an especially heated topic. For some, these multicultural "concessions" represented a problematic outcome of Québec's embrace of intercultural pluralism. The primary fear was a "monologic" one: That the pluralism inherent in official state policy was undermining the "Western values" and national identity of a Francophone, Québécois society embedded in a modern liberal worldview. It was not long until these "monologic" nationalist fears became the centerpiece for a struggling third-party in the Québec political hierarchy.

The *Action démocratique du Québec* (ADQ) was formed in 1994 by dissenting members of the PLQ, Jean Allaire and Mario Dumont. The party was founded on the twin ideals of liberalism and nationalism, supporting (neo)liberal economic reform and increased political autonomy from federal centralized authority. The party elected its first (and only) member of the *Assemblée nationale du Québec*, Mario Dumont, in 1994 and continued to struggle to achieve electoral success until 2002, when four additional *adéquistes*[5] joined Dumont in the *Assemblée nationale*. However, these gains were short-lived as all four lost their seats in the 2003 provincial elections (although three additional ADQ candidates were elected for the first time).

The ADQ remained mired in electoral mediocrity until the 2007 provincial elections in which the ADQ successfully re-elected its five incumbents and *thirty-six* new members of the Québec *Assemblée Nationale*. In one election, the ADQ rose from five to forty-one *Assemblée* members and superseded the established sovereigntist party, the *Parti Québécois* (PQ), to become the official opposition party in the minority PLQ government[6]. The extraordinary success of the ADQ is further illustrated by the fact that the 2007 election was the first time the party was officially recognized by the federal government[7].

Numerous explanations for the rapid rise of the ADQ have been given, including dissatisfaction with both PLQ and PQ party leadership, perceived mistakes made by Jean Charest's PLQ government, resistance to the tireless sovereigntist agenda of the PQ, and the charismatic leadership and electoral strategy of Mario Dumont. However, the dominant issue of the election, the "reasonable accommodation" of

---

[5] The vernacular term for members of the *Action démocratique du Québec* (ADQ).

[6] Interestingly, the 2007 Québec elections gave rise to the first minority government in the province since 1878.

[7] In order to be officially recognized as a political party in Québec, the respective party must elect at least twelve members to the *Assemblée nationale du Québec*, or gain twenty percent of the popular vote in a provincial election.

minority culture and customs, was successfully dominated by Mario Dumont and the ADQ. In short, the party was able to monopolize the debate on Québec national identity by advocating limited multicultural rights and defending the hegemonic position of "Old-stock European values[8]" Québécois (Dumont 2007). The remainder of this section examines the rise of the ADQ and their dual platforms of neoliberalism and the necessity for integrating essentialized national culture for the purpose of increased popular legitimacy.

The official platform of the ADQ centered on two main issues: autonomy and neoliberal reform. The latter represented the official stance on the traditional dichotomy of federalism and sovereignty, while the former established a clear political economic position articulating a greater role for private investment and decreased state regulation of social services including heath care and education (see Caldwell 2003; Pinard 2003; Petry 2005). While the Québec electorate was intrigued by Dumont's autonomist position, the neoliberalism of the ADQ remained deeply unpopular. Some, including as Béland and Lecours (2006, 84–84), have pointed to neoliberal platform initiatives promoted by the ADQ as specific reasons for its inability to garner more popular support. In order to circumvent this problem without rescinding its neoliberal platform, the ADQ was forced to find an alternative means of obtaining popular legitimacy. The popularized "reasonable accommodation" debate provided such an opportunity.

In November 2006, Mario Dumont deemed the previously mentioned CLSC issue "not reasonable," which signified the beginning of the ADQ's political defense of monolithic Québec national culture through public criticism of many "accommodation" measures taken by state institutions. The ADQ's support remained relatively stagnant until January 2007 when the town of Hérouxville issued a "Publication of Standards" that was geared towards potential immigrants and designed "to inform the new arrivals to our territory, how we live to help them make a clear decision to integrate into our area" (Municipalité

---

[8] Author's translations. The original quote in Dumont's open letter is, "De souche européenne de par l'origine de ceux et celles qui ont fondé le Québec," (Each and every one who founded Québec had their origins in old-stock European [values]), which is followed by "L'ADQ propose aux Québécois un programme étoffé pour protéger ces valeurs communes et affirmer notre personnalité collective" (The ADQ proposes to the Québécois, a program to protect community values and assert our collective personality.)

Hérouxville 2007). The "standards" included references to the fact that the stoning or burning of women would not be tolerated and that the covering of faces was only tolerated on special occasions, such as Halloween. The problematic nature of these statements has been justifiably critiqued (see Nieguth and Lacassagne 2009), but in the context of this essay the Hérouxville "standards" are understood as evidence of a political opportunity.

The publication of these "standards" set off a vociferous debate both provincially and internationally about the role of cultural pluralism and "reasonable accommodation." Dumont and the ADQ were quick to praise the Hérouxville document as a welcome statement in support of traditional values and normative culture. More importantly, the production of the "standards" outside of the electoral campaign and external to the ADQ allowed the party to argue that their opposition to "reasonable accommodation" was merely a reflection of organic, popular sentiment.

Shortly after the January 2007 publication of the Hérouxville document, Dumont published an "open letter" to the people of Québec in which his position on Québec national identity was solidified as a defender of "old-stock European" values. Dumont, through official ADQ channels, explicitly identified Québécois values in monolithic terms – those traditionally European ethno-cultural norms such as Christianity (or exclusively Catholic), the French language, and liberal democratic politics (Dumont 2007). He continued to articulate the official position of the ADQ as primarily concerned with the defense of these "vieille souche" values.

The response from the PLQ and PQ was defensive – the sitting PLQ Premier accused Dumont of "demagoguery" and of fostering ethnocultural divisions, while Andre Boisclair, then head of the PQ, attacked the letter's reactionary conservatism by arguing against any religious/ ethnic-centricity in contemporary Québec nationalism (Dougherty 2007). Despite these claims that Dumont and the ADQ were advocating an ethno-centric nationalism, the popularity of the ADQ began to rise precipitously. In fact, the vitriolic dismissals from the PLQ and PQ of this "defense of Québécois identity" worked to the direct benefit of Dumont and the ADQ – by establishing the ADQ as the de facto party willing to engage in a populist defense of the dominant ethno-culture in Québec. As the Montréal Gazette observes, "...the surge in ADQ support began late last year [2006] after Dumont took up the defense of Québec's values and identity against the supposed threat posed by the "reasonable accommodation" of non-Christian religious practices" (MacPherson 2007a).

It is important to note that the ADQ's critique of "reasonable accommodation" was effective to the extent that the party embraced a monolithic conceptualization of Québécois national identity. This is important for two reasons. The first is that the issue of "monologic" or *ethnic* nationalism in Québec was abandoned after 1995 by the PQ (traditionally the provincial party positively associated with Québécois nationalism). The party made a conscious decision in the early 2000s to emphasize civic nationalist strategies that would facilitate integration and de-emphasize the popular notion of a xenophobic national identity. This offered a political opportunity for the ADQ to revive a "monologic" version of Québec nationalism as a political mobilization strategy. Second, the timing of Dumont's definitional "defense" of national culture did not simply coincide with a provincial election, but also with a rising popular sentiment against support for protected cultural pluralism. Regardless of the dubious rationale for generating the Hérouxville documents (the small town is home to one migrant family), the perception among many Québécois, particularly outside of urban Québec, is that increased migration and the push to attract new arrivals to areas outside of the Montréal- Québec-Gatineau urban centers represent a threat to the dominance of "old-stock" Québécois culture. The reality of any large-scale policy shift or the insinuated claim that meeting the cultural requests of migrant groups was somehow more compromising is highly questionable (if not completely unsubstantiated). However, the role of the media in popularizing recent instances of "accommodation" and the existent cultural divisions between urban and rural Québec (Nieguth and Lacassagne 2009) combined to foster a critical mass of public perception.

In essence, the ADQ was able to exploit the vacated strategic platform of monolithic, ethnic nationalism and connect to a popular notion of cultural crisis. The result was politically efficacious: "... Dumont was blamed by some for exploiting xenophobia, but credited by more with 'saying out loud what many people have been saying to themselves'" (MacPherson 2007b). In fact, some observers point to a broader dissatisfaction with multiculturalism supported by opinion polls citing a significant majority of Canadians expressing dissatisfaction with additional cultural accommodations (Gordon 2007). The caveat, of course, is that there has not been a recent increase of immigrants into Québec, nor has there been an increase in public demands for increased accommodation. Several analysts have pointed to amplified media attention to issues of ethno-cultural conflict and exaggeration of accommodation activities as the causes for increased popular criticism of "reasonable accommodation" (Valpy 2007). This is an important point, as the ADQ did not achieve its status as the defender of a monolithic Québécois identity through confrontation of qualitative social change.

Instead, the ADQ was able to present itself as a defender of Québec national culture in a climate of popularized "angst." That is, the ADQ *discovered* the efficacy of a monolithic cultural protectionist strategy and, as a result, gained increased political legitimacy. Electoral success in this context must therefore be juxtaposed with the ADQ's former failures running on the platform of neoliberal reform. Thus, the ADQ intentionally seized-upon the abandoned strategy of defense/articulation of national monolithic cultural identity as a way to combat popular dissatisfaction with its sustained neoliberal platform.

Put another way, the ADQ was able to sustain its (unpopular) neoliberal platform through the integration of monolithic national cultural definitions.

The Branding of Canada

The rise of the ADQ in the 2007 provincial elections was a distinct Québec event – local in nearly every sense. That being said, the local never exists in isolation. The influence of global economic integration and the accompanying diversification of the labor force that is reflective of nearly all advanced capitalist societies substantially influences the efficacy of monologic nationalism. Québec is an increasingly diverse society that requires a shift in its national cultural definition: If it is to continue economic growth through an expansion of its labor force, it must incorporate a more pluralist definition of national identity. Despite the reality of an increasingly pluralist society, the realities of an accompanying neoliberal political ideology promote a countervailing feature: Neoliberalism reduces the ability of state actors (or potential actors) to promote economic protectionism – long an effective legitimation strategy. The search for alternative strategies can, as in the case of the ADQ, lead to a revival of monolithic national cultural definitions in direct response to globalization-facilitated cultural diversification.

This contradictory outcome (neoliberal globalization promoting cultural pluralism *and* monolithic nationalism) is largely contingent on the historical significance of a singular national identity – which clearly exists in the context of Québec. But how might a state without such a singular nationalistic identity response to the legitimation challenges posed by increased cultural diversification and neoliberal barriers to economic protectionism? The comparative case of federal Canada offers a distinct strategy to the same desired end of a singular national identity. The Canadian state's effort to develop and maintain a specific "brand" is a uniquely neoliberal effort to promote the seemingly timeless goal of monolithic national cultural definition.

To say that the Canadian federal government has struggled to even identify, much less promote, a singular nationalist ideology is beyond obvious. The failure of post-conquest assimilation and the resulting Québec Act in 1774 meant that nearly from the beginning, Canada would never be practically able to implement a monolithic national identity. This has not, however, stopped the state from trying. From the promotion of British roots throughout the 19th century (and arguably, through the World Wars) to the pluralist, yet reactionary, nationalism of the Trudeau era, the Canadian state has toiled (in vain) to articulate a common nationalism.

The question of why is simple and explicated throughout this essay: The legitimation of state authority. The question of how becomes complicated by myriad factors; not the least of which is the context of neoliberal globalization. "State branding" has become one of the more popular forms of national identity building and one emanating from the conditions of global market capitalism. With some arguing that the "branding" of a particular state is an exclusively market-oriented strategy to tie a political/geographic place to a particular product or environmental condition (Papadopoulos 2004), others have opted for the less market-deterministic definition that a "brand-state comprises the outside world's ideas about a particular country" (van Ham 2001, 2).

While theoretical work on state branding is predictably diverse, there are a few common concepts that can be easily identified. First, the practice of branding is explicitly tied to increased competition between states for the spoils of financial globalization, specifically, the goal of attracting *foreign direct investment*. As FDI remains a significant indicator of economic growth potential and active participation in the global economic system, clearly developing a brand that will encourage FDI is explicitly tied to the "financialization" of global capitalism.

Second, states are also competing for skilled and monied migrants and the promotion of a singular brand that is attractive to these population groups is desirable. This is particular relevant in a Canadian context as Canada has actively pushed itself as a unique option in comparison with its economically dominant southern neighbor (see Chapters Six and Seven). Finally, many scholars illustrate the market-orientation (read: neoliberal-friendly) of branding efforts is designed to enhance the very *idea* of a respective nation-state in the eyes of both the international community and among its own citizens. This latter point is particularly relevant as branding has emerged as a neoliberal form of state identity construction. While some argue that branding is distinct from (state ideological) nationalism due to its roots in "commercial ambition (Jansen 2008, 122), the case of Canada illustrates a much more integrated effort to utilize "Brand Canada" as a means to achieve a singular national cultural definition that is both pluralist, market-friendly, and facilitates state legitimacy as the "brand manager."

"Brand Canada" was first articulated by then-Prime Minister Jean Chrétien in the 1990s as a means to project a positive international image for the purpose of increasing foreign investment (see Nimijean 2006a; Potter 2002). The idea of producing an image for external consumption certainly fits with the overarching economic motivations of "place branding." In fact, the construction of "Brand Canada" has been widely used to promote foreign investment, immigration, and tourism (see Hudson and Ritchie 2009; Potter 2009); however, once the development of "Brand Canada" is linked to its neoliberal context a more domestic outcome becomes visible.

Richard Nimijean's (2006a; 2006b; 2005) work on the connection between the state construction of a singular national cultural definition and branding places the transition to a neoliberal state at the center of this process[9]. His perspective is particularly useful for the purposes of illustrating the efficacy of national cultural definitions in neoliberal state-building. Put simply, the construction of "Brand Canada" allowed the Chrétien government to implement neoliberal reforms (specifically, public spending retrenchment and privatization initiatives) without a

---

[9] Interestingly, while other scholars also illustrate the importance of neoliberalism to the general process of branding, they argue that it is distinct from nation-building practices of the past. For instance, Jansen (2008) argues that contemporary branding is intended to privatize and commodify the concept of a national place, rather than promote a "civic" understanding of common ownership and relationship to a national space.

withdrawal of public support and expected reductions of legitimate authority.

Chrétien's particular form of "Brand Canada" emphasized the ideological cornerstones of the traditional Canadian (Keynesian) welfare state model: A progressive emphasis on the collective, a compassionate outlook on aspects of Canadian social life, and an emphasis on peacemaking (that would be accentuated following the US invasion of Iraq in 2003) (Chrétien 2000). This emphasis on "common values" occurred within a specific historical context.

First, the Chrétien government was forced to deal with the 1995 Québec sovereignty referendum that nearly resulted in a victory for the sovereigntist movement. The build-up to the referendum saw heavy spending by the federal government in support of the "Non" campaign, but more to the point, the narrow defeat of the referendum gave the federal government an opportunity to push for reconciliation and a singular, pluralist conceptualization of Canadian identity. Second, the emergent neoliberal hegemony that accompanied increased global market integration created certain opportunities for state retrenchment and deficit reduction. Nimijean (2006a and 2005) points to the Canada Health and Social Transfer (CHST) as a significant neoliberal reform[10] although the partial privatization of Canadian multiculturalism infrastructure also points to the overall shift toward a neoliberal governance model in the 1990s.

With respect to the latter, the contradictory relationship between neoliberal state retrenchment and economic protectionism comes to the forefront of political identity. The irony of Chrétien's "Brand Canada" was that his (Liberal) government articulated a neoliberal version of fiscal restraint while at the same time arguing that it was protecting and managing the "common" values of the traditional Canadian nation-state, at least partially articulated in the language of the (now defunct) welfare state model. Realistically, the decline of state economic protectionist capacity and its transfer to private or decentralized entities meant that the Canadian state was divesting itself from the actual provision of these protections (and contributing to sub-state

---

[10] The Canada Health and Social Transfer (CHST) represented the decentralization of health and social welfare spending in Canada. Briefly, the federal government shifted management and administrative responsibility for these services to provincial governments. The role of the federal government shifted from service provision to fiscal payments to the provinces for their administration of these services.

autonomy at the same time); however, its relegation to "paymaster" also allowed it to shift responsibility for service provision – and blame for service reductions – to private entities and provincial states.

The former point, of building a singular national identity in the aftermath of the 1995 Québec referendum illustrates the sustained goal of a monolithic national cultural definition, yet the challenge of building a pluralist version in the globalization era. Put another way, the Chrétien version of "Brand Canada" emphasizes values, partially articulated in traditional economic protectionist terms, which circumvent local identities and emphasize an orientation that is, interesting "identity neutral." The emphasis on civic values couched in political economic terms transcended binational (Franco-Anglo) cultural affiliations as well as Allophonic demands for recognition. In Chrétien's version, identity was recognized and celebrated in a true multicultural sense; however, Canadian identity was centered on a common core of "compassion," "community," and "peacemaking."

Of course, governments come and go – however the persistence of "Brand Canada" is testament to the durability of the state as a legitimated Canadian political institution. The struggle now is less over a social democratic versus a neoliberal strategy for state-building – that debate is settled in favor of neoliberal hegemony. Rather, the struggle for power granted by leadership of the Canadian state is over articulation of "Brand Canada." The Liberal Party, the Conservative Party, and the New Democratic Party of Canada have all moved toward a varied embrace of a neoliberal political economic reality, yet they are also embracing the resurgent public effort to define and articulate "Brand Canada." Current Prime Minister Stephen Harper has made substantial efforts to redefine the brand to emphasize fiscal responsibility and deemphasize the role of the state in the provision of public services.

In the end, both Québec and Canadian state-building is increasingly contingent on the ability of state actors to define and articulate a national cultural definition. The current struggle is over the monolithic or pluralist form of those respective definitions. As both Canada and Québec further embed within the current neoliberal orthodoxy, their respective capacities to meet national protectionist demands through economic means will be eroded. The outcome of this institutional capacity reduction will be an increased emphasis on the definition of national culture (perhaps in a more singular direction as exemplified by the ADQ or in a pluralist direction as illustrated by the Chrétien government) as a means to maintain legitimate authority. The state is a requisite political economic institution; however, neoliberalism seeks to reduce the economic regulatory and participatory role of the state. The result is an awkward combination of uneven economic protectionist efforts and increased emphasis on defining an acceptable national cultural definition to sustain authority.

Reconceptualizing the "Double Movement"

The cases of Canada and Québec illustrate the role of culture and the importance of national populations in legitimizing culturally-oriented social policies. Respective policies of multiculturalism and interculturalism represent attempts by both state entities to ensure social stability by meeting the demands of national populations and global market proponents. The use of the "double movement" concept through this essay implies that a change has occurred in how states are able to these dual pressures.

As stated in Chapter Two, the Polanyian "double movement" is a specific process: Liberal capitalism in the form of a *laissez-faire* market system encroaches on a respective social group (i.e., national population) which in turn generates a national protectionist demand which is satisfied through the enacting of national *economic* protections. That is, in Polanyi's original conceptualization the "double movement" is an explicitly economic process unfolding through a specific historical process. Obviously, any theoretical extrapolation of the original concept must move beyond this explicit historicism; however, a reconceptualization of the double movement need not descend into the realm of murky generalization. On the contrary, as Block and Blyth (among others) have shown, the seemingly cyclical pattern of liberal ascendency and decline has dramatic effects on policy paradigms and political economic structural opportunities. Clearly, the rise of neoliberalism and the decline of Keynesian economic protectionism created a dramatic shift in policy options due to what Ruggie termed "international regimes."

The utility of a Polanyian double movement framework is that it is not exclusively contingent on historical conditions, rather it is based on social reaction. Regardless of the policy paradigm or international regime, the state must maintain legitimate authority from those it governs. Similarly, in any capitalist context, national populations will seek protection from the negative conditions created by capitalist operation; while capitalist proponents will seek increased autonomy from regulatory mechanisms that inhibit their accumulation capacities. The persistence of these reflexive conditions means that, regardless of larger political economic conditions, a static relational framework will exist and govern national, state, and capitalist interaction. Having said that, the mechanics of this interactive relationship can change with respect to larger political economic conditions and ideological regimes.

This essay concludes that state stability responsibilities inherent in the "double movement" can no longer be met with respect to national economic protections. Thus, an orthodox understanding and application of the "double movement" is problematic. I argue that this shift in empirical conditions requires a reconceptualization of the "double movement" while retaining its dynamic analytical capacities. This essay argues that the capacity of the state to ensure stability by national populations through economic means is reduced as global market integration increases. This does not negate the need for state institutions to ensure the stability necessary for optimal global market performance. Neither does it negate national demands for protection from the adverse effect of global market integration.

The dynamic foundation of the "double movement" remains. The conditions in which the process operates has changed, requiring more attention to the role of culture in the process of state adaptation and capacity to ensure required stability. This essay shows that the "double movement" continues to have significant methodological value, although clearly an orthodox conceptualization can no longer be used. Any extension of Polanyi's original concept must become more of an ideal type as opposed to a concrete theory. However, as the cases of Canada and Québec have shown, even ideal typical models can illuminate relational trends.

A reoriented "double movement" would retain the economic focus on predatory liberal market integration; however calls for national protection are increasingly reliant on socio-cultural means. This process, I argue, is the result of state adaptation in response to the pressures of the global economic system. That is, the role of the state, as the local control institution for ensuring social stability, remains constant. The means or capacities of the state to ensure social stability through explicit economic means is reduced as a result of global market integration (primarily the result of state adherence to neoliberal political economic stipulations). This political handicap results in the state seeking alternative means to ensure social stability – these means have been increasingly cultural. Therefore, the discursive interrelationship between state and nation has shifted from one of political economics to one of culture.

The potential implications of this shift will be briefly discussed in the following section. I argue that such a reconceptualized "double movement" could have substantial methodological value for future research. The analytical power of this approach is in its ability to integrate locally specific processes of cultural change or resistance with the macro socio-economic processes of a singular global economic system. It must be noted that while the global market system is a singular systemic entity, the process of global market integration by respective nation-states is an uneven process. Analytical approaches to this uneven process of integration should be able to reflect local variations.

The diversity of local cultural differences and the alternative avenues for national social protectionism using such cultural vehicles leads me to conclude that the "double movement" is valuable as a methodological tool but not as a theoretical framework. In other words, this reconceptualized understanding of the "double movement" views local cultural variants and responses as playing a dominant role in the nation/state dichotomy. That is, a general theory of "double movement" applicability is difficult given the relative cultural diversity of each case. We can, however, conclude that the realms of state policy capacity have expanded beyond traditional economic protections. This conclusion offers a useful foundation upon which future comparative analyses can be built.

The value of this perspective from a methodological perspective does, however, allow for future theoretical generalizations to be made. By using this reconceptualized methodological framework, we can then implement comparative case studies that will then, in turn, lead to general theoretical conclusions. This essay shows that this methodological approach is initially viable. The expansion of such a methodology would entail a major comparative case study, perhaps within regional political economic blocs (such as the EU or Latin America) or between divergent cases such as comparative core/periphery studies. Through additional comparative study we will be able to determine (1) whether culture plays an equally significant role in determining national protectionist strategies and (2) work toward a greater understanding of the contemporary state that is increasingly challenged by global market integration processes. The goal of advancing this methodological project would be to discover future potential directions for studies of the state and possibly develop a greater understanding of efficacious policies that allow national populations to effectively combat the predatory effects of globalization.

Future Directions

From the conclusions of this essay we can hypothesize four possible outcomes that will hopefully inspire additional study and theoretical development. This concluding section is the culmination of the theoretical project and offers avenues for future research on the state and the role of the "double movement" as an effective methodological framework. The outcomes are presented in their hypothetical form. I will add brief justification for their position as a potential outcome, but further analysis of each potential outcome will be left for future work.

1. *The state will increase its ability and skill in controlling national cultural symbols resulting in the increased domination of national populations through cultural manipulation and control.*

This outcome will occur due to alliance formation between national, state, and global market proponents. For instance, state capacity and ability to manage and define national culture is enhanced by cooperation from national groups who articulate a cultural vision or definition that supports state efforts. Leadership from the state can influence national culture, but this influence is most effective when it is supported by national popular leadership.

A contemporary example of this process is found in the alliance between the United States Republican Party and evangelical Christian groups in the late 1970s and early 1980s. The cooperative efforts of organized national (evangelical) groups assisted state efforts by the Reagan administration (1980–1988) to influence and manage national culture through the active redefinition of American political symbols as having specific affiliations and connotations. This example briefly illustrates the process of national cultural control as facilitated by a specific national group with a specific cultural definition that facilitates global market integration. In other words, the national cultural group (evangelical Christians) gains increased power with respect to the state and in turn promotes national compliance despite the presence of adverse effects of global market integration (deindustrialization, agricultural decline). The state was then able to ensure global systemic operation due to a stable national population that was controlled, in large part, through the redefinition of national culture.

This outcome results in contemporary stability in accordance with the Hegelian-Marxian concept of false consciousness and operates in much the same manner as Gramsci's concept of hegemony. We can assume that this outcome is probable in core states given the privileged position of its national populations with respect to abject and pervasive poverty. The relative affluence of core states facilitates additional control mechanisms in the form of mass media entertainment and material consumption promotion, both of which require tacit affirmation of the benefits resulting from global market integration and legitimate approval of existing control structures. This scenario clearly presumes a dominant position with respect to the global economic system. National populations, active in their own domination, are effectively controlled through state approved cultural definitions, symbols, and affiliations. These state controls are locally managed by co-operative national groups who stand to increase their power as they support the state project of global market integration. In this scenario, long-term stability is increasingly dependent on the state, its alliances with cooperative national groups, and its ability to manage and control national cultural definitions.

2. *The nation will gain greater understanding of cultural manipulative efforts on the part of the state and react negatively to this process of cultural control.*

The second possible outcome could result if the previously stated requisites collapse. If state capacity to influence or control national cultural definitions and symbols is reduced, national populations could increase their general power with respect to the state and the global economic system. In this scenario national groups will recognize the manipulative efforts of the state and react in a negative fashion weakening state control capacities. This outcome would decrease the dominant position of the global economic system due to the potential inability of the state to control national populations and ensure stability. The global economic system would have to address national protectionist concerns on a more direct level due to the inability of state cultural controls to meet protectionist demands.

An example of this process is arguably occurring in Latin America. Specifically, the most recent Bolivian election saw the rise of Evo

Morales, the first indigenous Aymara president of Bolivia, who was elected on a platform of emphasizing indigenous culture (as opposed to the Bolivian tradition of ignoring) and reasserting state control over national economic protections. In short, the initial promise of the Morales era in Bolivia is built on a rearticulation of national culture (from a political ideal of inclusivity, "we are all Indians" with the reality being massive economic stratification based largely on race – to a recognition of the racial basis for this economic stratification) which has allowed the state political discourse to shift again toward issues of national economic protection.

In this scenario, the national population has the opportunity to transcend state cultural definitions and controls, reestablish these controls from a cultural perspective, and potentially protect itself through economic means. This, of course, is contingent on the group that is able to actively redefine national cultural controls and their interest in reestablishing national economic protections from global market integration. The opportunity for such a shift is possible.

3. *The state will continue its relative decline in control capacities and be replaced with regional or global governing structures to ensure local stability.*

This scenario is predicated on the observation that the nation-state system, designed to originally maintain and control national economies and facilitate international trade, is undergoing qualitative change. The ability for the state to control or protect national economic interests is eroding in the face of neoliberal market demands. If cultural controls prove ineffective in ensuring long-term local stability, global market proponents will seek alternate forms of governance. Advocates of the global polity thesis argue that this process is already underway (Meyer 1980; Meyer et al. 1997; Boli and Thomas 1997). This theory argues that a global culture based on European models of rationality, liberal democracy, and liberal capitalism is pervasive enough to allow a common political discourse to occur. This common political discourse has the potential to produced shared governance structures.

Obvious examples of this process are institutions such as the United Nations, which has limited political and military authority granted through international cooperative unions. Another example of regional governance structure could be the European Union, which consists of several institutions of political control including the European Parliament and the ministerial Council of the European Union.

I would argue that this scenario is least likely due to the increased importance of national culture as a local control mechanism. Current levels of state-national cultural integration make it much more difficult to argue for the relinquishment of state power to supranational governance structures because national culture has been explicitly tied to the existing state. A nation-state joined by shared culture will lose this developed connection resulting in national instability. Resulting national instability will negatively affect global economic operation and therefore represents a significant disincentive for creating supranational governance at this time. One can look to recent history to see the function of the "double movement" in opposition to such an outcome.

The economic cooperation of the European Union has resulted in the world's strongest currency; however, the establishment of a singular constitutional system of governance has not matched this economic cooperation. In fact, the most recent attempt to ratify a European constitution was rejected by the national populations of France and the Netherlands. One of the more successful strategies in mobilizing support for constitutional reject was in appeals to national cultural sovereignty (Bordonaro 2005). Thus, while supranational governance structures are possible, the power of respective national populations and the ability of state and national actors to exploit cultural definitions, symbols, and histories for resistive purposes makes large-scale implementation unlikely. In fact, it seems more likely that attempts to implement regional supranational governance structures could follow the pattern of the EU, with powerful states or national populations resisting this impulse. Such a collapsed effort would likely lead to a return to either of the first two scenarios presented here. The deciding factor, it would seem, would be the strength of the state to manage and control national cultural structures (scenario one). Conversely, such a political collapse (failed regional governance) could present an opportunity for national populations to redefine or re-establish control over national cultural structures (scenario two).

4. *The power of national populations will increase beyond state capacities to control resulting in local instability. This instability could in turn result in increased regional or even global conflict.*

This scenario is the direct result of instability generated by an unbalanced "double movement." Local destabilization has the potential to degenerate into large-scale conflict due to the withdrawal of local structures of control and the inability of the global economic system to enforce stability through existing supranational institutions. This process can occur in two obvious ways.

First, the dominance of the global economic system grows beyond the ability of state cultural controls to pacify national populations. In this instance, the control of culture becomes irrelevant in the face of extreme economic inequalities and the inability for culture to mask such adverse economic conditions. In other words, discursive conflict centered on issues of national culture are overwhelmed by pervasive economic problems such as unemployment, poverty, and accompanying detrimental social conditions. This situation could result in social revolution or at least social instability that threatens global economic operation. In other words, the expansion of global market predation creates an imbalance in the "double movement" that overwhelms existing state protectionist capacities motivating local instability.

Second, national power increases to the point that it overwhelms state control mechanisms. Once control of the state is accomplished, the national group can choose to function in the way similar to the Morales administration. That is, usurped state power can be used to promote national economic health through diplomacy and renegotiated agreements within the global economic system. The possibility also exists that the dominant national group will chose not to protect its national populations within the context of the global market economy, but instead choose to expand its power through the forced acquisition of resources and capital of other nation-states.

Both of these outcomes can result in regional or even global conflict possibly promoting systemic collapse. This obviously is the most undesirable outcome, but unfortunately not the least likely. The negative potential for regional or global conflict seems more likely in peripheral regions due to their position within the global economic system. Core states and national populations will be less likely to contribute to the destabilization of a beneficial systemic arrangement. The motivation for systemic destabilization is possibly more attractive to peripheral states. This of course is an unproven hypothesis as one could argue that core state action taken in a unilateral fashion could be viewed as being systemically destabilizing. If a core state does not act in accordance with the systemic demands of the global market system, there could be ramifications for national popular destabilization. It seems unlikely, however, that core states will jeopardize their privileged position with anti-systemic actions on a large scale.

These possible outcomes are simply a few of the many directions for future comparative research on the nation-state using a reconceptalized "double movement" framework. This essay is designed to develop a greater understanding of the capacities and roles of the contemporary state with respect to national protection and global market integration.

Canadian multicultural policies and Québec intercultural policies offer the opportunity to observe and analyze state action as the result of both global market integration and in meeting national protectionist demands. The conclusions that are made from this study require that additional attention be played to the role of culture in understanding social policy strategies in Canada and Québec. The role of the Canadian and Québec state in the contemporary era cannot be adequately understood without attention to the role of culture as a stabilization tool or strategy. The efficacy of these strategies is also consistent with the "double movement" framework in that the ultimate success of multicultural and intercultural policies is determined by national popular legitimation as well as systemic global economic adherence.

The conclusions, that state capacity to protection national populations through economic means has waned resulting in increased state capacity to address national protectionist demands through cultural means, offer an opportunity to examine the complex interrelationships between nation, state, and global economy in a methodologically sound manner. I believe that this project provides a unique and promising foundation upon which a substantial research agenda can be built.

BIBLIOGRAPHY

Abowd, John M. and Richard B. Freemand. 1991. *Immigration, Trade, and the Labor Market*. Chicago: University of Chicago Press.

Abraham, David. 1977. "State and Classes in Weimar Germany." *Politics and Society* 7(3): 229–266.

Abu-Laban, Yasmeen. 2003. "For Export: Multiculturalism in an Era of Globalization." In *Profiles of Canada*, 2nd Edition, edited by Kenneth G. Pryke and Walter C. Soderlund. Toronto: Irwin Publishing.

Abu-Laban, Yasmeen and Christina Gabriel. 2002. *Selling Diversity: Immigration, Multiculturalism, Employment Equity, and Globalization*. Peterborough, ON: Broadview Press.

Abu-Lughod, Janet. 1997. "Going Beyond Global Babble." In *Culture, Globalization and the World System: Contemporary Conditions for the Representation of Identity*, edited by Anthony D. King. Minneapolis: University of Minnesota Press.

Abu-Lughod, Janet. 1989. *Before European Hegemony: The World System A.D. 1250–1350*. Oxford: Oxford University Press.

Aitken, Hugh. 1959. "Defensive Expansionism: The State and Economic Growth in Canada." In *The State and Economic Growth*, edited by Hugh Aitken. New York: Social Science Research Council.

Albouy, David. 2008. "The Earnings Gap between Francophone and Anglophones from a Canadian Perspective, 1970–2000." *Canadian Journal of Economics* 41(4): 1211–1238.

Albrow, Martin. 1996. *The Global Age: State and Society Beyond Modernity*. Stanford: Stanford University Press.

Alion-Souday, Galit and Gideon Kunda. 2003. "The Local Selves of Global Workers: The Social Construction of National Identity in the Face of Organizational Globalization." *Organization Studies* 24(7): 1073–1096.

Althusser, Louis. 2001. *Lenin and Philosophy and Other Essays*, translated by Ben Brewster. New York: Monthly Review Press.

Alvarez, Sonia; Evelina Dagnino, and Arturo Escobar. 1998. "Introduction: The Cultural and the Political in Latin American Social Movements." In *Cultures of Politics/Politics of Culture: Re-Visioning Latin American Social Movements*, edited by Sonia Alvarez, Evelina Dagnino, and Arturo Escobar. Boulder, CO: Westview.

Anastakis, Dimitry. 2005. *Auto Pact: Creating a Borderless North American Auto Industry*. Toronto: University of Toronto Press.

Anderson, Benedict. 1983. *Imagined Communities: Reflections on the Origins and Spread of Nationalism*. London: Verso Press.

Anderson, Fred. 2001. *Crucible of War: The Seven Years' War and the Fate of Empire in British North America, 1754–1766*. New York: Vintage Press.

Appadurai, Arjun. 1990. "Disjuncture and Difference in the Global Cultural Economy." *Public Culture* 2(2) 1–23.

Arbour, Pierre. 1993. *Quebec Inc. and the Temptation of State Capitalism*. Montreal: R. Davies Publishers.

Armour, Leslie. 1981. *The Idea of Canada and the Crisis of Community*. Ottawa: Steel Rail Publishing.

Aronowitz, Stanley and Peter Bratsis. 2002. "State Power, Global Power." In *Paradigm Lost: State Theory Reconsidered*, edited by Stanley Aronowitz and Peter Bratsis. Minneapolis: University of Minnesota Press.

Arrighi, Giovanni; Terence K. Hopkins; and Immanuel Wallerstein. 1989. *Antisystemic Movements*. London: Verso Press.

Ash, Amin. 1994. *Post-Fordism: A Reader*. Malden, MA: Blackwell.

Auger, Martin F. 2008. "On the Brink of Civil War: The Canadian Government and the Suppression of the 1918 Quebec Easter Riots." *Canadian Historical Review* 89(4): 503–540.

Bailyn, Bernard. 1986. *Voyagers to the West: A Passage in the Peopling of American on the Eve of the Revolution*. New York: Knopf.

Baiman, Ron; Heather Boushey; and Dawn Saunders. 2000. *Political Economy and Contemporary Capitalism: Radical Perspectives on Economic Theory and Policy*. Armonk, NY: M.E. Sharp.

Balthazar, Louis. 1995. "Quebec and the Ideal of Federalism." *The Annals of the American Academy of Political and Social Science* 538: 40–53.

Bamyeh, Mohammed. 1998. "Sociology, Civil Society, and the Unbound World." *Canadian Journal of Sociology* 23(2–3): 179–193.

Barbaro, Fred. 1995. "Rethinking 'Ethnic Pride.'" *Social Thought* 18(1): 75–92.

Barber, Benjamin. 1995. *Jihad vs. McWorld*. New York: Times Books.

Barrow, Clyde. 2005. "The Return of the State: Globalization, State Theory, and the New Imperialism." *New Political Science* 27(2): 123–145.

Barrow, Clyde. 2002. "The Miliband-Poulantzas Debate: An Intellectual History." In *Paradigm Lost: State Theory Reconsidered*, edited by Stanley Aronowitz and Peter Bratsis. Minneapolis: University of Minnesota Press.

Barrow, Clyde. 1993. *Critical Theories of the State: Marxist, Neo-Marxist, Post-Marxist*. Madison: University of Wisconsin Press.

Barry, Brian. 2001. *Culture and Equality*. Cambridge: Polity Press.

Bashevkin, Sylvia. 1991. *True Patriot Love: The Politics of Canadian Nationalism*. Toronto: Oxford University Press.

Baskaran, Thushyanthan. 2009. "Supranational Integration and Regional Reorganization: On the Maastricht Treaty's Impact on Fiscal Decentralization in EU Countries." *Constitutional Political Economy* (Online First -http://www .springerlink.com/content/n347013665786572/, Retrieved September 2, 2010).

Beauchemin, Jacques. 2004. "What Does It Mean to be a Quebecer? Between Self-Preservation and Openness to the Other." In *Québec: State and Society*, 3rd Edition, edited by Alain Gagnon. Peterborough: Broadview Press.

Béland, Daniel and André Lecours. 2008. *Nationalism and Social Policy: The Politics of Territorial Solidarity*. Oxford: Oxford University Press.

Béland, Daniel and André Lecours. 2006. "Sub-state Nationalism and the Welfare State: Quebec and Canadian Federalism." *Nations and Nationalism* 12(1): 77–96.

Béland, Daniel and André Lecours. 2005. "The Politics of Territorial Solidarity: Nationalism and Social Policy Reform in Canada, the United Kingdom, and Belgium." *Comparative Political Studies* 38(6): 676–703.

Bernard, André. 2000. *La Vie Politique au Québec et au Canada*, 2ᵉ édition. Sainte-Foy: Presses de l'Université du Québec.

Bernard, Mitchell. 1997. "Ecology, Political Economy, and the Counter-Movement: Karl Polanyi and the Second Great Transformation." In *Innovation and Transformation in International Studies*, edited by Stephen Gill and James H. Mittelman. Cambridge: Cambridge University Press.

Bell, David Victor John. 1992. *The Roots of Disunity: A Study of Canadian Political Culture*. Revised Edition. Toronto: Oxford University Press.

Best, Jacqueline. 2005. *The Limits of Transparency: Ambiguity and the History of International Finance*. Ithaca: Cornell University Press.

Bibby, Reginald. 1995. *The Bibby Report: Social Trends in Canadian Style*. Toronto: Stoddart.

Bibby, Reginald. 1990. *Mosaic Madness: The Poverty and Potential of Life in Canada*. Toronto: Stoddard.

Birchfield, Vicki. 1999. "Contesting the Hegemony of Market Ideology: Gramsci's 'Good Sense' and Polanyi's 'Double Movement.'" *Review of International Political Economy* 6(1): 27–54.

Birkland, Thomas A. 2001. *An Introduction to the Policy Process: Theories, Concepts, and Models of Public Policy Making.* Armonk, NY: M.E. Sharpe.

Bissoondath, Neil. 1994. *Selling Illusions: The Cult of Multiculturalism in Canada.* Toronto: Penguin Books.

Bitner, Ruth and Leslee Newman. 2005. *Saskatchewan History.* Saskatoon, SK: Saskatchewan Archives Board.

Block, Fred. 2007. "Understanding the Diverging Trajectories of the United States and Western Europe: A Neo-Polanyian Analysis." *Politics & Society* 35(1): 3–33.

Block, Fred. 2001. "Using Social Theory to Leap over Historical Contingencies: A Comment on Robinson." *Theory and Society* 30(2): 215–221.

Block, Fred. 1990. *Postindustrial Possibilities: A Critique of Economic Discourse.* Berkeley: University of California Press.

Block, Fred. 1988. *Revising State Theory: Essays in Politics and Postindustrialism.* Philadelphia: Temple University Press.

Block, Fred and Margaret Somers. 1984. "Beyond the Economistic Fallacy: The Holistic Social Science of Karl Polanyi." In *Vision and Method in Historical Sociology*, edited by Theda Skocpol. Cambridge: Cambridge University Press.

Blyth, Mark. 2002. *Great Transformations: Economic Ideas and Institutional Change in the Twentieth Century.* Cambridge: Cambridge University Press.

Boas, Franz. 1940. *Race, Language, and Culture.* New York: Macmillan.

Boli, John and George M. Thomas. 1997. "World Culture in the World Polity." *American Sociological Review* 62(2): 171–190.

Bonatto S.L. and F.M. Salzano. "A Single and Early Origin for the Peopling of the Americas Supported by Mitochondrial DNA Sequence Data." *Proceedings of the National Academy of Sciences* 94: 1866–1871.

Bordonaro, Frederico. 2005 (June 3). "The Rise of French Pro-Sovereignty Movements and their Geopolitical Consequences." *PINR: Power and Interest News Report.* www .pinr.com/report.php?ac=view_printable&report_id=308&language_id=1

Bothwell, Robert; Ian Drummond; and John English. 1989. *Canada Since 1945: Power, Politics, and Provincialism.* Revised Edition. Toronto: University of Toronto Press.

Bothwell, Robert; Ian Drummond; and John English. 1987. *Canada, 1900–1945.* Toronto: University of Toronto Press.

Bourdieu, Pierre. 1990. *The Logic of Practice*, translated by Richard Nice. Cambridge: Polity Press.

Bourdieu, Pierre. 1989. "Social Space and Symbolic Power." *Sociological Theory* 7: 14–25.

Bourdieu, Pierre. 1977. *Outline of a Theory of Practice*, translated by Richard Nice. Cambridge: Cambridge University Press.

Boyer, Marcel. 2001. *La performance économique du Québec: constats et défies.* Montréal: Centre universitaire du recherché en analyse des organizations.

Boyer, Robert and Daniel Drache, eds. 1996. *States against Markets: The Limits of Globalization.* London: Routledge.

Brace, C.L.; A. Russell Nelson; Noriko Seguchi; Hiroaki Oe; Leslie Sering; Pan Qifeng; Li Yongyi; and Dashtseveg Tumen. 2001. "Old World Sources of the First New World Human Inhabitants: A Comparative Craniofacial View." *Proceedings of the National Academy of Sciences of the United States* 98(17): 10017–10022.

Bradbury, John H. 1982. "State Corporations and Resource Based Development in Quebec, Canada: 1960–1980." *Economic Geography* 58(1): 45–61.

Braudel, Fernand. 1984. *Civilization and Capitalism.* Volume 3. New York: Harper and Row.

Braudel, Fernand. 1982. *Civilization and Capitalism.* Volume 2. New York: Harper and Row.

Braudel, Fernand. 1981. *Civilization and Capitalism*. Volume 1. New York: Harper and Row.

Breitkreuz, Clifford. 1997. "Reform Party: Federal Funding for Multiculturalism a Needless Expense." In *The Battle Over Multiculturalism: Does It Help or Hinder Canadian Unity*, edited by Andrew Cardozo and Louis Musto. Ottawa: PSI Publishing.

Brenner, Neil and Nik Theodore. 2002. "Cities and Geographies of 'Actually Existing Neoliberalism." *Antipode* 34(3): 349–379.

Brettell, Caroline B. and James F. Hollifield. 2000. "Introduction: Migration Theory." In *Migration Theory: Talking Across Disciplines*, edited by Caroline B. Brettell and James F. Hollifield. London: Routledge.

British Broadcasting Corporation (BBC). 2010. "Turkey's State-Dominated Past Goes Up in Smoke." http://news.bbc.co.uk/2/hi/europe/8579872.stm, Retrieved 22 March, 2010.

Brochmann, Grete and Tomas Hammar, eds. 1999. *Mechanisms of Immigration Control: A Comparative Analysis of European Regulation Policies*. Oxford: Berg.

Brooks, Stephen. 2002. *The Challenge of Cultural Pluralism*. Westport, CT: Praeger.

Brossard, Jacques. 1967. *L'immigration: les droits et pouvoirs du Canada et du Québec*. Montréal: Presses de l'Université Montréal.

Brown, George W. 1954. "Canadian Nationalism: An Historical Approach." *International Affairs* 30(2): 166–174.

Brown, Robert Craig and Ramsay Cook. 1974. *Canada 1896–1921: A Nation Transformed*. Toronto: McClelland and Stewart.

Brubaker, Rogers. 1992. *Citizenship and Nationhood in France and Germany*. Cambridge: Harvard University Press.

Buckner, Phillip. 1985. *The Transition to Responsible Government in British North America, 1815–1850*. Westport, CT: Greenwood Press.

Brun, Henri; Diane Demers; Patrice Garant; Andrée Lajoie; Marie Claude Prémont; and Daniel Proulx. 2005 (November 17). "Quebec Medicare Plan is not what the Supremes Ordered." *The Gazette*.

Cafik, Norman. 1977 (December 2). Speech given at the Conference on Third Language Teaching. Vancouver, British Columbia.

Caldwell, Gary. 2003. "Is the ADQ Quebec's Next Generational Party?" *Inroads* 13: 85–90. Retrieved December 4, 2007 http://findarticles.com/p/articles/mi_qa4014/is_200307/ ai_n9277714.

Cameron, Elspeth, ed. 2004. *Multiculturalism & Immigration in Canada: An Introductory Reader*. Toronto: Canadian Scholar's Press.

Canada. 1985. *Report of the Royal Commission on the Economic Union and Development Prospects for Canada*. Ottawa: Supply and Services.

Canada. 1982. *The Canadian Charter of Rights and Freedoms*. Department of Justice Canada. http://laws.justice.gc.ca/en/charter/.

Canada. 1973. *The Canadian Government Policy on Multiculturalism: Royal Commission Bilingualism and Biculturalism*. Canada National Archives. RG 6. Accession Number 89/90/319. Volume 5. File 3250-0.

Canada. 1970. *Royal Commission of Bilingualism and Biculturalism, The Cultural Contributions of other Ethnic Groups*. Ottawa: Information Canada.

Canadian Health Coalition. 2002. "Keeping Our Options for Reform Alive: Ten Actions to Restore Public Health Care." www.healthcoalition.ca/appendix.pdf.

Carens, Joseph, ed. 1995. *Is Quebec Nationalism Just? Perspectives from Anglophone Canada*. Montreal: McGill-Queen's University Press.

Castells, Manuel. 2004. *The Power of Identity*. 2nd Edition. Oxford: Blackwell Publishing.

Castells, Manuel. 1996. *The Rise of the Network Society*. Cambridge: Blackwell Publishing.

Castonguay, Claude. 2002 (May 7). "The Pension Plan and the Caisse de depot et placement du Québec." 30th Anniversary Lecture at the Institute for Research on Public Policy. Montréal, Canada. www.irpp.org/events/archive/castonguay.pdf .Ret. 8-29-2009.

CBC. 2004 (October 14). "Ottawa's Cup Runneth Over: Federal Budget Surpluses." CBC News Online. http://www.cbc.ca/news/background/budget/.

Cerny, Philip. 1996. "International Finance and the Erosion of State Policy Capacity." In Globalization and Public Policy, edited by Philip Gummett. Brookfield, VT: Edward Elgar.

Cerny, Philip. 1994. "The Dynamics of Financial Globalization: Technology, Market Structure, and Policy Response." Policy Sciences 27: 319–342.

Chanlat, Alain and Renée Bédard. 1991. "Managing in the Quebec Style: Originality and Vulnerability." International Studies of Management & Organization 21(3): 10–37.

Charbonneau, Hubert and Robert Maheu. 1973. Les aspects démographiques de la question linguistique. Québec: L'Editeur Officiel du Québec.

Chase-Dunn, Christopher. 1989. Global Formation: Structures of the World-Economy. Cambridge: Basil Blackwell.

Chodos, Robert; Rae Murphy; and Eric Hamovitch. 1993. Canada and the Global Economy. Toronto: James Lorimer.

Chrétien, Jean. 2000. "The Canadian Way in the 21st Century." Speech at the Conference "Progressive Governance for the 21st Century." June 2–3.

Chua, Amy. 2003. World on Fire: How Exporting Free Market Democracy Breeds Ethnic Hatred and Global Instability. New York: Doubleday.

Citizenship and Immigration Canada (CIC). 2007. "Canada Becoming the More Attractive North American Immigration Destination." CIC News: Canada Immigration Newsletter. http://www.cicnews.com/2007/08/canada-attractive-north -american-immigration-destination-0834.html. Ret. July 27, 2010.

Citizenship and Immigration Canada (CIC). 2003. Facts and Figures 2003: Immigration Overview. http://www.cic.gc.ca/english/pub/facts2003/permanent/12.html

Citizenship and Immigration Canada (CIC). 2000. Facts and Figures 2000: Immigration Overview. http://www.cic.gc.ca/english/pdf/pub.facts2000.pdf

Citizenship and Immigration Canada (CIC). 2000. Forging Our Legacy: Canadian Citizenship and Immigration, 1900–1977. Ottawa: Public Works and Government Sources Canada.

Clarkson, Stephen and Christina McCall. 1994. Trudeau and Our Times, Volume 2: The Heroic Delusion. Toronto: McClelland and Stewart.

Clarkson, Stephen and Christina McCall. 1990. Trudeau and Our Times, Volume 1: The Magnificent Obsession. Toronto: McClelland and Stewart.

Clawson, Dan; Alan Neustadtl; and Mark Weller. 1998. Dollars and Votes: How Business Campaign Contributions Subvert Democracy. Philadelphia: Temple University Press.

Cordero-Guzmán, Héctor R.; Robert C. Smith; and Ramón Grosfoguel. 2001. Migration, Transnationalization, and Race in a Changing New York. Philadelphia: Temple University Press.

Conrad, Margaret; Alvin Finkel; and Cornelius Jaenen. 1993. History of the Canadian Peoples: Beginnings to 1867. Toronto: Copp Clark Pitman.

Cox, Robert. 1997. "Economic Globalization and the Limits to Liberal Democracy." In The Transformation of Democracy?, edited by Andrew McGrew. London: Polity Press.

Cox, Robert. 1987. Production, Power, and World Order. New York: Columbia University Press.

Craib, Ian. 1993. Anthony Giddens. London: Routledge.

Dahl, Robert. 1961. Who Governs? Democracy and Power in an American City. New Haven: Yale University Press.

Dahl, Robert. 1958. "A Critique of the Ruling Elite Model." *American Political Science Review* 52(2): 463–469.

Dai, Shaing; David Ford; Shirley Roh; and Ravi Verma. 1996. *Fertility Projections for Canada, Provinces, and Territories, 1993–2016.* Demographic Documents Series, no. 1. Toronto: Statistics Canada.

Danysk, Cicilia. 1995. *Hired Hands: Labour and the Development of Prairie Agriculture, 1880–1930.* Toronto: McClelland and Stuart.

Dickason, Olive Patricia. 1997. *Canada's First Nations: A History of Founding Peoples from Earliest Times.* Toronto: Oxford University Press.

Dicken, Peter. 2003. *Global Shift: Reshaping the Global Economic Map in the 21st Century.* 4th edition. New York: Guilford Press.

Domhoff, G. William. 1987. "Corporate-Liberal Theory and the Social Security Act: A Chapter in the Sociology of Knowledge." *Politics and Society* 15(3): 295–330.

Domhoff, G. William. 1967. *Who Rules America?* Englewood Cliffs, NJ: Prentice-Hall.

Domke, David and Kevin Coe. 2007. "The God Strategy: The Rise of Religious Politics in America." *Journal of Ecumenical Studies* 42(1): 53–75.

Doran, Charles F. 2001. *Why Canadian Unity Matters and Why Americans Care: Democratic Pluralism at Risk.* Toronto: University of Toronto Press.

Doran, Charles F. and Ellen Babby, eds. 1995. *Being and Becoming Canadian.* Thousand Oaks, CA: Sage Publications.

Dougherty, Kevin. 2007. "Dumont Letter Smacks of Demagoguery, Charest Says." *Montreal Gazette*, January 19, pp. A20.

Duca, John V. and David D. van Hoose. 2001. "The Rise of Goods-Market Competition and the Fall of Nominal Wage Contracting: Endogenous Wage Contracting in a Multisector Economy." *Journal of Macroeconomics* 23(1): 1–29.

Dumont, Mario. 2007. "Une constitution québécoise pour encadrer les accommodements raisonnables." Lettre adéquiste http://bulletin.adq.qc.ca/bulletins/2007-01-17_25.html. Retrieved January 12, 2008.

Dunaway, Wilma. 2001. "The Double Register of History: Situating the Forgotten Woman and Her Household in Capitalist Commodity Chains." *Journal of World System Research* 7(1): 2–29.

Dunleavy, Patrick and Brendan O'Leary. 1987. *Theories of the State: The Politics of Liberal Democracy.* London: Macmillan Education.

Dunn, William N. 2003. *Public Policy Analysis: An Introduction.* 3rd Edition. Englewood Cliffs, NJ: Prentice-Hall.

Dye, Thomas R. 2002. *Who's Running America: The Bush Restoration.* Upper Saddle River, NJ: Prentice-Hall.

Eccles, W.J. 1972. *France in America.* New York: Harper and Row.

Eccles, W.J. 1969. *The Canadian Frontier, 1534–1760.* New York: Holt, Rinehart, and Winston.

Eden, Lorraine and Maureen Appel Molot. 1993. "Canada's National Policies: Reflections on 125 Years." *Canadian Public Policy* 19(3): 232–251.

Eisinger, Peter K. 1973. "The Conditions of Protest Behavior in American Cities." *American Political Science Review* 67: 11–28.

Eliofotou, Polyvios S. 2008. "Cyprus: Immigration, Wage Indexation and the Adjustment in EMU." *ECFIN Country Focus* 5(10): 1–7. http://ec.europa.eu/economy_finance/publications/countryfocus_en.htm, Retrieved 1/20/2011.

Endres, A.M. 2005. *Great Architects of International Finance: The Bretton Woods Era.* London: Routledge.

Escobar, Arturo. 2001. "Culture Sits in Place: Reflections on Globalism and Subaltern Strategies of Localization." *Geography* 20(2): 139–174.

Esping-Andersen, Gøsta. 1996. "After the Golden Age?" In *Welfare States in Transition: National Adaptations in Global Economies*, edited by Gøsta Esping-Andersen. London: Sage Publications.

Ess, Charles. 2002. "Liberation in cyberspace ... Or computer-mediated colonization? Introduction to "Global cultures: collisions and communication." *Electronic Journal of Communication/La Revue Electronique de Communication* 12(3–4): http://www .cios.org/www/ejc/v12n34.htm

Evans, Peter. 1997. "The Eclipse of the State? Reflections on Stateness in an Era of Globalization." *World Politics* 50(1): 62–87.

Evans, Peter. 1995. *Embedded Autonomy: States and Industrial Transformation.* Princeton: Princeton University Press.

Evans, Peter B; Dietrich Rueschemeyer; and Theda Skocpol. 1985. *Bringing the State Back In.* Cambridge: Cambridge University Press.

Falk, Richard. 1999. *Predatory Globalization: A Critique.* London: Polity Press.

Farazman, Ali. 1999. "Globalization and Public Administration." *Public Administration Review* 59(6): 509–522.

Featherstone, Mike, ed. 1990. *Global Culture: Nationalism, Globalization and Modernity.* London: Sage.

Fenwick, Rudy. 1982. "Ethnic Culture and Economic Structure: Determinants of French-English Earnings Inequality in Quebec." *Social Forces* 61(1): 1–23.

Ferguson, Adam. 1966 [1767]. *An Essay on the History of Civil Society,* edited by Duncan Forbes. Edinburgh: University of Edinburgh Press.

Fitzmaurice, John. 1985. *Quebec and Canada: Past, Present and Future.* London: C. Hurst & Company.

Foner, Nancy and Rubén G. Rumbaut, eds. 2000. *Immigration Research for a New Century: Multidisciplinary Perspectives.* New York: Russell Sage Foundation.

Forget, Claude E. 1984. *La Caisse de dépôt et placement du Québec: sa mission, son impact et sa performance.* Toronto: Institut C.D. Howe.

Francis, R. Douglas. 1993. "Regionalism and the Regions." In *Canada,* edited by Mel Watkins. New York: Facts on File.

Frank, Andre Gunder. 1998. *ReOrient: Global Economy in the Asian Age.* Berkeley: University of California Press.

Frank, Andre Gunder and Barry K. Gills. 1993. *The World-System: Five Hundred Years or Five Thousand?* London: Routledge.

Fraser, Matthew. 1987. *Quebec Inc.: French-Canadian Entrepreneurs and the New Business Elite.* Toronto: Key Porter Books.

Farazmand, Ali. 1999. "Globalization and Public Administration." *Public Administration Review* 59(6): 509–522.

Friedman, Thomas. 2000. *The Lexus and the Olive Tree.* New York: Farrar, Straus, and Giroux.

Frow, John. 1999. "Cultural Studies and the Neoliberal Imagination." *Yale Journal of Criticism* 12(2): 423–430.

Fry, Earl H. 2000. "Quebec Confronts Globalization: A Model for the Future?" *Québec Studies* 30: 57–69.

Fukuyama, Francis. 1992. *The End of History and the Last Man.* New York: Free Press.

Fuller, Colleen. 1998. *Caring for Profit: How Corporations are Taking over Canada's Health Care System.* Vancouver: New Star Books.

G7 Venezia Economic Declaration. 1987 (June 10). www.g7.utoronto.ca/summit/ 1987venice/communique/index.html

Gagnon, Alain and Raffaele Iacovino. 2004. "Interculturalism: Expanding the Boundaries of Citizenship." In *Québec: State and Society,* 3rd edition, edited by Alain Gagnon. Peterborough: Broadview Press.

Games, Alison. 1999. *Migration and the Origins of the English Atlantic World.* Cambridge: Harvard University Press.

Geertz, Clifford. 1983. *Local Knowledge: Further Essays in Interpretive Anthropology.* New York: Basic Books.

Geertz, Clifford. 1973. *The Interpretation of Cultures: Selected Essays.* New York: Basic Books.

Gellner, Ernest. 1983. *Nations and Nationalism.* Oxford: Blackwell Publishers.

Gendron, Pierre and Michel Sarra-Bournet. 1998. *Le Pays de tous les Québécois: diversité culturelle et souveraineté.* Montréal: VLB.

Gereffi, Gary and Miguel Korzeniewicz, eds. 1994. *Commodity Chains and Global Capitalism.* Westport, CT: Praeger.

Giddens, Anthony. 2003. *Runaway World: How Globalisation is Reshaping our Lives.* London: Routledge.

Giddens, Anthony. 1990. *The Consequences of Modernity.* Stanford: Stanford University Press.

Giddens, Anthony. 1984. *The Constitution of Society: Outline of the Theory of Structuration.* Berkeley: University of California Press.

Gill, Stephen. 1990. *American Hegemony and the Trilateral Commission.* Cambridge: Cambridge University Press.

Gilpin, Robert. 2000. *The Challenge of Global Capitalism: The World Economy in the 21st Century.* Princeton: Princeton University Press.

Gilpin, Robert. 1987. *The Political Economy of International Relations.* Princeton: Princeton University Press.

Gilroy, Paul. 2008. "Race, Rice and the Info-war." In *Cultural Politics in a Global Age: Uncertainty, Solidarity, and Innovation,* edited by David Held and Henrietta L. Moore. Oxford: Oneworld.

Godin, Pierre. 1991. *La Révolution tranquille: La fin de la grande noirceur.* Montréal: Boreal.

Goodwin, Jeff; James M. Jasper; and Francesca Poletta, eds. 2001. *Passionate Politics: Emotions and Social Movements.* Chicago: University of Chicago Press.

Gordon, Milton. 1964. *Assimilation in American Life: The Role of Race, Religion, and National Origins.* New York: Oxford University Press.

Gordon, Sean. 2007. "Quebec Town Spawns Uneasy Debate." *Toronto Star.* February 5. Retrieved February 5, 2008. http://www.thestar.com/article/178262.

Gorz, André. 1994. *Capitalism, Socialism, Ecology,* translated by Chris Turner. London: Verso.

Gramsci, Antonio. 1999. *Selections from the Prison Notebooks,* edited and translated by Quintin Hoare and Geoffrey Nowell Smith. New York: International Publishers.

Granatstein, J.L. 1975. *Canada's War: The Politics of the Mackenzie King Government, 1939–1945.* Toronto: Oxford University Press.

Granovetter, Mark. 1985. "Economic Action, Social Structure, and Embeddedness." *American Journal of Sociology* 91: 481–510.

Green, Alan G. 1994. "International Migration and the Evolution of Prairie Labour Markets in Canada, 1900–1930." In *Migration and the International Labor Market 1850–1939,* edited by Timothy J. Hatton and Jeffrey G. Williamson. London: Routledge.

Green, Alan G. and David Green. 2004. "The Goals of Canada's Immigration Policy: A Historical Perspective." *Canadian Journal of Urban Research* 13(1): 102–139.

Green, Alan G. and David Green. 1999. "The Economic Goals of Canada's Immigration Policy: Past and Present." *Canadian Public Policy* 25(4): 425–451.

Guéhenno, Jean-Marie. 1995. *The End of the Nation-State,* translated by Victoria Elliot. Minneapolis: University of Minnesota Press.

Gwyn, Richard. 1995. *Nationalism Without Walls: The Unbearable Lightness of Being Canadian.* Toronto: McClelland and Stewart.

Habermas, Jürgen. 2001. *The Postnational Constellation: Political Essays,* translated and edited by Max Pensky. Cambridge: MIT University Press.

Habermas, Jürgen. 1998. *Between Facts and Norms: Contributions to a Discourse Theory of Law and Democracy.* Cambridge: MIT University Press.

Habermas, Jürgen. 1987. *The Theory of Communicative Action,* Volume Two: Lifeworld and System: A Critique of Functionalist Reason. Boston: Beacon Press.

Habermas, Jürgen. 1984. *The Theory of Communicative Action*, Volume One: Reason and the Rationalization of Society. Boston: Beacon Press.

Habermas, Jürgen. 1975. *Legitimation Crisis*, Translated by Thomas McCarthy. Boston: Beacon Press.

Halli, Shiva S. and Leo Driedger, eds. 1999. *Immigrant Canada: Demographic, Economic, and Social Challenges*. Toronto: University of Toronto Press.

Hallowell, Gerald. 2005. *The Oxford Companion to Canadian History*. Oxford: Oxford University Press.

Hamelink, Cees J. 1994. *The Political of World Communication: A Human Rights Perspective*. London: Sage.

Hannerz, Ulf. 1997. "Scenarios for Peripheral Cultures." In *Culture, Globalization, and the World-System: Contemporary Conditions for the Representation of Identity*, edited by Anthony D. King. Minneapolis: University of Minnesota Press.

Hansen, Marcus Lee. 1940. *The Atlantic Migration, 1607–1860: A History of the Continuing Settlement of the United States*. Cambridge: Harvard University Press.

Hardy, Cynthia and Nelson Phillips. 1998. "No Joking Matter: Discursive Struggle in the Canadian Refugee System." *Working Paper in Human Resource Management and Industrial Relations* 11. Melbourne: University of Melbourne Department of Management.

Harris, Nigel. 1995. *The New Untouchables: Immigration and the New World Worker*. London: I.B. Tauris.

Harris, Richard and Melinda J. Seid, eds. 2000. *Critical Perspectives on Globalization and Neoliberalism in the Developing Countries*. Boston: Brill Publishing.

Harrison, Trevor. 1996. "Class, Citizenship, and Global Migration: The Case of the Canadian Business Immigration Program, 1978–1992." *Canadian Public Policy* 22(1): 7–23.

Hart, Michael; Bill Dymond; and Colin Robertson. 1994. *Decision at Midnight: Inside the Canada-U.S. Free-Trade Negotiations*. Vancouver: University of British Columbia Press.

Harvey, David. 2007. "Neoliberalism as Creative Destruction." *The Annals of the American Academy of Political and Social Science* 610(1): 21–44.

Harvey, David. 2005. *A Brief History of Neoliberalism* New York: Oxford University Press.

Hawkins, Frieda. 1988. "Canadian Multiculturalism: The Policy Explained." In *Canadian Mosaic: Essays on Multiculturalism*, edited by A.J. Fry and Charles Forceville. Amsterdam: Free University Press.

Hawkins, Frieda. 1972. *Canada and Immigration: Public Policy and Public Concern*. Montreal: McGill-Queen's Press.

Head, Keith and John Ries. 1998. "Immigration and Trade Creation: Econometric Evidence from Canada." *Canadian Journal of Economics* 31(1): 47–62.

Held, David. 1995. *Democracy and the Global Order: From the Modern State to Cosmopolitan Governance*. Stanford: Stanford University Press.

Held, David. 1991. "Democracy, the Nation-State and the Global System." In *Political Theory Today*, edited by David Held. Stanford: Stanford University Press.

Held, David; Anthony G. McGrew; David Goldblatt; and Jonathan Perraton. 1999. *Global Transformations: Politics, Economics, and Culture*. Stanford: Stanford University Press.

Held, David and Anthony McGrew, eds. 2007. *Globalization Theory: Approaches and Controversies*. Cambridge: Polity Press.

Held, David and Henrietta L. Moore. 2008. "Introduction: Cultural Futures." In *Cultural Politics in a Global Age*, edited by David Held and Henrietta L. Moore. Oxford: Oneworld Press.

Heller, Patrick. 2001. "Moving the State: The Politics of Democratic Decentralization in Kerala, South Africa, and Porto Alegre." *Politics & Society* 29(1): 131–163.

Hertel, Thomas W. and Roman Keeney. 2006. "What Is at Stake: The Relative Importance of Import Barriers, Export Subsidies, and Domestic Support." In *Agricultural Trade Reform and the Doha Development Agenda*, edited by Kym Anderson and Will Martin. New York: Palgrave Macmillan.

Hirst, Paul Q. and Grahame Thompson. 1996. *Globalization in Question: The International Economy and the Possibilities of Governance*. Cambridge: Polity Press.

Hobsbawm, Eric. 1992. "Nationalism: Whose Fault-line is it Anyway?" Anthropology Today.

Hobsbawm, Eric.1990. *Nations and Nationalism since 1780*. Cambridge: Cambridge University Press.

Hobson, John M. 2000. *The State and International Relations*. Cambridge: Cambridge University Press.

Hobson, John M. 1997. *The Wealth of States: A Comparative Sociology of International Economic and Political Change*. Cambridge: Cambridge University Press.

Hobson, John M. and M. Ramesh. 2002. "Globalisation Makes of States What States Make of It: Between Agency and Structure in the State/Globalisation Debate." *New Political Economy* 7(1): 5–22.

Hobson, John M. and Leonard Seabrooke. 2001. "Reimagining Weber: Constructing International Society and the Social Balance of Power." *European Journal of International Relations* 7(2): 239–274.

Holden, Michael. 2008. "Overview of Canadian Direct Investment." In *Brief, PRB 08-33E*. Ottawa: Parliamentary Information and Research Service. http://www2 .parl.gc.ca/Content/LOP/ResearchPublications/prb0833-e.pdf, Ret. July 12, 2010.

Hollifield, James, F. 2000. "The Politics of Labor Migration: How Can We "Bring the State Back In"?" In *Migration Theory: Talking Across Disciplines*, edited by Caroline B. Brettell and James F. Hollifield. London: Routledge.

Horsman, Matthew and Andres Marshall. 1994. *After the Nation-State*. London: Macmillan.

Hudson, Simon and J.R. Brent Ritchie. 2009. "Branding a Memorable Destination Experience: The Case of 'Brand Canada'" *International Journal of Tourism Research* 11(2): 217–228.

Hunter, Floyd. 1953. *Community Power Structure*. Chapel Hill: University of North Carolina Press.

Intellectuels pour le souveraineté du Québec (IPSQ). 1999. "Quebec Sovereignty: A Legitimate Goal." Position Paper for the Bloc Québécois. http://www.rocler.qc.ca/ turp/eng/Intellectuals/Intel.htm

Jansen, Clifford J. 2005. "Canadian Multiculturalism." In *Possibilities & Limitations: Multicultural Policies and Programs in Canada*, edited by Carl E. James. Halifax: Fernwood Publishing.

Jansen, Sue Curry. 2008. "Designer Nations: Neo-liberal Nation Branding – Brand Estonia." *Social Identities* 14(1): 121–142.

Jasper, James M. 1997. *The Art of Moral Protest: Culture, Biography, and Creativity in Social Movements*. Chicago: University of Chicago Press.

Jenkins, J. Craig and Charles Perrow. 1977. "Insurgency of the Powerless: The Farm Worker Movements, 1946–1972." *American Sociological Review* 42: 249–268.

Jennings, Francis. 1988. *Empire of Fortune: Crown, Colonies, and Tribes in the Seven Years' War in America*. New York: Norton.

Jessop, Bob. 2002. "Globalization and the National State." In *Paradigm Lost: State Theory Reconsidered*, edited by Stanley Aronowitz and Peter Bratsis. Minneapolis: University of Minnesota Press.

Jessop, Bob. 1994. "The Transition to Post-Fordism and the Schumpeterian Workfare State." In *Towards a Post-Fordist Welfare State?* Edited by Roger Burrows and Brian Loader. London: Routledge.

Jessop, Bob. 1993. "Towards a Schumpeterian Workfare State? Preliminary Remarks on Post-Fordist Political Economy." *Studies in Political Economy* 40: 7–39.

Jessop, Bob. 1990. *State Theory: Putting the Capitalist State in its Place*. Oxford: Polity Press.

Jessop, Bob. 1982. *The Capitalist State*. New York: New York University Press.

Johnson, Jon R. 2002. "How Will International Trade Agreements Affect Canadian Health Care?" Discussion Paper No. 22. Published by the Romanow Commission on the Future of Health Care in Canada. Ottawa: National Library of Canada.

Joppke, Christian. 2004. "The Retreat of Multiculturalism in the Liberal State: Theory and Policy." *The British Journal of Sociology* 55(2): 237–257.

Kaldor, Mary. 2003. *Global Civil Society: An Answer to War*. Cambridge: Polity Press.

Kaplan, Robert D. 2000. *The Coming Anarchy: Shattering the Dreams of the post Cold War*. New York: Random House.

Keating, Michael. 2001. "Nations without States: The Accommodation of Nationalism in the New State Order." In *Minority Nationalism and the Changing International Order*, edited by Michael Keating and John McGarry. Oxford; Oxford University Press.

Keating, Michael. 1995. *Nations against the State: The New Politics of Nationalism in Quebec, Catalonia, and Scotland*. New York: St. Martin's Press.

Keating, Michael and John McGarry. 2001. "Introduction." In *Minority Nationalism and the Changing International Order*, edited by Michael Keating and John McGarry. Oxford; Oxford University Press.

Kedourie, Elie. 1960. *Nationalism*. London: Hutchinson.

Kelner, Marrijoy and Evelyn Kallen. 1974. "The Multicultural Policy: Canada's Response to Ethnic Diversity." *Journal of Comparative Sociology* 2: 21–34.

Kennedy, Paul. 1993. *Preparing for the Twenty-First Century*. New York: Random House.

Keynes, John Maynard. 1920. *The Economic Consequences of the Peace*. New York: Harcourt, Brace, and Howe.

King, Laura. 2005 (January 14). "Venture Well: Northern Exposure." *Grand Banks Capital Press Release*. Newton Center, MA: Grand Banks Capital.

King, Russell. 1996. "Migration in a World Historical Perspective." In *The Economics of Labour Migration*, edited by Julien van den Broeck. Cheltenham, UK: Edward Elgar.

Klein Goldewijk, C. G. M., and J.J. Battjes. 1997. "A Hundred Year (1890–1990) Database for Integrated Environmental Assessments." *National Institute of Public Health and the Environment*, Bilthoven, Netherlands. RIVM-Report no. 422514002.

Koch, Max. 2006. *Roads to Post-Fordism: Labour Markets and Social Structures in Europe*. Aldershot: Ashgate.

Kramer, Eric Mark, ed. 2003. *The Emerging Monoculture: Assimilation and the "Model Minority."* Westport, CT: Praeger.

Kriesi, Hanspeter. 1995. "The Political Opportunity Structure of New Social Movements: Its Impact on Their Mobilization." In *The Politics of Social Protest*, edited by J. Craig Jenkins and Bert Klandermans. Minneapolis: University of Minnesota Press.

Kroeber, A.L. and C. Kluckhohn, eds. 1952. *Culture: A Critical Review of Concepts and Definitions*. Cambridge: Peabody Museum of American Archaeology and Ethnology.

Kukathas, Chandran. 1998. "Liberalism and Multiculturalism: The Politics of Indifference." *Political Theory* 26(5): 686–99.

Kukathas, Chandran. 1992. "Are there Any Cultural Rights?" *Political Theory* 20(1): 105–39.

Kurien, Prema. 2004. "Multiculturalism, Immigrant Religion, and Diasporic Nationalism: The Development of an American Hinduism." *Social Problems* 51(3): 362–385.

Kymlicka, Will. 1995. *Multicultural Citizenship: A Liberal Theory of Minority Rights*. Oxford: Clarendon Press.

Kymlicka, Will. 1989. *Liberalism, Community, and Culture*. Oxford: Oxford University Press.

Lacoursière, Jacques. 1997. *Histoire populaire du Québec, 1896–1960*. Sillery: Septentrion.

Lampert, Allison. 2005 (April 5). "Students at 9 CEGEPs Reject Preliminary Offer." *The Gazette*, A6.

Lanctôt, Gustave. 1967. *Canada and the American Revolution*. Toronto: Clarke and Irwin.

Lehman, Marc. 1999. "Canadian Multiculturalism" Current Issue Review 93-6E. Ottawa: Parliamentary Research Branch, Library of Parliament.

Lell, J.T.; R.I. Sukernik; Y.B. Starikovskaya; B. Su; L. Jin; T.G. Schurr; P.A. Underhill; and D.C. Wallace. 2002. "The dual origin and Siberian affinities of Native American Y-chromosomes." *American Journal of Human Genetics* 70: 192–206.

Lenin, Vladimir Il'ich. 1939. *Imperialism, the Highest Stage of Capitalism: A Popular Outline*. New York: International Publishers.

Levi, Margaret. 1988. *Of Rule and Revenue*. Berkeley: University of California Press.

Lévi-Strauss, Claude. 1963. *Structural Anthropology*, translated by Claire Jacobson and Brooke Grundfest Schoepf. New York: Basic Books.

Levine, Marc V. 1990. *The Reconquest of Montreal: Language Policy and Social Change in a Bilingual City*. Philadelphia: Temple University Press.

Li, Peter. 2003. *Destination Canada*. Oxford: Oxford University Press.

Light, Ivan Hubert and Parminder Bhachu. 1993. *Immigration and Entrepreneurship: Culture, Capital, and Ethnic Networks*. New Brunswick, NJ: Transaction Publishers.

Linteau, Paul-André; René Durocher; Jean-Claude Robert. 1983. *Québec: A History, 1867–1929*. Toronto: James Lorimer and Company.

Linteau, Paul-André; René Durocher; Jean-Claude Robert; and François Richard. 1991. *Québec since 1930*. Toronto: James Lorimer and Company.

Lobao, Linda. 2005. "Decentralization and the Neo-Liberal Roll Out: Are Communities Racing to the Bottom?" Paper presented at the Annual Meeting of the American Sociological Association, Philadelphia, PA. 12 August.

Long, Norton E. 1958. "The Local Community as an Ecology of Games." *American Journal of Sociology* 64: 251–261.

Long, Norton E. and George Belknap. 1956. "A Research Program on Leadership and Decision-making in Metropolitan Areas."

Lovink, Geert. 2002. *Dark Fiber: Tracking Critical Internet Culture*. Cambridge: MIT University Press.

Lowi, Theodore. 2005. "Politics, Economics, and Justice: Toward a Politics of Globalizing Capitalism." In *Mastering Globalization: New Sub-States' Governance Strategies*, edited by Guy Lachapelle and Stéphane Paquin. New York: Routledge.

Lukes, Stephen. 2005. *Power: A Radical View*. 2nd edition. London: Macmillan.

Maclure, Jocelyn. 2003. *Québec Identity: The Challenge of Pluralism*. Montréal: McGill Queen's University Press.

MacPherson, Don. 2007a. "Dumont Makes it Respectable Again: Surge in ADQ Support Began after It Took Up the Defence of Quebec's Identity." *Montreal Gazette*, April 5, pp. A21.

MacPherson, Don. 2007b. "Reasonable Accommodation Soft-Peddled." *Montreal Gazette*, February 24, pp. B7.

Malinowski, Bronislaw. 1960. *A Scientific Theory of Culture and Other Essays*. New York: Oxford University Press.

Mann, Michael. 1997. "Has Globalization Ended the Rise and Rise of the Nation-State?" *Review of International Political Economy* 4(3): 472–496.

Mann, Michael. 1984. "The Autonomous Power of the State: It's Origins, Mechanisms, and Results." *European Journal of Sociology* 25(2): 185–213.

Mann, Susan. 1982. *The Dream of Nation: A Social and Intellectual History of Quebec*. Toronto: Macmillan.

Marshall, T.H. 1964. *Class, Citizenship, and Social Development*. New York: Doubleday.

Marx, Karl. 1964. *Early Writings*, edited and translated by Tom Bottomore. New York: McGraw Hill.

Marx, Karl and Frederich Engels. 1955. *The Communist Manifesto*, translated by Samuel Moore. Chicago: H. Regnery.

Massey, Douglas S. 1995. "The New Immigration and Ethnicity in the United States." *Population and Development Review* 21(3): 631–652.

Massey, Vincent and Georges-Henri Lévesque. 1951. *Report of the Royal Commission on National Development in the Arts, Letters and Sciences: 1949–1951*. Ottawa: Edmond Cloutier Press. http://www.collectionscanada.gc.ca/massey/h5-400-e .html, Ret. July 12, 2010.

Mathieu, Jacques. 1991. *La Nouvelle-France: Les Français en Amérique du Nord, XVIe– XVIIIe siècle*. Ste-Foy, Québec: Les presses de l'Université Laval.

McEwen, Nicola. 2006. *Nationalism and the State: Welfare and Identity In Scotland and Quebec*. Brussels: P.I.E. Peter Lang.

——. 2005. "Globalization, Welfare Solidarity, and Sub-State Governance." In *Mastering Globalization: New Sub-States' Governance and Strategies*, edited by Guy Lachapelle and Stéphane Paquin. New York: Routledge.

McEwen, Nicola and Richard Parry. 2005. "Devolution and the Preservation of the United Kingdom Welfare State." In *The Territorial Politics of Welfare*, edited by Nicola McEwen and Luis Moreno. London: Routledge.

McGhee, Robert. 1996. *Ancient Peoples of the Arctic*. Vancouver: University of British Columbia Press.

McGhee, Robert. 1978. *Canadian Arctic Prehistory*. Toronto: Van Nostrand Reinhold.

McGuire, Randall H.; Joan Smith; and William G. Martin 1986. "Patterns of Household Structures and the World-Economy." *Review* 10(1): 75–97.

McInnis, Marvin. 1994. "Immigration and Emigration: Canada in the Late Nineteenth Century." In *Migration and the International Labor Market 1850–1939*, edited by Timothy J. Hatton and Jeffrey G. Williamson. London: Routledge.

McMahon, Fred. 2003. "Quebec Prosperity: Taking the Next Step." *Studies in Economic Prosperity: An Occasional Paper from the Centre for Budgetary Studies*. Vancouver: The Simon Fraser Institute.

McRoberts, Kenneth. 1997. *Misconceiving Canada: The Struggle for National Unity*. Oxford: Oxford University Press.

McRoberts, Kenneth. 1988. *Quebec: Social Change and Political Crisis*. Toronto: McClelland and Stewart.

Mestrovic, Stjepan. 1998. *Anthony Giddens: The Last Modernist*. London: Routledge.

Meyer, John W. 2000. "Globalization: Sources and Effects on National States and Societies." *International Sociology* 15(2): 233–248.

Meyer, John W. 1980. "The World Polity and the Authority of the Nation-State." In *Studies of the Modern World-System*, edited by A. Bergesen. New York: Academic Press.

Meyer, John W.; John Boli; George M. Thomas; and Francisco O. Ramierez. 1997. "The World Society and the Nation-State." *American Journal of Sociology* 103(1): 144–181.

Migué, Jean-Luc. 1998. *Étatisme en déclin du Québec*. Montréal: Varia.

Miliband, Ralph. 1977. *Marxism and Politics*. New York: Oxford University Press.

Miliband, Ralph. 1969. *The State in Capitalist Society*. New York: Basic Books.

Mills, C. Wright. 1956. *The Power Elite*. New York: Oxford University Press.

Mitchell, Katharyne. 2004. *Crossing the Neoliberal Line: Pacific Rim Migration and the Metropolis*. Philadelphia: Temple University Press.

Mitlin, Diana. 2001. "Civil Society and Urban Poverty: Examining Complexity." *Environment and Urbanization* 13(2): 151–173.

Mittelman, James H. 1997. "The Dynamics of Globalization." In *Globalization: Critical Reflections*, edited by James H. Mittelman. Boulder: Lynne Rienner.

Moore, Henrietta L. 2008. "The Problem of Culture." In *Cultural Politics in a Global Age*, edited by David Held and Henrietta L. Moore. Oxford: Oneworld Press.

Morton, William L. 1964. *The Critical Years: The Union of British North America, 1857–1873*. Toronto: McClelland and Stewart.

Mosley, Layna. 2007. "The Political Economy of Globalization." In *Globalization Theory: Approaches and Controversies*, edited by David Held and Anthony McGrew. Cambridge: Polity Press.

Municipalité Hérouxville. 2007. "Publication of Standards" January 25. Retrieved April 30, 2008. http://municipalite.herouxville.qc.ca/Standards.pdf.

Nash, June C. and María Patricia Fernández-Kelly, eds. 1983. *Women, Men, and the International Division of Labor*. Albany: State University of New York Press.

National Democratic Party. 2005. *Party Platform on Jobs*. http://www.ndp.ca/page/3001.

Nieguth, Tim and Aurélie Lacassagne. 2009. "Contesting the Nation: Reasonable Accommodation in Rural Quebec." *Canadian Political Science Review* 3(1): 1–16.

Nimijean, Richard. 2006a. "Brand Canada: The Brand State and the Decline of the Liberal Party." *Inroads* 19(Summer): 84–93.

Nimijean, Richard. 2006b. "The Politics of Branding Canada: The International-Domestic Nexus and the Rethinking of Canada's Place in the World." *Mexican Journal of Canadian Studies* 11: 67–85.

Nimijean, Richard. 2005. "Articulating the 'Canadian Way:' Canada and the Political Manipulation of Canadian Identity." *British Journal of Canadian Studies* 18(1): 26–52.

O'Brien, Robert and Marc Williams. 2004. *Global Political Economy: Evolution and Dynamics*. Houndmills: Palgrave.

O'Connor, James. 1973. *The Fiscal Crisis of the State* New York: St. Martin's Press.

Ohmae, Kenichi. 1995. *The End of the Nation-State: The Rise of Regional Economies*. New York: Free Press.

Ongley, Patrick and David Pearson. 1995. "Post-1945 International Migration: New Zealand, Australia and Canada Compared." *International Migration Review* 29 (3): 765–93.

Owram, Doug. 1992. *The Promise of Eden: The Canadian Expansionist Movement and the Idea of the West, 1856–1900*. 2nd Edition. Toronto: University of Toronto Press.

Pacom, Diane. 2001. "Being French in North America: Quebec Culture and Globalization." *American Journal of Canadian Studies* 31(3): 441–450.

Panitch, Leo. 1994. "Globalisation and the State." In *Socialist Register, 1994*, edited by Ralph Miliband and Leo Panitch. London: Merlin Press.

Panitchpakdi, Supachai. 2002. "The WTO System and the Promotion of Peace." Turkish *Policy Quarterly* 1(4).

Papadopoulos, Nicolas. 2004. "Place Branding: Evolution, Meaning and Implications." *Place Branding* 1(1): 36–49.

Paquet, Gilles. 1999. *Oublier la Révolution tranquille*. Montréal: Liber.

Pâquet, Martin. 1997. *Toward a Quebec Ministry of Immigration, 1945–1968*. Ottawa: Canadian Historical Association.

Parekh, Bhikhu. 1997. "Dilemmas of a Multicultural Theory of Citizenship." *Constellations* 4(1): 54–62.

Parkman, Francis. 1983. *France and England in North America*. New York: Viking Press.

Parkman, Francis. 1962. *Montcalm and Wolfe: The French and Indian War*. New York: Collier Books.

Parizeau, Jacques. 1995. "The Case for a Sovereign Quebec." *Foreign Policy* 99: 69–77.

Passaris, Constantine. 1986. "Canada's Demographic Outlook and Multicultural Immigration." *Effects of Demographic Shifts on Economic Activities* (Project No. 0004-001) – Report of Western Opinion Research Inc. File 36, Volume 3317, Demographic Review Secretariat.

Peck, Jamie and Adam Tickell. 2002. "Neoliberalizing Space." In *Spaces of Neoliberalism: Urban Restructuring in North America and Western Europe*, edited by Neil Brenner and Nik Theodore. Malden, MA: Blackwell Publishing.

Peck, Jamie; Nik Theodore; and Neil Brenner. 2010. "Postneoliberalism and Its Malcontents." *Antipode* 41(1): 94–116.

Pelletier, Gérard. 1983. *Le temps des choix, 1960–1968*. Montréal: Stanké.

Pelletier, Mario. 1989. *La machine à millards: l'histoire de la Caisse du dépot et placement du Québec*. Montréal: Editions Québec/Amérique

Perry, Ross. 1982. *The Future of Canada's Auto Industry: The Big Three and the Japanese Challenge*. Toronto: James Lorimer.

Petry, Francois. 2005. "Comparison chiffrée des plateformes de l'ADQ, du PLQ et du PQ aux élections de 1993, 1998 et 2003." Paper presented at the conference, *Bilan des réalizations du gouvernement Charest*, December 9–10, Québec City, Québec.

Pickel, Andreas. 2003. "Explaining, and Explaining With, Economic Nationalism." *Nations and Nationalism* 9(1): 105–127.

Pinard, Maurice. 2003. "A Great Realignment of Political Parties in Quebec." (The CRIC Papers: Special Edition). Retrieved December 18, 2007. Montreal: Centre for Research and Information on Canada (http://www.cric.ca/pdf/cahiers_special/cahier_spec_mars 03_eng.pdf).

Pincus, Stephen. 1999. "Nationalism, Universal Monarchy, and the Glorious Revolution." In *State/Culture: State Formation after the Cultural Turn*, edited by George Steinmetz. Ithaca: Cornell University Press.

Piven, Frances Fox. 1995. "Globalizing Capitalism and the Rise of Identity Politics." In *The Socialist Register 1995: Why Not Capitalism?*, edited by Leo Panitch. London: Merlin Press.

Piven, Frances Fox and Richard Cloward. 1993. *Regulating the Poor: The Functions of Public Welfare*. 2nd Edition. New York: Vintage Books.

Plourde, Michel. 2000. *Le Français au Québec: 400 Ans d'Histoire et de Vie*. Fides, Québec: Publications du Québec.

Polanyi, Karl. 2001[1944]. *The Great Transformation: The Political and Economic Origins of Our Time*. Boston: Beacon Press.

Polsby, Nelson W. 1960. "How to Study Community Power: The Pluralist Alternative." *The Journal of Politics* 22(3): 474–484.

Pool, John Charles and Stephen C. Stamos. 1989. *International Economic Policy: Beyond the Trade and Debt Crisis*. Lexington, MA: Lexington Books.

Portes, Alejandro, ed. 1998. *The Economic Sociology of Immigration: Essays on Networks, Ethnicity and Entrepreneurship*. New York: Russell Sage Foundation.

Portes, Alejandro. 1997. "Neoliberalism and the Sociology of Development: Emerging Trends and Unanticipated Facts." *Population and Development Review* 23(2) 229–259.

Portes, Alejandro. 1978. "Introduction: Toward a Structural Analysis of Illegal (Undocumented) Immigrants." *International Migration Review* 12(4): 469–484.

Potter, Evan. 2009. *Branding Canada: Projecting Canada's Soft Power through Public Diplomacy*. Montréal: McGill-Queen's University Press.

Potter, Evan. 2002. "Canada and the New Public Diplomacy." *Discussion Papers in Diplomacy* 81 http://ccges.apps01.yorku.ca/old-site/IMG/pdf/05_Potter.pdf Ret. August 15, 2010.

Potts, Lydia. 1990. *The World Labour Market: A History of Migration*, translated by Terry Bond. London: Zed Books.

Poulantzas, Nicos. 1980. *State, Power, Socialism*. London: Verso Books.

Poulantzas, Nicos. 1978. *Classes in Contemporary Capitalism*. London: Verso Books.

Przeworski, Adam. 1985. *Capitalism and Social Democracy*. Cambridge: Cambridge University Press.

Québec. 1990. *Au Québec pour bâtir ensemble: énoncé de politique en matière d'immigration et de l'intégration.* Québec: Ministère des communautés culturelles et de l'immigration du Québec.

Québec. 1984. *Québec Policy on Cultural Development: Introduction to Volume I.* Archives Canada. Record Group 6, File No. 3250-0 v.2

Québec. 1981. *Autant de façons d'être Québécois: plan d'action du gouvernement du Québec a l'intention des communautés culturelles.* Québec: Développment culturel et scientifique.

Québec. 1975. *Charte des droits et libertés de la personne.* R.S.Q., Chapter C-12. Québec: Editeur official du Québec.

Reid, Malcolm. 1972. *The Shouting Signpainters: A Literary and Political Account of Quebec Revolutionary Nationalism.* New York: Monthly Review Press.

Reifer, Thomas, ed. 2004. *Globalization, Hegemony, and Power: Antisystemic Movements and the Global System.* Boulder: Paradigm Publishers.

Renan, Ernest. 1882. *Qu'est-ce qu'une nation? Conférence faite en Sorbonne, le 11 mars.* Paris: Calmann Lévy. Reprinted in Henriette Psichari (ed.) *Oeuvres completes de Ernest Renan:* Tome I. Paris: Calmann-Lévy, 1947–61.

Renault, Alain. 1991. "Logiques de la nation." In *Théories du nationalisme; Nation, nationalité, ethnicité,* edited by Gil Delannoi and Pierre-André Taguieff. Paris: Editions Kime.

Richler, Mordecai. 1992. *Oh Canada! Oh Quebec! A Requiem for a Divided Country.* New York: A.A. Knopf.

Rioux, Marcel. 1974. *Les Québécois.* Paris: Seuil.

Ritzer, George. 1999. *Enchanting a Disenchanted World: Revolutionizing the Means of Consumption.* Thousand Oaks, CA: Pine Forge Press.

Ritzer, George. 1993. *The McDonaldization of Society.* Thousand Oaks, CA: Pine Forge Press.

Robertson, Roland. 1995. "Glocalization: Time-Space and Homogeneity-Heterogeneity." In *Global Modernities,* edited by Mike Featherstone, Scott Lash, and Roland Robertson. London: Sage.

Robertson, Roland. 1992. *Globalization: Social Theory and Global Culture.* London: Sage.

Robertson, Roland and Frank J. Lechner 1985. "Modernization, Globalization, and the Problem of Culture in World-System Theory." *Theory, Culture, and Society* 2(3): 103–117.

Robinson, William I. 2004. *A Theory of Global Capitalism: Production, Class, and State in a Transitional World.* Baltimore: Johns Hopkins University Press.

Robinson, William I. 1996. *Promoting Polyarchy: Globalization, U.S. Intervention, and Hegemony.* Cambridge: Cambridge University Press.

Robson, Terry. 2000. *The State and Community Action.* London: Pluto Press.

Roby, Yves. 1976. *Les Québécois et les investissments américains, 1918–1929.* Québec: Les presses de l'Université Laval.

Rosenberg, Justin. 2005. "Globalization Theory: A Post Mortem." *International Politics* 42(1): 2–74.

Rosenberg, Justin. 2000. *The Follies of Globalisation Theory.* London: Verso Books.

Rudometof, Victor. 2003. "Glocalization, Space, and Modernity." *The European Legacy* 8(1): 37–60.

Ruggie, John G. 1982. "International Regimes, Transactions, and Change: embedded Liberalism in the Postwar Economic Order." *International Organization* 36(2): 379–415.

Salt, John. 1989. "A Comparative Overview of International Trends and Types, 1950–80." *International Migration Review* 23(3): 431–456.

Santos, F.R.; A. Pandya; C. Tyler-Smith; S.D.J. Pena; M. Schanfield; W.R. Leonard; L. Osipova; M.H. Crawford; and R.J. Mitchell. 1999. "The Central Siberian Origin for Native American Y-chromosomes." *American Journal of Human Genetics* 64: 619–628.

Sassen, Saskia. 1996. *Losing Control? Sovereignty in an Age of Globalization.* New York: Columbia University Press.

Sassen, Saskia. 1991. *The Global City: New York, London, Tokyo.* Princeton: Princeton University Press.

Sassen, Saskia. 1988. *The Mobility of Labor and Capital: A Study in International Investment and Labor Flow.* Cambridge: Cambridge University Press.

Schaeffer, Robert K. 2005. *Understanding Globalization: The Social Consequences of Political, Economic, and Environmental Change.* 2nd Edition. Lanham, MD: Rowman & Littlefield Publishers.

Scharpf, Fritz. 1999. *Governing in Europe: Effective and Democratic?* Oxford: Oxford University Press.

Schiller, Herbert I. 1992. *Mass Communication and American Empire.* 2nd Edition. Boulder, CO: Westview Press.

Schiller, Herbert I. 1976. *Communication and Cultural Domination.* White Plains, NY: International Arts and Sciences Press.

Schmidt, Alfred. 1981. *History and Structure: An Essay on Hegelian-Marxist and Structuralist Theories of History,* translated by Jeffrey Herf. Cambridge: MIT University Press.

Schneider, Jane. 1977. "Was There a Pre-Capitalist World-System?" *Journal of Peasant Studies* 6(4): 20–29.

Scholte, Jan Aart. 2000. *Globalization: A Critical Introduction.* London: Palgrave.

Scholte, Jan Aart. 1997. "Global Capitalism and the State." *International Affairs* 73(3): 427–452.

Scott, James C. 1998. *Seeing Like a State: How Certain Schemes to Improve the Human Condition Have Failed.* New Haven: Yale University Press.

Scott, James C. 1990. *Domination and the Arts of Resistance: Hidden Transcripts.* New Haven: Yale University Press.

Scott, James C. 1985. *Weapons of the Weak: Everyday forms of Peasant Resistance.* New Haven: Yale University Press.

Scott, James C. 1976. *The Moral Economy of the Peasant: Rebellion and Subsistence in Southeast Asia.* New Haven: Yale University Press.

Seabrooke, Leonard. 2002. "Bringing Legitimacy Back in to neo-Weberian State Theory and International Relations." Working Paper Series No. 2002/6. Canberra: Australian National University, Department of International Relations.

See, Scott. 2001. *The History of Canada.* Westport, CT: Greenwood Press.

Seglow, Jonathan. 1998. "Universals and Particulars: The Case of Liberal Cultural Nationalism." *Political Studies* 46(5): 963–77.

Sen, Amartya. 2002. "How to Judge Globalism." *The American Prospect* 13(1): http://www.prospect.org/print/V13/1/sen-a.html.

Shannon, Thomas. 1989. *An Introduction to the World-System Perspective.* Boulder: Westview Press.

Sharma, Chanchal Kumar. 2005. "Why Decentralization? The Puzzle of Causation." *Synthesis* 3(1): 1–17.

Shefner, Jon; George Pasdirtz; and Cory Blad. 2006. "Austerity Protests and Immiserating Growth in Mexico and Argentina." In *Latin American Social Movements: Globalization, Democratization, and Transnational Social Networks,* edited by Hank Johnston and Paul Almeida. Lanham, MD: Rowman & Littlefield.

Siggins, Maggie. 1994. *Riel: A Life of Revolution.* Toronto: Harper-Collins.

Sklair, Leslie. 2001. *The Transnational Capitalist Class.* Oxford: Basil Blackwell.

Sklair, Leslie. 1995. *Sociology of the Global System.* 2nd Edition. Baltimore: Johns Hopkins University Press.

Skocpol, Theda. 1985. "Bringing the State Back In: Strategies of Analysis in Current Research." In *Bringing the State Back In*, edited by Peter B. Evans, Dietrich Rueschemeyer, and Theda Skocpol. Cambridge: Cambridge University Press.

Skocpol, Theda. 1979. St*ates and Social Revolutions: A Comparative Analysis of France, Russia, and China*. Cambridge: Cambridge University Press.

Slaughter, Stephen. 2005. *Liberty Beyond Neo-liberalism: A Republican Critique of Liberal Governance in a Globalising Age*. Houndmills: Palgrave Macmillan.

Smith, Adam. 1981[1776]. *An Inquiry into the Nature and Causes of the Wealth of Nations*. New York: Oxford University Press.

Smith, Allen. 1981. "National Images and National Maintenance: The Ascendancy of the Ethnic Idea in North America." *Canadian Journal of Political Science* 14(2): 227–257.

Smith, Anthony D. 1971. *Theories of Nationalism*. New York: Harper & Row.

Smith, David, Dorothy J. Solinger, and Steven C. Topik, eds. 1999. *States and Sovereignty in the Global Economy*. London: Routledge.

Smith, Joan and Immanuel Wallerstein, eds. 1992. *Creating and Transforming Households: The Constraints of the World-Economy*. Cambridge: Cambridge University Press.

Soderberg, Susanne. 2004. *The Politics of the New International Financial Architecture: Reimposing Neoliberal Domination in the Global South*. New York: Zed Books.

Sowell, Thomas. 2002. *A Conflict of Visions: Ideological Origins of Political Struggles*. New York: Basic Books.

Spruyt, Hendrik. 2002. "The Origins, Development, and Possible Decline of the Modern State." *Annual Review of Political Science* 5: 127–149.

Stark, David and Laszlo Bruszt. 1998. *Postsocialist Pathways: Transforming Politics and Policies in East Central Europe*. Cambridge: Cambridge University Press.

Statistics Canada. 2005 (May 17). "Foreign Direct Investment." *The Daily*. http://www.statcan.ca/Daily/English/050517/d050517a.htm.

Statistics Canada. 2003 (June 12). "Births." *The Daily*. http://www.statcan.ca/english/dai-quo/adaily.htm.

Statistics Canada. 1996. *CANSIM Socio-economic Database*. Table 109-0011. Urban population as a proportion of total population, Canada, provinces, territories and health regions, 1996, every 5 years (Percent).

Statistics Canada. 1992 (March 27). "Foreign Direct Investment." *The Daily*. www.statcan.ca/Daily/English/050517a.htm.

Steinmetz, George. 1999. "Introduction: Culture and the State." In *State/Culture: State-Formation after the Cultural Turn*, edited by George Steinmetz. Ithaca: Cornell University Press.

Steward, Julian. 1955. *Theory of Culture Change: The Methodology of Multilinear Evolution*. Urbana: University of Illinois Press.

Straubhaar, Thomas. 1988. *On the Economics of International Labor Migration*. Bern: Verlag Paul Haupt Bern und Stuttgart.

Straubhaar, Thomas. 1986. "The Causes of International Labor Migrations – A Demand-Determined Approach." *International Migration Review* 20(4): 835–855.

Strange, Susan. 1996. *The Retreat of the State: The Diffusion of Power in the World Economy*. Cambridge: Cambridge University Press.

Strange, Susan. 1985. "Protectionism and World Politics." *International Organization* 41: 233–259.

Stiglitz, Joseph; José Antonio Ocampo, Shari Spiegel, Ricardo Ffrench-Davis, and Deepak Nayyar. 2006. *Stability with Growth: Macroeconomics, Liberalization, and Development*. Oxford: Oxford University Press.

Sutton, Francis X. 1956. *The American Business Creed*. Cambridge: Harvard University Press.

Swank, Duane. 2002. *Global Capital, Political Institutions, and Policy Change in Developed Welfare States*. Cambridge: Cambridge University Press.

Sweezy, Paul. 1970. *The Theory of Capitalist Development: Principles of Marxian Political Economy*. New York: Modern Reader Paperbacks.

Tarrow, Sidney. 1983. "Struggling to Reform: Social Movements and Policy Change during Cycles of Protest." *Western Societies Paper 15*. Ithaca, NY: Cornell University.

Taylor, Charles. 1994. "The Politics of Recognition." In *Multiculturalism*, edited by Amy Gutmann. Princeton: Princeton University Press.

Taylor, Charles. 1992. *The Ethnics of Authenticity*. Cambridge: Harvard University Press.

Taylor, Charles. 1989a. *The Sources of the Self: The Making of the Modern Identity*. Cambridge: Harvard University Press.

Taylor, Charles. 1989b. "Cross-Purposes: The Liberal-Communitarian Debate." In *Liberalism and the Moral Life*, edited by Nancy L. Rosenblum. Cambridge: Harvard University Press.

Thompson, E.P. 1978. *The Poverty of Theory and Other Essays*. New York: Monthly Review Press.

Thompson, E.P. 1968. *The Making of the English Working Class*. Harmondsworth: Penguin.

Thompson, John Herd and Allen Seager. 1985. Canada 1922–1939: Decades of Discord. Toronto: McClelland and Stewart.

Tomlinson, John. 2003. "Globalization and Cultural Identity." In *The Global Transformations Reader: An Introduction to the Globalization Debate*. 2nd Edition, edited by David Held and Anthony McGrew. Cambridge: Polity Press.

Thomson, Dale C. 1984. *Jean Lesage and the Quiet Revolution*. Toronto: Macmillan.

Trudeau, Pierre Elliott. 1971. "Announcement of Implementation of Policy of Multiculturalism within Bilingual Framework." *Canadian House of Commons*. Ottawa, October 8, 1971.

Ukrainian Canadian Committee (UCC). 1968. *White Paper on the Final Report of the Royal Commission on Bilingualism and Biculturalism*. Winnipeg: Ukrainian Canadian Committee.

Urmetzer, Peter. 2003. *From Free Trade to Forced Trade: Canada in the Global Economy*. Toronto: Penguin Canada.

Vachon, Robert and Jacques Langlais. 1983. *Who is Quebecois?* Ottawa: Tecumseh Press.

Vaillancourt, François. 1996. "Language and Socioeconomic Status in Quebec: Measurement, Findings, Determinants, and Policy Costs." *International Journal of the Sociology of Language* 121: 69–92.

Vaillancourt, François. 1985. *Income Distribution and Economic Security in Canada*. Toronto: University of Toronto Press.

Valpy, Michael. 2007. "A Shortage of Accommodation: Is the Rise of Quebec's ADQ a Bad Omen for Multiculturalism?" *The Globe and Mail*, March 31, pp. F1.

Van Ham, Peter. 2001. "The Rise of the Brand State: The Postmodern Politics of Image and Reputation." *Foreign Affairs* 80(5): 2–6.

Vincent, Andrew. 1987. *Theories of the State*. Oxford: Basil Blackwell.

Vincent, Carol. 1997. "Community and Collectivism: The Role of Parents' Organizations in the Educational System." *British Journal of Sociology of Education* 18(2): 271–283.

Waisman, Carlos. 1999. "Civil Society, State Capacity, and the Conflicting Logics of Economic and Political Change." In *Markets and Democracy in Latin America*, edited by Philip Oxhorn and Pamela Starr. Boulder: Lynne Riennier.

Waite, J.B. 1971. *Canada, 1874–1896: Arduous Destiny*. Toronto: McClelland and Stewart.

Wallerstein, Immanuel. 1999. "Globalization or the Age of Transition? A Long-Term View of the Trajectory of the World-System." Papers of the Fernand Braudel Center, State University of New York, Binghamton. http://fbc.binghamton.edu/iwtrajws .htm.

Wallerstein, Immanuel. 1997. "The National and the Universal: Can There Be Such a Thing as World Culture?" In *Culture, Globalization, and the World-System: Contemporary Conditions for the Representation of Identity*, edited by Anthony D. King. Minneapolis: University of Minnesota Press.

Wallerstein, Immanuel. 1988. "Development: Lodestar or Illusion." *Economic- and Political Weekly* 23(29): 2017–2023.

Wallerstein, Immanuel. 1979. *The Capitalist World Economy*. Cambridge: Cambridge University Press.

Wallerstein, Immanuel. 1974. *The Modern World-System I: Capitalist Agriculture and The Origins of the European World-Economy in the Sixteenth Century*. New York: Academic Press.

Ward, Kathryn. 1993. "Reconceptualizing World-System Theory to Include Women." In *Theory on Gender/Feminism on Theory*, edited by Paula England. New York: Aldine.

Warner, W.W. Lloyd, ed. 1943. *Yankee City*. New Haven: Yale University Press.

Wassman, Jürg. 1998. *Pacific Answers to Western Hegemony: Cultural Practices of Identity Construction*. Oxford: Berg.

Waters, Mary C. 1999. "Sociology and the Study of Immigration." *American Behavioral Scientist* 42(9): 1264–1267.

Weede, Erich. 2004. "The Diffusion of Prosperity and Peace by Globalization." *The independent Review* 9(2): 165–186.

Weimer, David and Aidan R. Vining. 2004. *Policy Analysis: Concepts and Practice*. 4th Edition. Englewood Cliffs, NJ: Prentice-Hall.

Weiss, Linda. 2003. "Introduction: Bringing Domestic Institutions Back In." In *States in the Global Economy: Bringing Domestic Institutions Back In*, edited by Linda Weiss. Cambridge: Cambridge University Press.

Weiss, Linda. 1998. *The Myth of the Powerless State*. Ithaca: Cornell University Press.

Went, Robert. 2001-2002. "Globalization: Towards a Transnational State? A Skeptical Note." *Science and Society* 65(4): 484–491.

Williamson, John. 1993. "Development and the 'Washington Consensus'" *World Development* 21(8): 1329–1336.

Wonnacott, Paul. 1965. "Canadian Automotive Protection: Content Provisions, The Bladen Plan, and Recent Tariff Changes." *Canadian Journal of Economics and Political Science* 31(1): 98–116.

Woods, Ngaire. 2000. "The Political Economy of Globalization." In *The Political Economy of Globalization*, edited by Ngaire Woods. London: Macmillan.

Wuthnow, Robert. 1987. *Meaning and Moral Order: Explorations in Cultural Analysis*. Berkeley: University of California Press.

Wuthnow, Robert; James Davison Hunter; Albert Bergesen; and Edith Kurzweil. 1984. *Cultural Analysis: The Work of Peter L. Berger, Mary Douglas, Michel Foucault, and Jürgen Habermas*. Boston: Routledge & Kegan Paul.

Yúdice, George. 2005. *The Expediency of Culture: Uses of Culture in the Global Era*. Durham: Duke University Press.

INDEX